SWAT TEAMS

Other Books by Captain Robert L. Snow

The Militia Threat

Stopping the Stalker

Family Abuse

SWAT TEAMS

Explosive Face-Offs with America's Deadliest Criminals

Captain
ROBERT L. SNOW

PERSEUS PUBLISHING

Cambridge, Massachusetts
A Member of the Perseus Books Group

Library of Congress Catalog Card Number: 99-06680
ISBN 0-7382-0262-2

Perseus Publishing is a Member of the Perseus Books Group.

4   5   6   7   8   9   10——03
First printing, November 1999

Visit us on the World Wide Web at www.perseuspublishing.com

To Alan F. Wolfe,
who dedicated his first book to me

Acknowledgments

A book about a subject as complex as police SWAT teams could never be written without help, and many kind people assisted me in the completion of this book. A particularly heartfelt thank you goes to Plenum's Senior Editor Linda Greenspan Regan, who saw the value of my book and immediately acquired it. I also want to express my thanks and appreciation to Melicca McCormick, Ms. Regan's assistant, whose careful editing and thoughtful suggestions turned my ideas into a polished manuscript. A special thank you also goes to my agent, Fran Collin, for her hard work and constant faith in me. And I especially want to thank my wife, Melanie, and my children, Alan and Melissa, for giving me both the encouragement and the time I needed to write.

I naturally received a large amount of information and technical assistance from other police agencies while writing this book. Many police SWAT teams kindly agreed to assist me. I want to thank my brother and sister officers not just of the Indianapolis Police Department, but also of the Federal Bureau of Investigation, the Los Angeles Police Department, the Los Angeles County Sheriff's Department, the San Bernardino County Sheriff's Department, the New York City Police Department, the Richmond (Virginia) Police Department, the Columbia (Missouri) Police Department, and the Angier (North Carolina) Police Department. Also, a thank you goes to Steve Gentry, formerly of the U.S. Army's elite SWAT team, the Delta Force.

Finally, I want to extend my deepest appreciation to Lieutenant Stephen Robertson, tactical commander of the Indianapolis Police Department SWAT team, for his very careful and thoughtful critique of my manuscript.

Contents

Why Have a SWAT Team?

It took less than ninety minutes to change America forever.

On August 1, 1966, an atrocity occurred in Austin, Texas, an incident that first stunned the country and then forever vanquished any feelings of safety and security the American public may have enjoyed. In less than ninety minutes, a man named Charles Joseph Whitman leaped from obscurity to infamy, becoming one of America's worst mass murderers when, using a high-powered rifle, he randomly killed over a dozen people and wounded over thirty more from his perch atop the University of Texas clock tower building in Austin.

The Texas Tower sniper, as he became known as, stunned America because this wasn't some deviant criminal creeping into a building in the middle of the night and senselessly killing people, as Richard Speck had done just weeks before in Chicago when he murdered eight nurses. This was a random slaughter of people committed in the middle of the day, in the bright sunlight, with dozens of people nearby, a slaughter committed in an area where people felt they should be safe. But even worse was the fact that the murders were not committed by a career criminal with a long record of violence; they were committed by a least expected person: a University of Texas honors student. The Texas Tower sniper incident stunned the country because it showed Americans that

1

there was no place a person could really feel safe any longer and no person they could really feel safe from. But more than just the magnitude of the atrocity and what it meant to America's feeling of security, this event would also usher the country into a new era, an era in which events such as this would become more and more commonplace, until finally Americans would no longer be stunned or even surprised when they heard of them.

At a little after 11:00 A.M. on August 1, 1966, posing as a maintenance worker, twenty-five-year-old Charles Whitman used a dolly to roll a footlocker into the clock tower building on the campus of the University of Texas at Austin. At 308 feet high, the clock tower was the tallest building in Austin in 1966 and gave a commanding view not only of the campus but also of the surrounding business area, a fact that would fit well into Whitman's plans. Not arousing any suspicion in the lobby of the clock tower building, Whitman wheeled the dolly into an elevator and up to the twenty-seventh floor. He had earlier that morning rented the dolly because he very likely found he could no longer lift and carry the footlocker. In preparation for his eventual slaughter, he had packed the footlocker with three rifles, a sawed-off shotgun, two handguns, hundreds of rounds of ammunition, a five-gallon container of water, some sandwiches, and a container of gasoline.

Charles Whitman's bloody rampage, however, didn't start at the clock tower; it actually began several hours before. Earlier, before coming to the clock tower building, Whitman, a former altar boy and Eagle Scout, had visited his mother at her apartment. Mrs. Whitman, married to Charles's father for twenty-five years, had recently separated from her husband and now lived alone. While visiting her, Charles shot his mother in the back of the head and killed her. Leaving a note pinned to her apartment door saying that Mrs. Whitman was ill and wouldn't be in for work that day, he returned to his own apartment and stabbed to death his wife, Kathleen, as she lay in their bed. In a letter left behind and found by the police, Whitman wrote of how much he loved both his wife and his mother but said that he had to kill them to save them from the embarrassment of what he was about to do. At the bottom of the letter he made the chilling notation: "3 A.M. Both mother and wife dead."

Although unknown to the authorities Whitman had recently been seeing a psychiatrist, and had told him that he'd been experiencing periods of intense anger. He related to the doctor that, though he loved his wife, he had on two recent occasions physically assaulted her. He also told the psychiatrist that he often thought about going up into the clock tower with a deer rifle and shooting people.

The psychiatrist, Dr. Maurice D. Heatly, later said that Whitman's moods would range from overt hostility to weeping, that he had admitted having overwhelming periods of hostility with very minimal provocation. "This massive muscular youth seemed to be oozing with hostility," Dr. Heatly said. "Most of this hostility was directed toward his father" (Waldron, 1966, A1).

Indeed, in a second letter Whitman left behind, he ranted for two pages about how much he hated his father. However, in addition to Whitman's quick-tempered hostility and hate for his father, there was something just as important that neither he nor anyone close to him knew about. Whitman also had a rapidly growing brain tumor, already the size of a pecan, which the coroner said would have killed him soon.

On the twenty-seventh floor of the clock tower building, a woman who maintained the visitor's register became Whitman's third victim. The police would find her shot to death at her station near the stairway to the observation deck, and they theorized that she may have challenged Whitman, who had told the people downstairs he had maintenance work to do on the observation deck.

The observation deck of the clock tower building sat five floors above the twenty-seventh floor and could be reached only by the stairway, up which Whitman lugged the heavy footlocker. At the top of the stairs, he encountered a woman and two small children, who were viewing the campus below from the observation deck. Whitman methodically shot all three of them. Then, with the bodies lying nearby, he took up a position with one of his rifles at the ledge that ran around the observation deck.

At a half past eleven on the morning of August 1, 1966, the temperature in Austin had already climbed into the nineties, but still, the area below the clock tower building, both on campus and in the nearby business area, teemed with people, many on their lunch hour, giving Whitman dozens of targets to choose from. Although, while serving in the U.S. Marine Corps, Whitman had been only a mediocre shot, his aim from atop the clock tower suddenly became deadly accurate. He first shot a young black man riding a bicycle across the campus and then hit a young girl in the head. After this, he shot a pregnant woman in the abdomen, killing her eight-month-old unborn child, and then began shooting people as they hid in doorways or looked out of windows trying to see what was happening. The area below the clock tower quickly became filled with his victims, and, as if in a game, several times Whitman allowed would-be rescuers to get close to the dead and wounded and then shot the rescuers.

Down on the ground below, no one at first knew what was happening. The cracks of gunfire seemed to come from far away, and it wasn't until the people started falling and not getting back up that the lunch crowd suddenly began racing for cover. Within a few moments, the switchboard at the Austin Police Department lit up with call after call about gunfire on the campus of the University of Texas. Officers from the Texas Highway Patrol, the University of Texas Police Force, the Capitol Grounds Police Force, and the Austin Police Department responded immediately from all directions, but because of the heavy gunfire coming from the tower, they couldn't get close enough to do anything to stop the shooting. They couldn't even get close enough to assist the wounded who lay bleeding and crying for help in the ninety-eight-degree heat.

It was August 1, 1966, and while these kinds of incidents were not completely unheard of then, they hadn't yet begun occurring with such frequency that the police felt the need to make specific plans on how to deal with them. In 1966, America had not yet reached the point where events like the Texas Tower sniping had become commonplace enough to warrant worrying about them. In an Associated Press article on August 2, 1966, the day after the incident, Austin Police Chief Robert Miles admitted that the police had no specific plans for the handling of a sniper incident. "In a situation like this," the chief said, "it all depended on independent action by the officers" (Heavily armed, 1966, 1).

For an hour and thirty minutes, the carnage continued on the campus of the University of Texas at Austin, with Whitman firing from all sides of the observation deck. The independent action that Chief Miles spoke of consisted mostly of uncoordinated handgun and rifle fire at the sniper, which had no effect other than to chip away at the sandstone facing of the tower and to puncture the clock face. At one point, though, the police did manage to fly overhead in an airplane and shoot down at Whitman, but they were quickly driven away by his gunfire. This independent action Chief Miles spoke of also included commandeering armored cars that were delivering money and using them to rescue the wounded. But during the ninety very long and bloody minutes, Whitman fired over a hundred shots and killed over a dozen innocent people.

Finally, some officers came up with a plan they thought might work. Officers Ramiro Martinez and Houston McCoy realized that they had to get to the top of the tower if they were going to stop the gunman. But they also realized that they couldn't get to the tower along the walkways. The sniper was too accurate, as the tragic number of dead and wounded attested. Instead, their plan was to use the underground tunnels that connected the buildings on campus.

With the large number of people shot already, the officers knew they had to move immediately, and so they quickly put their plan into action. They and two other men entered the tunnel system and were able to safely gain entry to the clock tower building, where they cautiously made their way up to the twenty-seventh floor, finding the body of the woman who had manned the visitor's register, Whitman's first victim at the tower. Seeing that she was beyond help, the men then crept up the five flights of stairs. As they neared the observation deck, they were advised of the sniper's position by walkie-talkie transmission from the Department of Public Safety airplane that still flew overhead, though now staying far enough away to avoid being shot at.

Once outside, the officers began edging their way around the observation deck, coming at Whitman from different directions and hoping to catch him by surprise. But a few moments later, as they advanced on him, Whitman suddenly turned, saw the men, and fired his weapon at them. Officer Martinez didn't hesitate. He shot Whitman six times with his service revolver, while Officer McCoy shot him twice with a shotgun. Although mortally wounded, Charles Whitman simply wouldn't give up and continued moving. Officer Martinez grabbed Officer McCoy's shotgun and shot Whitman again, finally killing him.

The officers didn't advance on the sniper right away; instead, they watched Whitman's body for a few moments to be certain he was really dead. When they were sure, Officer Martinez waved a green flag to those below. It was finally over.

Events such as the Texas Tower sniping, though unusual, were not completely unheard of in America before 1966. At least once every ten years since the turn of the century, some demented person had committed a wholesale slaughter of some type. But things suddenly began changing in America in the middle 1960s. Events such as this were now beginning to occur much more frequently. In a matter of only a few years, it seemed, the pace of violence in our country had begun to grow at a sickening speed. On the day of the Texas Tower incident, for example, the country was still reeling from Richard Speck's brutal murder of eight nurses in Chicago only a few weeks before. But more than this, police chiefs all across the country in 1966 were on edge from the recent riots in Watts, and from the simmering violence they knew was ready to erupt at any moment in many of America's inner-city neighborhoods. On top of all this, the growing antiwar feeling in the country in 1966 threatened to turn violent any day.

The incident in Austin, however, because it was so blatant and had shattered the last myth of safety Americans enjoyed, was the final impetus these chiefs of police needed to make them decide they had to have plans ready to handle events like the Texas Tower sniping. And they needed teams of police officers equipped and trained to carry out these plans. They needed Special Weapons and Tactics (SWAT) teams.

Even though the police in Austin had finally been able to neutralize Charles Whitman, their efforts had been completely uncoordinated and had taken ninety minutes—precious time during which many innocent people had been killed or wounded. And the officers' success in Austin, the chiefs of police realized, had depended on a large element of luck. The country's police chiefs knew they couldn't always depend on luck. They needed a unit that could be called in at a moment's notice and plans that could be carried out immediately.

"Special weapons and tactics teams moved into a new era after Charles Whitman climbed into a tower on the first day of August 1966 and shot forty-six people, fifteen of whom died," said Lieutenant Sid Heal of the Los Angeles County Sheriff's Department in an article in the SWAT magazine *The Tactical Edge*. "This marked the birth date of the modern police SWAT concept. Since that day, almost every major police department in the United States has formed a special response team to handle similar situations."

Retired captain John A. Kolman, also of the Los Angeles County Sheriff's Department, agrees in his book *A Guide to the Development Of Special Weapons and Tactics Teams* when he says: "Prior to 1966, few, if any, law enforcement agencies staffed specialized teams to deal with armed, barricaded suspects. Generally speaking, these assignments were left to the uniformed patrol officer who may or may not have been prepared or equipped to resolve the matter."

Following the Texas Tower incident many police SWAT teams, groups of officers specially trained and equipped to handle dangerous and unusual criminal incidents, began being formed in communities all across the United States. The acronym *SWAT* is believed to have first been used by the Los Angeles Police Department, whose team, formed just after the Texas Tower incident, carried out operations against both the Black Panthers in 1969 and the Symbionese Liberation Army (SLA, the group that kidnapped Patty Hearst) in 1973, operations which encouraged police departments that had been hesitating to form similar units. These similar units were given many different names and acronyms, including Special Response Team (SRT), Emergency Response Team (ERT), and Special Emergency Response Team (SERT). But regardless of the names and acronyms that police departments gave these units, they all performed a similar function: to take over whenever events had gone beyond the capability of ordinarily trained and equipped police officers to handle and resolve, as the following incident demonstrates.

Indianapolis police officer Jerry Griffin, just four days short of his thirtieth birthday, lay on the grass behind a carport as Officer Pat Young feverishly attempted CPR on him, even though she knew he was dead. The smell of gunpowder hung heavy and thick around the carport.

Minutes before, a seemingly ordinary "disturbance" run had come out over the police radio on a seemingly ordinary November evening. (A "run" is police terminology for an assignment given to a police officer by the radio dispatcher.) Officer Griffin and Officer Amos Atwood, both only a few blocks from the address and each operating as a one-officer unit, told the dispatcher they would take the run. A few moments later, arriving first, Officer Griffin slipped his dark blue Ford Crown Victoria to the curb in front of 4702 West 36th Street.

The neighborhood of mostly post–World War II tract houses only occasionally saw trouble serious enough to require the police. The homes, occupied largely by retired people or factory workers, might occasionally be the site of a family fight that got loud enough for someone to call the police, and there might occasionally be a burglary or two in the neighborhood, but nothing like the bloodbath that evening would see.

Officer Griffin climbed out of the police car and walked into the carport on the west side of the house. Officer Atwood, who arrived only moments later, saw him knock on a door in the carport. A second later, Atwood heard Griffin shout, "Man, don't do it!" Almost immediately came the blast of a shotgun. After a second of shock, Atwood raced to the carport, where he saw Officer Griffin, who had been shot in the chest and was mortally wounded, stagger out of the carport and into the rear yard of the house. Officer Atwood fired several shots at the man with the shotgun, but he missed as the man dashed back into the house. Officer Atwood then ran back to his car and radioed for an ambulance and more police officers.

The gunman would later be identified as forty-seven-year-old Richard Moore, whose ex-wife's parents, it turned out, lived at the address. Interestingly, though Mr. Moore would kill three people that night and wound as many, he had had only one other encounter with the police before this, on a minor shoplifting charge over a decade before.

Officer Roy Potter, arriving just moments after the shooting of Officer Griffin, ran around to the east side of the house to look for Griffin. As Officer Potter reached the southeast corner of the house, he saw Lieutenant Cicero Mukes, an eighteen-year veteran and the highest-ranking police officer on the district that evening, pulling up in front of the house. When Lieutenant Mukes stepped out of his police car, a shotgun blast from the house struck him in the face.

Seeing this, Officer Potter raced to get out of the line of fire, but another shotgun blast from the house struck him in the left side. Falling to the ground, Potter lay still and played dead. The ploy would save his life.

While this entire incident, which had begun simply as an ordinary police run, took less than a minute, Mr. Moore had already killed one police officer and wounded two others. As the SWAT team was being requested, and as more police officers, answering the call of "Officer down," began arriving and pulling the wounded to safety, Mr. Moore began barricading himself inside the house. What the police didn't know at the time was that in the minutes before the first officers arrived, Mr. Moore, apparently outraged over the divorce decree that had become final the day before, had already killed his ex-wife (purposely shooting her in the groin with the shotgun), her father, and the family dog, their bodies found strewn throughout the house on West 36th Street. He had also critically wounded his ex-wife's mother with two blasts from the shotgun (though she would later recover from her wounds, as would Lieutenant Mukes and Officer Potter).

This incident, which began as simply an ordinary police run, just like any of the thousands of other ordinary runs officers go on every year, had in just a few moments erupted into a situation that plainly called for more resources than the ordinary police officer has at his or her disposal. It called for the specialized equipment, expertise, and training that only a police SWAT team can provide; it had all of the elements necessary for a SWAT call-up.

Since large local police departments, however, are independent of each other and answer to no central authority, there are no national guidelines for when and what a police SWAT team should be called up and used for. Each police department must decide for itself when and where to use SWAT. However, there are a number of incident types and criminal activities that usually meet the criteria for a call-up of a police department's SWAT team. These include hostage incidents, in which someone is being held captive and whose safe release is usually contingent on meeting certain demands of the hostage taker. They also include barricaded-person incidents, in which usually distraught and often unbalanced people have fortified a location and are harming others or threatening to, and high-risk arrests, such as stakeouts for a robbery, a contract murder, a gang fight, or a rape. SWAT is also used by many police departments for the service of high-risk arrest and search warrants. This high-risk warrant service, while usually involving drug dealers, who in the past decade or so have begun arming themselves with high-tech, high-destruction weapons and demonstrating a propensity to use them, may also include any incident in which the police believe the person the warrant is to be served on will react violently. As stated above, though, since most police departments in the United States are independent of each other, the exact criteria that would warrant a call-up of the SWAT team cannot be universally stated. However, since police SWAT teams are trained and equipped to handle high-risk incidents and therefore often carry high-destruction weaponry, their use is usually, but not always, tightly controlled.

Just how often do the types of events that generally require a police SWAT team occur?

Since there are also no national reporting requirements for these types of incidents, no national statistics are kept on their rate of occurrence, but according to the Miami Police Department SWAT manual: "At an ever increasing rate, situations involving 'special threats' are confronting law enforcement agencies.... Experience has indicated that when inadequate resources and tactics are used, deaths and injuries may result unnecessarily among police, hostages, innocent civilians, and suspects."

Almost everyone involved in law enforcement would agree that events which generally require the calling up of a SWAT team are occurring at an alarmingly increasing rate each year, and most police officers know the reason why. Although undoubtedly not as clear to ordinary citizens as to the police, the deadly incident on West 36th Street in Indianapolis clearly demonstrates, as I will show, how the evolving technology of news distribution has radically changed the world of law enforcement. The police today must face many types of crime they have never had to face before—and probably wouldn't have to face if not for the crime reports now appearing in the news media.

Crime news today is no longer simply the reporting of crime in the local community or the mention of one or two criminal incidents in another part of the state. Because of the increased ability to distribute news, crime today often receives in-depth coverage from all over the world, coverage that reveals every gory detail. In addition, crime news today is no longer old by the time it reaches the public. Because of its rapid distribution, crime news today is often so fresh that the blood of the victims hasn't even had time to dry.

All of this is a radical change from only three or four decades ago, when mostly just local crimes were reported in the news. Now, nearly every heinous crime committed anywhere in the United States, and often the world, is covered in depth both in the newspapers and on television, often fueling unbalanced people with criminal possibilities never before considered. Moore's actions on West 36th Street, it turned out, down to the killing of the family dog, were simply a plot taken from a half dozen similar incidents which had occurred that year around the country, incidents reported in depth in the news media.

Anyone who doubts this assertion about crime imitation has only to remember the mass killing at a post office in Edmond, Oklahoma, in 1986 and then the subsequent killings at other post offices, including same-day killings at postal facilities in California and Michigan, the killing of three postal workers in New Orleans, the killing of two people in a New Jersey post office, and the postal worker in Royal Oak, Michigan, who, after telling people "he would make Edmond look like a tea party," killed three co-workers (*The Tactical Edge*, 1992, p. 62). And if this isn't enough to convince skeptics, one only has to remember the killing of twenty-one people at the McDonald's restaurant in San Ysidro, California, in 1984 and then the subsequent killings at other fast-food restaurants, including the McDonald's in Kenosha, Wisconsin, where the killer left behind a videotape praising famous serial killers. Another incident which shows how a mass killing like this can obsess people occurred in Los Angeles, where the police department had to use tear gas to flush out a man who had barricaded himself with fourteen firearms and had told family members he wanted to emulate James Huberty, the killer at the McDonald's in San Ysidro. And readers will recall the more recent bombing of the World Trade Center in New York City in 1993, an act that the perpetrators carried out by parking a vehicle there containing a bomb made of fertilizer and diesel fuel. This event naturally received enormous news coverage. Two years later, the federal building in Oklahoma City was also bombed, this act too carried out by parking a vehicle there containing a bomb made of fertilizer and diesel fuel.

However, probably the best example of how news distribution inadvertently spawns crime is the Dan Cooper case. Before Dan Cooper (erroneously identified in the media as D. B. Cooper) hijacked Northwest Orient Flight 305 out of Portland in 1971, aircraft hijackings were practically unknown to the general public, and very, very few law enforcement agencies had ever had to deal with one. Yet, the intense coverage of the crime by the news media quickly spread word of Mr. Cooper's escapade to hundreds of newspapers and television stations all around the world. Every detail of the crime soon became known to people living in even the most remote areas. Unfortunately, because of this intense, almost suffocating, news coverage, over the next decade hundreds of aircraft were similarly hijacked, and law enforcement agencies were forced to learn quickly how to deal with a type of crime practically unheard of before. In October 1977, for example, Thomas Hannan hijacked a Frontier Airlines Boeing 737 and demanded $3 million and parachutes, a crime with a very close resemblance to the Cooper case, with the exception that, unlike Mr. Cooper, Mr. Hannan was not successful and ended the hijacking by killing himself with a shotgun.

But that was the 1970s, and most law enforcement authorities were surprised then by the magnitude of the copycat crimes. Today, we are much less surprised.

Today, if a person walks into his place of employment and kills six co-workers with an assault rifle and then takes hostages and waits to shoot it out with the authorities, police all across the country brace themselves, knowing with certainty because of news distribution capabilities that somewhere, and probably in several locations, copycat crimes will cost other lives. Today, if a person under some kind of emotional stress stockpiles an arsenal and then barricades himself inside his house, taking his family hostage and shooting at anyone who happens to come near, the police can bet that the massive and widespread news coverage of this event will spawn a half dozen similar crimes.

This copycat syndrome, though, isn't just an effect of the

increased distribution capabilities of the news media. It is also an effect of Hollywood's compulsion to rush into production movies about any heinous crime that has enough gory details to attract viewers.

"The treatment amounts to glorification," said *Washington Post* TV critic Tom Shales, writing about the made-for-TV movie *Murder in the Heartland*, a film about mass murderer Charles Starkweather. "The film might as well have been called *Charlie Starkweather, Superstar*" (Leo, 1993, A6).

But as if the effects of news media and Hollywood coverage weren't deadly enough, they have given birth to another especially disturbing and deadly side effect. Any person contemplating a copycat crime knows that to get into the national news media, or perhaps even into a *Movie of the Week*, there has to be a large amount of carnage. The more blood and innocent victims there are, the better the chances.

The psychology of why people would want to do this, why people would want to murder, mutilate, and torture innocent victims just for the notoriety, is beyond the scope of this book. The unfortunate fact is that they do, and that the way Hollywood and the news media treat these people and their crimes has a large effect on their motivation and numbers, which seem to be growing.

"Increasingly, the media cover the most violent murderers in the same way they cover TV stars or baseball players," complained syndicated columnist John Leo (1993, A6).

However, it is not only Hollywood productions that have this effect on unstable people. In 1977, under the pseudonym Richard Bachman, Stephen King published a book titled *Rage*. This book, whose plot deals with a high school student who kills his teacher and then takes his classmates hostage, sold a respectable number of copies under the pen name. But once it was discovered that Richard Bachman was actually Stephen King and the book was republished, its sales multiplied many times, and it was read by many more people, some of them very likely unstable.

Since the republication of *Rage*, there have been a number of incidents very similar to this plot, including one in Cuba City, California, where a former student murdered a history teacher and three students and then took the class hostage. A young man at Loara High School in Anaheim, California, shot another student and then held a drama class hostage. In Rapid City, South Dakota, a student with a gun walked into his math class and took it hostage.

Deputies James Morgan and Ann Burge of the San Bernardino County Sheriff's Department conducted a study several years ago in which they collected reports of crimes from around the United States that followed the plot of *Rage*. "We found that, within a very short time of the republication of *Rage*, we had five or six incidents right out here in California," said Deputy Morgan in a telephone interview (October 18, 1994). "We couldn't be certain that the book motivated the acts, but they all followed a similar plot."

Is any of this Stephen King's fault? Should he share any of the blame for these incidents if it could be shown that the people committed the acts after reading his book? Of course not. No one can hold someone responsible for what unstable people do with information directed toward the general public. As both a police officer and a writer, I firmly believe that no government agency should be able to tell the news media, Hollywood, or writers what to produce or how to produce it. Through my years as a law enforcement officer, I have come to realize that our continued freedom demands a free and unrestricted press. The media's job is to report the news, and crime has always been news, particularly gory or spectacular crimes. And incidentally, I am one of Stephen King's biggest fans.

This increase over the last few decades in vicious and often complex crimes, crimes that many people would never even have thought to commit, is simply an unfortunate by-product of a growing technology that allows for the rapid and far-reaching distribution of news and information, and most police departments realize that they simply have to learn how to live and cope with it. Just as it is the obligation of the media to report the news, it is the obligation of the police to stop crime, protect innocent people, and arrest criminals, no matter where the idea for the crime originated.

And yet, while average police officers, in their traditional role as peace keepers, are trained and equipped to handle any number of aberrant human behaviors, they are simply not trained and equipped to handle every kind of aberrant human behavior, particularly the more bizarre and violent behaviors. They are not trained and equipped to handle incidents in which people with high-destruction weapons have taken hostages and are holed up in a fortified location. Nor are they trained and equipped to handle incidents in which the slightest slip could cost many lives.

And so, as the world, through its news coverage, becomes smaller, and as its inhabitants, through the increasing availability of high-tech weapons, become more violent, incidents will undoubtedly continue to occur and then to recur that the average police officer is simply not trained or equipped to handle without putting himself or herself, along with many innocent bystanders, in extreme danger.

To fill this void, most medium-sized and large-sized police departments have formed SWAT teams: squads of police officers trained extensively in hostage rescue, high-risk entry, and threat neutralization. But does this threat that police SWAT teams are formed to fight exist only in large metropolitan areas? The answer, unfortunately, is no. While these types of incidents do often occur in large cities, they also occur in places like Apple Valley, Minnesota; Terre Haute, Indiana; Everett, Washington; Lumberton, North Carolina; and hundreds of similar small communities.

"The need for special weapons and tactics teams within small rural and municipal police departments becomes more evident each day," said Jeffrie Jacobs in the introduction to his book *SWAT Tactics* (1983). "The majority of officers working in these less populated geographical areas have been doing so with a false sense of security. When they read about fellow officers being slain during confrontations with barricaded suspects or snipers or in hostage situations, they view these as big-city crime problems. Such confrontations and violent crimes are no longer confined to the big cities. They are spreading to the suburbs and to the rural areas at an alarming rate" (p. ix). To deal with such incidents, many small police departments either have contracted for SWAT services from large police departments or have formed mutual-aid SWAT teams with other small police departments.

As was demonstrated in the incident on West 36th Street in Indianapolis, SWAT can, through high-tech equipment and disciplined team action, bring deadly and volatile situations quickly under control. An hour after SWAT had taken up tactical positions around the house on West 36th Street, the incident was resolved with no further officers injured. The reason is that SWAT brought the equipment and expertise necessary to contain the situation without putting the officers at high risk. Moore, realizing the futility of his situation, first tried unsuccessfully to kill himself with a shotgun blast to the stomach and then came out and surrendered. (He is now serving a life sentence at Indiana's maximum-security prison at Michigan City.) As this incident demonstrated, calling for SWAT can often be the answer to successfully resolving high-risk situations with the lowest risk to both those involved and innocent bystanders.

Qualities and Selection of SWAT Team Members

On the morning of Friday, March 26, 1993, the California State Board of Equalization Building in Sacramento was seeing its usual influx of workers arriving to begin their day. However, March 26 would not turn out to be just another workday. It would instead be a day few of the people employed at the building would ever forget.

The twenty-four-story building, which houses 2,300 workers and is responsible for receiving and disbursing tax money, had been set up with an elaborate security system, and employed over a dozen security guards. All employees working in the building wore large identification badges and were required to pass through security doors and checkpoints in order to reach the elevators and stairways. In addition to controlling access to the building, the security system also included a glass pod that sat in the center of the lobby, where three of the guards watched activity throughout the building on video monitors.

A little past 9:30 A.M., one of the security guards noticed a heavy-set middle-aged man attempting to slip into the building with a group of employees, and the guard stopped and questioned him. The security guards had seen this man hanging around the outside of the building for the past week, and so the guard was immediately suspicious. When questioned, the man couldn't explain why he was trying to get into the building, and so the guard escorted him back outside.

Suspicious of the attempted intruder's intentions because of the evasive answers he had given, the security guard followed the man to a van parked close by and attempted to question him about why he was trying to get into the building. The interrogation didn't get far, though, because, instead of answering the guard's questions, the man reached into a large canvas bag he had inside the van and pulled out a .357 Magnum revolver, disarming the security guard and then handcuffing him to a parking meter. When the security guard attempted to reason with him, the man fired a shot at the security guard's feet.

The attempted intruder, the police would later find, was James Ray Holloway, a former police officer with eighteen years' experience as a California highway patrol officer and as an agent for the California State Board of Alcohol Beverage Control. Holloway, the police discovered however, had left both of these jobs because of drinking and discipline problems. When the police searched his house in nearby Manteca, California, later that day, they found on a table a stack of the legal papers that would be necessary to settle his estate and a copy of the Stockton (California) Police Department's General Orders Manual, open to the section that gave guidelines for when police officers could use deadly force. Several sections had been highlighted.

After firing the shot at the security guard's feet, Holloway put the revolver away, picked up the canvas bag, which contained a 30–30 rifle, a 12-gauge shotgun, two .357 Magnum revolvers, and hundreds of rounds of ammunition, and headed back for the lobby of the California State Board of Equalization Building. Again, Holloway attempted to slip into the building with a group of employees, and again, one of the security guards, unaware that Holloway had handcuffed the other security guard nearby, stopped him and led him back outside.

Holloway, however, appeared determined to get into the building. He had apparently been planning for a long time what he was going to do that day. It was later discovered that he had carried a list in his pocket with the names of fifteen people on it, people who he believed worked in the building and who he intended to kill. Reportedly, Holloway had been receiving tax bills for his wife, who was deceased, and no amount of calling or writing had stopped these bills from coming. Soon, Holloway apparently began believing that the people involved in sending out these tax bills, the fifteen people on his list, were persecuting him, and he began blaming his failed business ventures and personal problems on them.

Standing on the sidewalk for a few moments after being put out of the building for the second time, Holloway finally yanked his shotgun out of the canvas bag and began blasting away at the glass doors and windows, creating an access hole into the lobby, through which he then raced with the canvas bag. On his way through the lobby, apparently wanting to discourage any thoughts of stopping him, Holloway fired several blasts from the shotgun at the glass-enclosed security pod; the sound of the gunfire was deafening inside the building as the sheets of safety glass exploded into thousands of sharp little pieces that flew through the lobby.

As soon as the shooting erupted and glass started exploding, the people in the lobby began screaming and running en masse for the exits. In the confusion, Holloway raced to the nearest open elevator, an express elevator, and headed toward the upper floors of the building, where the workers were not yet aware that anything was wrong.

It was raining in Sacramento at 10:00 A.M. on that Friday, but the employees of the Communications Center of the Sacramento Police Department didn't have time to think about the weather. Hundreds of calls about a madman shooting up the State Board of Equalization Building down on N Street suddenly deluged the center. During some of the calls, dispatchers could hear the sounds of gunfire and screaming in the background.

The call for officers to respond to the shooting quickly went out, both to the Sacramento Police Department SWAT team and to the main police station just a dozen blocks north of the State Board of Equalization Building. Officers began responding immediately, but as the first police arrived they were confronted by a scene of mass panic. All of the building's 2,300 workers seemed to be trying to get out at the same time, hundreds of employees screaming as they shoved their way out of the building. And even worse, cars racing to get out of the area jammed the streets and delayed many of the regular police and SWAT team members from getting to the building.

Finally, the first uniformed officers at the scene were able to get into the building and question several of the panicky employees, finding that the man who had shot up the lobby had apparently got off the elevator on the eighteenth floor and was now holding a large number of employees hostage there. When the first three SWAT officers managed to get through the traffic jam and arrive at the scene, they made certain that the area was secured and contained as well as it could be; they then rode up to the eighteenth floor and began the next step in any SWAT incident, a very quiet, careful reconnaissance. It didn't take long for them to locate the man they were looking for. They found him sitting in a hallway of the huge, almost mazelike architecture of work cubicles, surrounded by hostages.

Quietly slipping in around the cubicles, two of the SWAT officers began covertly evacuating some of the hostages who were farthest away from the man, while the third SWAT member, the team leader, contacted police headquarters and gave a quick account of the situation. Within a few minutes, another SWAT officer arrived on the eighteenth floor, while below, newly arriving officers began covering all exits to prevent the hostage taker's escape.

Interestingly, the SWAT officers noticed, the hostage taker, while heavily armed, and from the extensive damage he had done so far to the building—obviously not adverse to using his weapons—now seemed very casual and almost nonchalant, not appearing to notice when the hostages began slowly sliding away from him, finally leaving him standing alone in the hallway that ran between the work cubicles. The SWAT officers realized that they might never get a better opportunity. After a telephone call by the team leader to advise police headquarters of what they were going to do, as well as a quick strategy meeting among the SWAT members, the officers circled around and took positions of cover near Holloway. Then, when everyone was ready, the team leader called out to him: "Police Department! Drop your weapon and put your hands in the air!"

Holloway, however, rather than surrendering, spun the shotgun he carried around toward the voice of the team leader, his face contorted into an expression of intense anger and hatred. The SWAT officer who was positioned for the best shot, and who had been designated as the first shooter, followed the plan, took aim, and squeezed the trigger of his automatic weapon. However, in events such as this, things do not always go as planned, and the weapon malfunctioned. For a moment, nothing happened as the team leader dove for cover and everyone else waited. Finally, the other SWAT officers began firing, hitting Holloway twelve times. None of the shots were fatal, however, and Holloway gave no indication of wanting to surrender. Instead, he stumbled down the hallway and, once out of view of the officers, ducked into a small work cubicle.

Advancing in a coordinated, flanking movement, yet unsure which cubicle Holloway had run into, the SWAT officers began carefully searching the work areas, finding employees hiding in several of them. The SWAT officers continued the cautious search until finally they heard Holloway begin shouting: "I'm going to kill them all!"

Now aware of the hostage taker's location, the nearest SWAT officer, his automatic weapon set on three-round-burst mode, peeked into the cubicle where the shouting had come from. He found Holloway lying on the floor facing away from him, his shotgun aimed toward the area where the SWAT team leader had been a few moments earlier. A hostage sat at Holloway's feet, hands raised and trembling.

"Drop your weapon and don't move!" the SWAT officer ordered as he stepped into the cubicle and aimed his weapon at Holloway.

Holloway again refused to surrender and instead attempted to swivel around and get up into a sitting position, while bringing the shotgun around toward the SWAT officer. The officer fired three bursts, killing Holloway, the only fatality during the incident.

The police later discovered through the video monitoring system that Holloway had apparently already gained access to the building at around 7:30 A.M. that morning, and that he had been in the building for at least an hour and a half. Although it is unknown exactly what he was doing during this time, investigators believe he was performing a reconnaissance, looking for the work locations of the fifteen people whose names he had on his list. It is also unknown why he left the building and then tried to return at 9:30 A.M., but it may have been to check some records or information in his van, since he hadn't found any of the people on his list. While Holloway had apparently planned for a long time what he was going to do that day and had been seen by the security guards scouting the building during the previous week, he had targeted the wrong building. None of the fifteen people on his list worked at the California State Board of Equalization Building.

The selection of individuals to become police officers is not a perfect system, as the case of James Ray Holloway clearly demonstrates. Holloway worked twice as an officer, even though he had serious drinking and discipline problems. A number of people like Holloway become police officers every year but quickly find they cannot handle the job. Law enforcement is not a job that just anyone can do well, and that few can do very well. It takes a special type of individual to be able to handle the immense power and authority that goes with the position, particularly when dealing with disagreeable, disgruntled, or just plain hostile people. It takes a special kind of person to be able to do the job very well and still make the public happy.

It's true that many people could handle the job of a police officer if they had to deal only with polite, nice citizens who treated them with respect. However, police officers find that this is seldom the case. Instead, an officer's patience and professionalism are almost daily pushed to the limit because most of the people the police have to deal with are angry, upset, or hostile. While they are often not upset at the police, they still feel the need to take their anger out on someone, and the police are there. Still, these people must be dealt with professionally by the police, and that takes a special type of person.

While police department personnel units try their best to weed out individuals who are unfit to be police officers, who cannot deal with hostility, or who have other serious personality problems, every year people like Holloway still manage to slip through. Even conducting thorough background checks, having intensive psychological exams, and holding tough oral interviews cannot catch all of the unfit people because many of them don't show their unfitness until they're on the job.

Anyone who has worked in a police department personnel unit (as I did) will testify that the job of a law enforcement officer, because of its status and power, attracts not just people with a desire for public service, but also a lot of people who suffer from personality inadequacies. These people hope that, if they don the uniform of a police officer, they will be seen as powerful and will consequently be treated with more respect. However, they find soon after joining a police department that not everyone respects the uniform, that not everyone is impressed by their power and authority. Every run becomes a challenge to the power of these new officers with personality inadequacies. Sergeants and lieutenants quickly discover who these officers are because they are constantly involved in confrontations with citizens, and they soon begin piling up large numbers of disorderly-conduct and resisting-arrest cases.

When I was in charge of the personnel branch of the Indianapolis Police Department, we went to great lengths to keep these kinds of people out of the police department. We knew they would give us nothing but grief. Still, some slipped through.

And so, if these people can cause problems for law enforcement in a regular police officer's position, imagine what they could do with the enhanced power that comes with being on a SWAT team. It is for this reason that SWAT teams have stringent entry requirements, much more stringent than a police department's general entry requirements.

"We always look at the SWAT applicant's service record," said Indianapolis Police Department SWAT Commander, Captain Dennis Hawkins. "We don't want any disciplinary problems."

This is vitally important because a SWAT officer carries and uses weapons much more destructive than the average police officer carries and uses, and while the average officer only very occasionally becomes involved in an incident where taking a life is a possibility, most SWAT call-outs involve this possibility. Every SWAT team commander knows that, if an officer does manage to become a SWAT team member and yet is unfit to be one, his presence is likely to do tremendous damage to the SWAT team and to the police department, both in lives lost and in reputations damaged.

A person has only to consider what James Ray Holloway was able to accomplish with just his training and experience as a regular police officer. It could have been much worse, and very likely more deadly, particularly for the officers attempting to apprehend him, if he had had the training and experience of a SWAT officer. Regardless, he was still able to rather easily get by a strong security setup. Sacramento Deputy Police Chief Fred Arthur is quoted as saying, "Quite frankly, he had the wherewithal to take the whole building hostage" (Former CHP officer, 1993, p. 58).

Police departments know they must keep unqualified officers like Holloway off of SWAT teams. Since SWAT team members are so often involved in life-and-death situations and always carry high-destruction weaponry, only the very best officers, only those with the most self-discipline, only those with the coolest heads, and only those officers who are able to work well with others can make the team a successful, smoothly operating unit. A police SWAT team will not succeed if it has officers who are discipline problems or hotheads, and it will not succeed if it has officers who are not able to function well with the other team members. Police departments have therefore set up strict guidelines for evaluating officers who apply to become SWAT team members.

While conducting research for this book, I was able to obtain the entry requirements for over thirty municipal and state police department SWAT teams and found that most look for the same qualities and attributes. The first and most important attribute they all look for, and the one that might keep even an outstanding regular police officer from becoming a good SWAT officer, is the ability to function as a team member. Being part of a strongly disciplined team is difficult for many police officers, especially good police officers, because most police work, by its nature, requires an officer to think and act independently, with little. supervision by or coordination with other officers. Most police officers work as a one-person unit. But this simply can't work on a SWAT team. On a police SWAT team, the members' lives often depend on the officers' looking out for each other as the team takes a coordinated action. To be effective and to keep casualties to a minimum, police SWAT teams must work with strict, disciplined coordination. There is absolutely no room on a police SWAT team for a "hotdog," which is police jargon for an officer who likes to go crashing into incidents like a bulldozer, seldom with any plan and usually without waiting for backup or assistance.

"There is no 'I' in the word *team*," said Sergeant Robert Givan, a long-time member and training officer of the Indianapolis Police Department SWAT team. "I know this saying is not original with me, but it's the essence of what makes a good SWAT officer."

Robert P. Chappel, in his book *S.W.A.T. Team Manual* (1979), agrees when he says, "There can be no individual on a SWAT team" (p. 3).

John A. Kolman, retired captain from the Los Angeles County Sheriff's Department, and for many years editor of the SWAT magazine, *The Tactical Edge*, says in his book *A Guide To The Development of Special Weapons and Tactics Teams* (1982), "Teamwork and discipline are the very essence of SWAT team success. There is no room for the glory seeker or egotist on a professional SWAT team" (p. 27).

Also, it should almost go without saying that all members of a police SWAT team, along with being able to function within a team environment, should be volunteers. While police work on its own is inherently dangerous, SWAT work is much more dangerous, so everyone on the team expects all the members to look out for each other. No SWAT officer would relish the thought that the officer who is supposed to be looking out for him or her really doesn't want to be there or to take part in the team operation. Fortunately, I've never heard of a police department that has a shortage of officers applying for SWAT.

And yet, while a SWAT team member must always be ready to work in coordination with other team members and carry out any plans or functions decided by the SWAT team leader, often the unexpected event occurs, the unexpected event that changes everything and throws the original plan into disarray. So, along with the ability to function as a team member, another important attribute needed in candidates for SWAT positions is above-average intelligence. SWAT requires a person who can see a situation, quickly review all of the possible alternatives, and then come to a sound decision about what must be done, and who must be able to do all of this while under tremendous stress. SWAT officers many times encounter incidents that are beyond the experience of most regular police officers, and therefore, they are not able to fall back on past experience. For this reason, most SWAT commanders want intelligent officers who can make good, solid decisions in unusual situations. Intelligence, however, should not be confused with education. Many highly educated individuals cannot make good decisions under stress, particularly the high stress experienced during a SWAT confrontation.

Along with above-average intelligence, SWAT commanders also want officers on the SWAT team who are emotionally stable.

Most SWAT incidents involve confrontations with individuals who have little or no respect for others, who are usually in a very excitable state, and whose emotions are on a roller-coaster. To deal effectively with these situations, an officer must have his or her own emotions under control. Otherwise, the SWAT commander will have two hotheads shooting at each other. Also, hostage takers occasionally do terribly inhumane things to their hostages, and a SWAT officer must be able to deal emotionally with this. No SWAT commander wants an officer who is so emotional that he or she is always heavy-handed with suspects and always seems to have to fight with them. In addition, an officer who does not have control of his or her emotions will often want to rush into an incident without thinking and evaluating the situation.

"You can use various scenarios to pressure SWAT applicants into showing how they will really respond under stress," said Cal Black, former FBI SWAT team commander and now security manager for the National Bank of Detroit, in a telephone interview (January 24, 1995). "This can really help weed out those you don't want." To do this, SWAT training officers often re-create real-life SWAT situations to see how well the SWAT applicants can function under stress. Some police departments, in order to make the scenarios more lifelike and stressful, even go so far as to recruit actors from local theater groups to play parts in these real-life SWAT scenarios. The SWAT team applicants are then confronted with these scenarios and must demonstrate not necessarily an in-depth knowledge of SWAT operations, since they are not yet trained SWAT officers, but a cool head and the ability to function and think well under high stress.

Besides being team players, emotionally stable, and above average in intelligence, SWAT team members are also expected to be physically fit. But this doesn't mean just being healthy, though a number of police departments do require a medical examination before accepting new members on the SWAT team. Most police departments also want prospective SWAT officers to display considerable upper body strength and stamina, and many have torturous physical agility courses to test these. This requirement is justified by the often demonstrated need for SWAT officers to rappel down building sides, climb many flights of stairs at full speed, carry heavy loads (such as bodies), and wrestle and subdue combative suspects. This requirement has kept most female police officers from applying for or being accepted onto police SWAT teams, but not completely. There are teams that do have female members, and Lieutenant Kathleen Brennan of the Pima County (Arizona) Sheriff's Department became in 1989 one of the first women in the United States to be named the head of a police SWAT team.

Nearly as important as physical strength and stamina in a prospective SWAT officer is the ability to fire a weapon, almost any weapon, accurately, and to be able to do this while running, while under high stress, and in close quarters. SWAT officers must be able to rush into a room, assess who is the perpetrator and who is the hostage, shoot the correct person if the need arises, and be able to do all of this without being shot themselves. In addition, SWAT officers must be able to shoot accurately with innocent people standing close to the perpetrator.

All of these attributes—teamwork, emotional stability, above-average intelligence, physical strength, and shooting ability—have been found through experience to be crucial to the success of SWAT officers. To be able to effectively assess these qualities in candidates, various police departments have developed different mechanisms. I have reviewed the SWAT selection criteria of over thirty police departments, and I have found that almost all have some type of physical fitness exam, usually in the form of a physical agility course. Most also demand that the candidates display firearms proficiency, and most have officers appear before an oral interview board. About half of the police departments conduct in-depth background investigations into the officer's disciplinary record and past performance, wanting to weed out hotheads and poor performers. Several of the police departments also require a psychological exam, some require a written test, and one even demands that all SWAT officers be nonsmokers. Five of the police departments, apparently in pursuit of a cohesive team, require that successful candidates receive a unanimous vote of approval from the present SWAT team members. A number of police departments, in order to create stress and anxiety, keep the nature of their selection process confidential. As a result, the evaluators can see how well the candidates function under the stress of not knowing what to expect, something that happens often in SWAT incidents.

But more important than all of these selection processes and procedures is the necessity that the SWAT team selection be honest, objective, and fair. The process, if it is to attract only the best candidates, must reflect the spirit of the team and inspire confidence in those who undertake it.

In his book *SWAT* (1979), Phillip L. Davidson of the Metropolitan Police Department of Nashville–Davidson County, Tennessee, says, "If a team is selected on the basis of personality, cronyism, or because they are 'good ole boys' the results will be disastrous. If there is ... a favorite fair-haired son, or an incompetent to put up with on the team, morale will disintegrate and efficiency will cease" (p. 5).

While all of the attributes and qualities discussed above are vital for the basic SWAT officer, there are also a number of specialty positions within a SWAT team that require even more stringent qualifications. For example, on every police SWAT team, there are officers who are designated as snipers. These officers rarely take part in the physical storming of a site (with the exception of laying down covering fire for the advancing officers). They are instead usually set up close to the incident scene with high-powered rifles and binoculars. And until the word comes down for them to neutralize (SWAT jargon for making an adversary incapable of aggressive action) the suspect, they act simply as intelligence gatherers who report back to the incident commander everything they see happening at the SWAT incident site.

Being a sniper requires tremendous discipline because the officer must often spend hours lying in cramped positions in uncomfortable locations, simply waiting and watching. Many times, snipers have the opportunity to shoot the suspect and end the incident, but they usually cannot shoot until they receive permission from the SWAT incident commander. When the order to shoot does come down, often because the suspect is harming or is about to harm the hostages, the sniper must be able to stop the suspect with one shot. And the sniper must be able to do all of this at a moment's notice, many times after lying in an uncomfortable position for several hours.

Another specialty position at a SWAT incident is that of hostage negotiator. Hostage negotiators (sometimes called *crisis negotiators*) are the officers who make verbal contact with the perpetrator at a SWAT incident and attempt to convince him or her that a peaceful surrender is in his or her best interests. Negotiators may or may not, depending on the police department, be part of the SWAT team. In some police departments, they have a separate unit of their own. Some police departments, though, require that their hostage negotiators train with the regular SWAT officers so the negotiators will understand the tactical side of SWAT. Then, in the event that a tactical resolution is decided on, the hostage negotiators will be aware of what they need to do in order to make the tactical assault successful, such as distracting the suspect, drawing him or her to a particular area of the site, or being able to identify what part of the site he or she is in. The qualities and attributes necessary for successful hostage negotiators, however, are very different from those for regular SWAT officers, and I will discuss these in more depth in the chapter on hostage incidents.

In addition to snipers and negotiators, there are a number of other positions on a police SWAT team, such as the point officer and the rear guard, who provide front and rear security for advancing SWAT officers; the cover officer, who provides covering fire during an operation; and the gas officer, who is responsible for the use of chemical weapons. However, the positions of point officer, rear guard, cover officer, and gas officer are usually considered interchangeable, as all SWAT officers are trained to perform them, and so the selection process for these is the same as for a regular SWAT officer.

Another crucial consideration, in addition to the careful process for the selection of SWAT officers, is the recognition that some officers who have been on a SWAT team for a long time may eventually become unfit to continue in the position. While this can also be true of regular police officers because their job is highly stressful, SWAT officers' jobs are even more so. SWAT officers more often face situations in which they may be killed, they may have to kill someone, or they may have to witness innocent people being killed. All of this causes stress and anxiety, which, over time, may adversely affect a SWAT officer's performance.

To deal with this, most police departments have debriefing sessions after SWAT incidents, and many have their department psychologist attend these in order to look for any signs of unresolved stress as the officers recall what happened during the incident and what they had to do. Usually, if the psychologist sees any signs of stress effects, or if the team leader sees any signs at other times, an appointment is made for the SWAT officer to see the department psychologist. The psychologist then determines if the officer is suffering from any long-term stress effects that could impair his or her performance as a SWAT team member and police officer.

The signs of stress effects that SWAT team leaders look for include avoiding other SWAT team members when not on a call, finding fault in everything the team does, skipping training, and showing irritation at being called out, as well as increased health problems that relate to stress and domestic problems. Of course, any of these symptoms may have causes other than SWAT team burnout or stress, but they should still make a SWAT team leader cautious and observant of the officer. A police SWAT team is much too dangerous a place for a person who no longer wants to be there, but who stays anyway because he or she doesn't want to look like a quitter.

In the last thirty years, all large and many medium-sized cities in the United States have formed police SWAT teams. Most of these teams have proved their worth time and time again by their ability to save lives and resolve high-risk situations peacefully. However, the worth of any police SWAT team depends almost totally on the caliber of the officers that make it up. Crucial to the continued success of these police SWAT teams, therefore, is their ability to continue to attract and recruit only the very best officers, with the necessary traits to be good SWAT officers. This can only happen by continuing the careful and diligent screening of SWAT applicants.

Snipers

At around 2:15 on the morning of September 15, 1992, the lobby of the Gateway Tower II apartments in Chattanooga, Tennessee, sat quiet and still. The building, a high-rise housing mostly elderly people and individuals on disability incomes, seldom saw any of its tenants up at this hour. The night watchman, an eighty-year-old man who lived in the apartment building and worked as the night watchman in order to supplement his income, had spent many quiet, peaceful nights sitting alone in the lobby. Tonight, however, would not be one of those nights.

Suddenly, the elevator door opened, and a man the night watchman recognized as a resident of the building stepped out and walked across the lobby. It wasn't until the man got close to where he was sitting that the night watchman noticed the man carried a blue-steel revolver in one hand and a police scanner and a package in the other. Pointing the revolver at him, the man ordered the night watchman to get up, then ushered him into a room just off the lobby, where there was a telephone. The gunman, later discovered by the police to be a diagnosed paranoid schizophrenic who had recently been refusing to take his medicine, had a long history of mental illness.

"I want you to call the police and tell them that I'm holding you hostage here," the man told the night watchman as he pointed the revolver at him. "And you tell them that I've got a bomb, and that I'm not afraid to use it!" (Williams, 1993, pp. 32–33).

With trembling hands, the night watchman, who had heart and respiratory problems, made a 911 call and told the police dispatcher exactly what the man with the gun told him to say. When the night watchman hung up, the gunman, apparently satisfied that the police were on the way, turned on the police scanner, which had been set to pick up the Chattanooga Police Department's frequency. As the two men waited for the police to arrive, the gunman told the hostage, "You'd better start praying because I'm going to start killing people soon, and this is as good a place as any to start."

Seconds after the elderly night watchman called 911 and told the police dispatcher that he was being held hostage, the dispatcher sent uniformed police officers to verify the call. The uniformed officers, who arrived on the scene within minutes, at first saw only an empty lobby, but then, the armed hostage taker and the hostage stepped out of the room off the lobby for a few moments, and the officers realized they had a serious situation developing. After calling back in on the radio and telling the dispatcher what they had found, the uniformed officers set up an inner and outer perimeter around the incident site and then waited for the SWAT team.

As the SWAT officers arrived, they began replacing the uniformed officers on the inner perimeter, which is the perimeter that encloses the area of greatest danger around any SWAT incident. The uniformed officers then continued to maintain the outer perimeter, which is the perimeter beyond which danger is minimal. When the SWAT incident commander arrived soon afterward, he set up the command post in a nearby firehouse and then began considering how to position his snipers, who would act first as observers and information gatherers, and then possibly as a means of neutralizing the threat in the event it became necessary. There were only two entry points on the first floor of the apartment building that the SWAT team found, both with good fields of fire, and so snipers were set up to cover both of these. Reconnaissance scouts soon reported back to the command post that both entry points on the first floor were locked and that there were several emergency exit doors that could be opened only from the inside. The command post had police cars block these exits to keep the hostage taker from escaping.

The command post, as it began formulating an emergency rescue plan, found through information gathered on the incident that the hostage was both elderly and had serious health problems. The SWAT incident commander and others formulating the rescue plan realized that this information and the fact that most of the residents of the building were either elderly or had serious health problems precluded the use of any chemical weapons. The emergency rescue plan decided on, therefore, would have the SWAT team access the building through windows on the second floor. They would immediately secure the elevators and stairways so that the hostage taker could not go up, nor the residents go down during the rescue attempt. A team would then storm the first floor and rescue the hostage.

In an attempt to bring about a peaceful settlement if at all possible but, if not possible, at least to buy time so that a more detailed rescue plan could be developed, the hostage negotiators went to work immediately, but with little result. They made initial contact with the hostage taker by telephone, but soon afterward, he dropped the telephone and then left it lying off the hook. When the negotiators found they could no longer use the telephone, they walked to the northwest corner of the building and, using a bullhorn, tried to establish contact again with the hostage taker. During this time, explosive ordnance experts rigged up explosives on the south side of the building, explosives that would blow out a large plate glass window in the event an emergency entry into the building was needed.

During the first two hours of the incident, the hostage negotiators had almost no contact with the hostage taker. At a little after 5:00 A.M., the hostage negotiators called out to the hostage taker on the bullhorn, asking him to come out and talk with them. Soon afterward, the gunman, holding the hostage in front of him, stepped out of the room he had been keeping the hostage in and walked through the apartment building's lobby. Still using the hostage as a shield, the hostage taker exited the building through the north doors, his arms wrapped around the hostage. In his right hand, he still held the revolver and, in his left hand, the package he claimed was a bomb.

"Drop your weapon!" the hostage negotiator called out over the bullhorn.

"You didn't keep your promise!" the hostage taker shouted back, the statement's meaning known only to him. Finally, he obeyed the police order and dropped the revolver and continued a few steps forward with the hostage. The hostage taker stopped, however, when he saw several police officers coming toward him. He let go of the hostage and turned around and picked up the revolver, pointing it at the police, who scurried for cover. He then grabbed the hostage again and pointed the revolver at the elderly man's head.

The hostage taker never got the chance to shoot. A sniper positioned to watch the north side of the building had him in his sights. The sniper could see that the revolver was cocked and that the hostage taker had his finger on the trigger. The hostage taker appeared agitated and was trembling, and the sniper knew it didn't take much of a pull to make a cocked revolver fire. Sighting on the hostage taker's head, the sniper squeezed off a round that entered the hostage taker's right ear canal and destroyed his brain stem. Because of the point of the bullet's impact, all motor activity in the hostage taker's body ceased, including movement in the finger he had on the trigger. He instantly fell to the ground dead. The hostage, though terrified and shaking uncontrollably, had been unharmed.

Snipers armed with high-powered rifles and telescopic sights are an integral part of any police SWAT team. Besides saving lives with carefully aimed and placed shots, as was done in the above incident, snipers also perform many other vital tasks. One crucial part they play happens once the decision is made to mount a tactical assault on a SWAT incident site. The assault-and-rescue team must be able to approach and gain entry into the site without being picked off by the suspects inside. Snipers are used to make this possible. Snipers can create diversions with gunfire that allow a SWAT assault-and-rescue team to gain safe entry into an incident site. This is done either by shooting from the side opposite the one from which the assault will take place, to divert the suspect's attention away from the side the assault is actually coming from, or by the snipers laying down a heavy line of fire that forces the suspects to take cover, allowing the SWAT assault-and-rescue team to gain access to the site during the firing. Snipers also monitor a SWAT assault-and-rescue team's progress as the team storms an incident site, watching from their vantage point for any dangers that the team may be unaware of. Usually, as an assault-and-rescue team is approaching an incident site, the SWAT officers listen over the radio to the snipers' comments about what they see. Snipers must also protect emergency medical and fire service personnel who need to go into the SWAT incident area.

But often, and just as important as using their firearms, snipers are used as observers and information gatherers, since they usually have an excellent view of the incident scene and have access to sight enhancers such as binoculars and night vision devices. Binoculars in particular are needed because, although a sniper has to get close enough to a site to observe, he doesn't want to get so close that he can be seen by the perpetrator and consequently ambushed. Snipers must observe without being observed. They therefore must know how to blend into the background and camouflage themselves (see photo on page 40). For maximum coverage at any SWAT incident site, the SWAT commander, if possible, sets up at least two snipers in two different positions. This strategy not only gives two chances for a clear shot if needed but also gives two views for information gathering. Snipers usually, but not always, are put onto high ground somewhere near the SWAT incident scene, which gives them a better field of view for shooting, for covering the SWAT assault-and-rescue team, and especially for gathering information.

Sniper camouflage suit (photo by Lieutenant Stephen Robertson).

"A sniper can collect enormous amounts of really good data and can give us ongoing information about what's happening at the site," said Lieutenant Larry Beadles, commander of the Richmond (Virginia) Police Department's SWAT team, in a telephone interview (January 24, 1995). "A good sniper can also tell us about the building's construction, what kind of locks it has, the best way in, and other information our tactical people need."

What types of information are snipers looking for when they observe a SWAT incident site? They are looking for any information that will assist the tactical planners at the command post. They observe and report on such things as the number of suspects they see at the site, their description, their locations, and what weapons they are carrying. They also report on the number of hostages, their description, and where they are located. From their positions, snipers can also often provide information on the suspect's stronghold, such as the best possible entry points into it, and any dangers the assault-and-rescue team will face during its approach, particularly any items that will delay the team from quickly gaining access to the incident site. These delays include vehicles purposely parked so as to block an entrance, cement blocks piled in front of doors, steps purposely removed, or obstructions placed on a stairway. This information is vital because the longer it takes for the assault-and-rescue team to gain entry into an incident site, the longer they are exposed to possible gunfire from those barricaded inside or nearby. Snipers also look for and warn the SWAT assault-and-rescue team of any possible booby traps around an incident site. These include trip wires that, when activated by being walked into, set off explosives or firearms, or pits dug on the approach route and camouflaged. These are often more easily seen from a high vantage point than they are from the ground.

But as important as this information is to providing a solution to an incident, the snipers themselves are often the solution. As in the incident in Chattanooga above, snipers many times resolve a life-threatening problem and do it without having to expose themselves or other police officers to the dangers inherent in a site assault. But to do so, snipers must have "cold shot accuracy." This means that they must be able to hit and incapacitate a target with the first shot, or what is known as a *cold shot*. This incapacitation must be done with the first shot because there will often not be time for a second, and because, even if there is time, during the first and second shot a suspect can easily kill a hostage or other innocent person. The sniper must be able to stop *with certainty* the life-threatening activity of suspects before they have a chance to carry out their intentions. This can be done only by an officer who has spent many hours at the firing range perfecting his or her marksmanship. SWAT snipers must practice until they can hit exactly where they aim on the very first shot and can do this after hours of sitting or lying in a cramped position waiting for the order to shoot. It is for this reason that being a sniper on a police SWAT team takes an exceptional individual who not only has tremendous self-discipline but is also willing to put in many extra hours in order to perfect his or her shooting skill.

However, a number of dangers are inherent in having a

sniper shoot a suspect who is threatening someone, particularly if the suspect has a finger on the trigger and the gun aimed at the person. In the case in Chattanooga described above, for example, a slight jerk when the hostage taker was shot would very likely have caused the revolver to fire. There is also the very real danger that, if the hostage and hostage taker are moving quickly or perhaps struggling, the sniper will accidently hit the hostage rather than the hostage taker, which unfortunately has happened. But snipers are almost always given the order to fire only when a situation has reached the point where an innocent person's life is in imminent danger, and so the risk must be taken.

What a sniper must do to end these kinds of situations safely is to bring about not just rapid, but instant, incapacitation of the threatening person. And not just any shot will do this. For example, shots that cause severe and rapid blood loss (a hit somewhere in the human vascular system) will usually cause unconsciousness within ten to fifteen seconds. But much can happen in that ten to fifteen seconds. The suspect can shoot and kill a half dozen people during this time. All hunters know of cases in which animals have run fifty yards or more after having been shot directly through the heart.

But in certain instances the threatening person has left the police no choice. If the police don't do something immediately, an innocent person is going to die. And so, even though snipers shoot only as a last resort, they must be ready to take an action if it is necessary to save a life, and often this means they must produce instant incapacitation. Snipers know that the proper placement of a shot that will produce instant incapacitation and will not cause a jerking reflex is a shot, from the back, in the spine just above the shoulder blades. This is where the brain stem, or medulla oblongata, is located. A shot here will drop a person without a quiver. From the side, this shot must be at just about the ear canal, while from the front, the shot needs to be between the nose and upper lip. I realize this all sounds very cold and inhuman, and that some people feel very uncomfortable about killing a person who has only threatened to kill but has not yet killed anyone, as in the

Chattanooga case above. The police, however, cannot wait until someone is killed before they do something. Sometimes, saving a life calls for the use of deadly force.

Over a decade ago, the U.S. Supreme Court, in the case of *Garner v. Tennessee*, severely restricted the instances in which police officers can use deadly force. While at one time the police in many states could use deadly force to stop any felon, this is no longer the case. Now suspects must present a real and imminent threat to the lives of others before the police can use deadly force to stop them. The *Garner v. Tennessee* decision, however, did not have much effect on incidents involving police SWAT teams. The perpetrators in these cases have usually already demonstrated that they are a serious risk to innocent people, and they are usually about to kill or seriously injure someone when the order is given for a SWAT sniper to fire. In these instances, the police really have no choice. They simply can't wait until the perpetrators actually kill someone before responding. The police have an obligation to save the lives of innocent people, and often, they must do this by lethal methods. And if, in stopping a person from killing or seriously injuring someone else, the police can do it with a shot placement that prevents any threat to innocent people nearby, as discussed above, shouldn't the police do that? Most people would answer yes (see photo on page 44).

"To have to use a sniper is always a last resort," said former FBI SWAT commander Cal Black. "Snipers shoot to kill, and SWAT is meant to save lives."

But moral considerations aside, even when a sniper is given the go-ahead for a shot, physical variables can affect the good shot placement needed. Gravity acts on the bullet to pull it down, air resistance slows the bullet's forward speed and power, and wind can move the bullet to either side. But these problems can be easily overcome by well-trained snipers who know how to compensate for them. A bigger problem presents itself when a bullet must be fired through some barrier, such as glass. Light-weight bullets, such as the .223 caliber used in some assault rifles, will often disintegrate on striking glass. This is why a survey of fifty-three

SWAT sniper using a .308 Remington 700 Action in McMillan stock (photo by Robert L. Snow).

police SWAT teams (Survey results 1994, 58) found that the majority favored .308-caliber ammunition for their sniper rifles. A .308-caliber bullet will penetrate glass and still have enough power to kill. The Remington 700 rifle and the Leupold telescopic sight, because of their high accuracy and reliability, were also favored by a majority of the SWAT teams.

However, when a bullet, such as a .308-caliber, has enough power to penetrate glass, this also presents problems. It has been found that, when bullets penetrate glass at an angle, they are deflected at an angle on the other side of the glass, so precise shot placement is very difficult. For this reason, SWAT snipers try to shoot as close as possible to perpendicular when firing through glass. If a bullet must be fired at an angle, the *cold shot* rule is broken, and snipers fire two bullets in rapid succession, the first to break the glass and the second to hit the target.

Shooting through glass also presents a problem called *spalling*. Spalling is a cone-shaped explosion of glass shards and particles that follows the bullet's path after it penetrates glass. These "secondary missiles" can cause serious injury or even death to hostages or other innocent people standing close to the glass being shot through.

But regardless of these dangers or problems, there often comes a time when a well-placed shot from a sniper is the only alternative, and the command to shoot is given (in most police SWAT teams, snipers can shoot without permission only if they see that a life is in imminent danger). The command for a sniper to shoot, incidentally, is usually given over the radio in code so that anyone listening in on a police scanner, such as the news media or the perpetrator, won't know in advance what is going to happen. To be effective, a sniper's shot should be unexpected, and, as shown in the following incidents, these shots can often save lives.

In Lupton, Arizona, state police officers forced a car containing a man and a woman he had abducted from California to the side of the road. Earlier, the suspect had been seen driving on Interstate 40 holding a gun up to the woman's head. The man, however, refused to come out of the car and also refused to let the woman out. Instead, he simply sat in the car with the gun to the woman's head. When negotiations failed, and the police felt certain that the man would kill the woman before giving up, the SWAT incident commander gave a police sniper the "green light" to shoot. The sniper had a clear view through the car's rear window and fired one shot, killing the man. The woman suffered only minor cuts from flying glass.

In Alhambra, California, a young man stormed into an office supply company, confronted the employees with a semiautomatic pistol, and demanded that they open the safe. As the manager led the gunman to the store safe, one of the employees slipped out the front door and called the police. Finding the safe empty, the suspect ran from the store but then stopped when he saw the police pulling into the parking lot. Racing back into the store, the gunman took the store manager hostage and attempted to escape using the manager as a shield. The police, however, blocked his route from the parking lot.

For the next hour, the police attempted to negotiate the gunman's surrender. During the negotiations, however, the gunman held the pistol up to the hostage's head, making numerous threats to kill him. It was later found that the gun contained special rounds that explode on impact. These rounds are designed to do devastating and lethal damage to human tissue. Without a doubt, if he had been shot in the head, the manager would have died. After an hour, with the negotiations going nowhere, the gunman suddenly cocked the hammer of the pistol. Believing he was preparing to kill the hostage, a sniper fired one shot, killing the gunman instantly. The hostage escaped unharmed.

In an apartment in Washington, D.C., a man shot a woman to death, stabbed a man, and then took another woman hostage. The police, responding to the murder, pursued the man and his hostage as they sped away from the apartment in a yellow van. The hostage taker crashed the van but then commandeered a car at gunpoint, forced the hostage inside, and sped off again. He also finally crashed this car. Several times during the pursuit, the man fired a gun out the window at the police. At the final crash scene, the police attempted to persuade the man to surrender, but without success. The hostage, the police noticed, appeared to be seriously injured and was drifting in and out of consciousness. Realizing that the hostage needed immediate medical attention, the incident commander gave the go-ahead to a sniper, who then shot and killed the man. The police rushed the hostage to the hospital in time to save her life.

Late one evening in Albuquerque, New Mexico, a man, after beating up his live-in girlfriend, snatched their eleven-month-old daughter and drove off. Later, he crashed into a police vehicle near a bridge over the Rio Grande. The man then got out of his car with the baby and ran out onto the bridge. As the police converged on him, he dangled his baby over the edge of the bridge and threatened to drop her; he later clutched her to him as he leaned over the bridge railing, screaming that he was going to jump off of the bridge and kill them both. Several police officers ran down under the bridge with a blanket, hoping to catch the child if he dropped her.

For a half hour, the police tried unsuccessfully to talk the man into giving them the baby, but he refused and continued threatening to kill her. Suddenly, he began moving away from the police and toward a darkened section of the bridge, toward an area where the police would not be able to see what he was doing. Since he had already placed the baby in extreme danger with no apparent thought about the consequences, the police could not allow him to move away from where they could control or at least see and try to respond to what he was doing. The baby's life was their responsibility. A police sniper shot and killed him. The police then returned the baby, unharmed, to her mother.

While some readers might wonder why the police couldn't have perhaps just rushed the man or maybe simply had the sniper wound him, these are both completely unacceptable options. If the police had rushed him, it would have taken at least several seconds to reach and overpower him, and he could easily have jumped off the bridge with the baby or tossed the baby off the bridge during this time. And shooting to wound, as discussed earlier, is extremely risky. Even mortally wounded individuals are capable of amazing feats. If the police had wounded him, the man could easily have jumped off the bridge with the baby or tossed the baby off before the police could do anything. And for those who might think that no parent would purposely toss his or her own child off a bridge, I have only to mention the Susan Smith case in Union, South Carolina—the mother who pushed her car into a lake with her two young children still strapped inside. Parents killing their own children, while certainly horrible and repulsive, is not that uncommon at all.

A final incident demonstrates how using a SWAT sniper is occasionally the only viable tactic a SWAT commander has. In the following incident, the use of a sniper ended one of America's worst mass-murder sprees. The use of a SWAT sniper in this incident very likely saved many lives.

On July 18, 1984, everything seemed to be fine with forty-one-year-old James Huberty. Although described by his neighbors as unfriendly, brooding, hotheaded, and always angry at someone, Huberty had on this day taken his wife and two daughters to the San Diego Zoo, and then for lunch at the McDonald's in Claremont Mesa. While Huberty had acted that day as if he didn't like anyone, this was normal behavior for him, and so everything seemed fine. However, at around 4:00 P.M., carrying a bag, he left his apartment in San Ysidro, California, a small community just south of San Diego. When his wife asked him where he was going, he told her, "I'm going to hunt humans." She said that at the time she didn't know what he meant (Price, 1984, p. 1).

Something, however, obviously brooded and festered inside Huberty. Earlier in the year, he and his family had moved to California from Ohio after he lost his job when the Babcock and Wilcox power generating plant in Canton, Ohio, closed down. He told people then that, if this was the end of his making a living for his family, he was going to take everyone with him. Things weren't going any better for Huberty in California, however, because earlier that week he had been laid off from his job as a security guard.

Walking to the McDonald's restaurant two hundred yards from his apartment, Huberty, dressed in camouflage pants and a dark shirt, stepped inside, pulled out a firearm, and suddenly screamed, "Freeze!" He then ordered everyone in the restaurant to get down on the floor. When they did, he opened fire on them with a 12-gauge shotgun, a 9-mm semiautomatic pistol, and an Uzi submachine gun, shooting until the guns went empty and then reloading and shooting again.

Screaming "I killed thousands in Vietnam and I'll kill thousands more!" Huberty shot and killed two eleven-year-old boys as they rode their bicycles up to the McDonald's playground. (The

Pentagon would later say it had no record of Huberty's ever having served in the military.) Huberty also shot and killed an elderly couple walking by the restaurant.

Uniformed police officers and the San Diego Police Department SWAT team responded immediately to the report of the shooting and quickly sealed off the area, but they weren't able to get close enough right away to stop the killing. "The suspect was firing at everyone, at anything that moved," said San Diego police officer Arthur Velasquez (Gunman massacres 1984, 1). In addition to shooting at citizens in and around the McDonald's, Huberty also fired several times at the police.

The scene of carnage at the McDonald's was unbelievable even to hardened police officers. "It was a sickening massacre," San Diego Chief of Police Bill Kolender told reporters. "It's the most terrible thing I've ever seen in my life, and I've been in the business twenty-eight years" (Coast man 1984, A1).

The police SWAT team at first attempted to negotiate with Huberty, but he wouldn't respond. Since there were still people alive inside the McDonald's, the police knew they had to do something—and do it quickly. Two snipers were set up, one atop a post office close by and one atop an apartment building. They were given the green light to stop the rampage if the opportunity presented itself.

By the time the snipers got into position, nine customers sitting in the eating area of the McDonald's had been shot and killed, as had five standing at the counter and three employees behind the counter. Outside the restaurant, four people had been killed. "People lying on the floor were moaning," said a witness to the killing. "He would go through the crowd picking them off one by one" (Gunman massacres 1984, 1).

But it would soon end.

The sniper atop the post office caught a glimpse of Huberty in the restaurant with the dozen or so hostages who were still alive. The sniper fired one shot, hitting Huberty and shattering his heart and spine. After the shot, officers close to the restaurant reported that Huberty was down but still moving. However, when the police SWAT team entered the restaurant minutes later, they found Huberty dead. Thus ended one of America's worst mass murders: twenty-one people killed and nineteen wounded. Interestingly, the only police record Huberty had had before this day was one arrest in Ohio for drunk and disorderly conduct.

Luckily, the incident in San Ysidro is an extreme case. Most SWAT incidents, though often involving violence and even death, aren't this extreme. Still, they are extraordinarily dangerous both to those involved and to the police, and they must be dealt with and resolved. Often, unfortunately, the use of a SWAT sniper is the only option available that will resolve an incident without increasing the risk of death and serious injury to innocent people. While police snipers are usually called on only as a last resort, their use has saved many lives and is an option all SWAT commanders must have.

4

Intelligence and Planning

The officers at the SWAT command post could see the sun just coming up over the horizon on Mother's Day 1993 in Riverside County, California. The SWAT team had been on duty now at the Paso de Lago Mobile Home Park since before midnight, and it appeared they were going to be needed there for a quite a while longer. The SWAT officers yawned and stretched while the hostage negotiators continued trying, as they had all night, to persuade a man inside one of the mobile homes to release his two sons and girlfriend, but with little result.

The incident had begun around 11:00 P.M. the previous evening, when the police responded to a call about a domestic disturbance at one of the mobile homes. The resident of the mobile home, a heavy user of drugs, specifically methamphetamines, had reportedly been hyperactive all day, threatening his girlfriend and sons, and positioning firearms from his large collection in strategic spots inside his home. Police officers answering the domestic disturbance call knocked on the door of the mobile home, but the man refused to allow the officers to come in or his girlfriend and two young sons, ages nine and twelve, to leave. When the officers wouldn't go away, the man threatened them with one of his weapons, then ducked back inside and locked the door. Following this development, and when the police discovered that the man had both a large supply of guns and a strong disposition toward violence, the officers called for SWAT.

Because of the man's reported heavy drug use that day and his threats against his girlfriend and sons, the SWAT team, recognizing the strong possibility of violence, developed very early in the incident a tactical rescue plan, should they have to make a dynamic entry into the home in order to save the three hostages. After the command post approved the plan, the SWAT team members rehearsed it in order to work out any problems or unseen complications. According to the plan, the assault-and-rescue team would force the front door of the mobile home while diversions were created at two corners of the home with flashbang devices. Flashbang devices are grenades that explode with a brilliant flash and an extremely loud bang, but that do little damage. The overload on the human sensory organs caused by the flash and the bang tends to confuse and disorient those closeby for several seconds.

The assault-and-rescue team would immediately, on gaining entry, set off another flashbang device in the living room and then begin securing the inside of the mobile home. Chemical agents would be used to flush the man out if the assault-and-rescue team found that he was hiding inside the home. The SWAT team also developed an alternate plan in the event the man fell asleep and the hostages managed to escape on their own, something that happens quite often, especially when the hostage taker is a heavy drug user.

Even though, at a number of times throughout the morning, the negotiators thought they were going to win the release of the hostages without having to resort to violence, the assault-and-rescue team continued to rehearse the plan, looking both for problems and for ways to improve it. However, after much rehearsing, and just when the assault-and-rescue team felt they had the plan as well developed as possible, the hostage negotiators suddenly came into possession of some new and extremely important intelligence about the incident. *Intelligence*, in SWAT jargon, means any information that relates to, and could have a bearing on, the resolution of the incident the SWAT team has been called out to resolve. In this case, when the negotiators talked with the female hostage on the telephone (hostage negotiators often ask to speak with the hostages in order to be assured they are OK), they found that the hostage taker had access to two automobiles parked nearby, and, more important, that he had placed heavy furniture in front of the door that the SWAT assault-and-rescue team planned to use as their entry point.

The problem of the two automobiles was easy to deal with. The officers simply blocked the vehicles with police cars so they couldn't be moved. The difficulties involved in the placement of the furniture required much more. They meant that, now, the tactical plan the assault-and-rescue team had developed, rehearsed, and refined had to be modified. The door was no longer the best possible entry point, because the element of surprise would be taken away by the time required to push through the furniture blocking the door.

Their new entry point for the assault, the SWAT team decided, would have to be the large window next to the door. Diversions just before the assault began would still be created outside the mobile home at the corners, and a flashbang would be tossed in through the broken window as the team entered. This plan, though, the SWAT team realized, was going to be much more difficult to implement. Extra precautions would have to be exercised, since going through a window is not as easy as going through a door. When officers smash open a door the way of entry is of a known size. When officers smash out a window, large shards of glass often remain that can be extremely dangerous to those trying to get through. Along with having to worry about the threat of being shot, SWAT officers now also had to worry about the threat of being sliced as they leaped through the broken window.

Negotiations continued into the afternoon, but still with little result. At a quarter to three in the afternoon, in order to add stress and speed up the man's surrender, the SWAT team shut off the electrical power to the mobile home. About forty-five minutes later, the man finally told the negotiators that he was ready to release the hostages and come out and surrender. A SWAT arrest team stood by to take the man into custody, while the SWAT assault-and-rescue team stood by to search and clear the mobile home.

For five minutes, the SWAT officers waited; there was no activity and no one coming out of the mobile home. Suddenly, a muffled gunshot came from inside the home, and then the sound of screaming. The assault-and-rescue team raced for the mobile home, putting into action the revised entry plan. While flashbangs exploded outside the home, the assault-and-rescue team smashed out the window and then tossed in a flashbang.

Within a few seconds, the assault-and-rescue team cleared the window and gained entry into the mobile home, finding the living room filled with the smell of gunpowder, but also finding the hostage taker on the floor struggling with his girlfriend over a firearm. The SWAT officers quickly subdued and handcuffed the hostage taker, then found that the man's twelve-year-old son had been shot almost point blank with a shotgun just under his left arm and had a gaping six-by-twelve-inch hole in his chest. Fortunately, on the scene were several physicians who were reserve deputies with the SWAT team, and these physicians quickly administered lifesaving care. A helicopter transported the young boy to Loma Linda University Medical Center. Although he was seriously injured, the care he received at the scene saved his life, and doctors gave him a good prognosis for full recovery. Because of the quick action of the SWAT team, the other two hostages escaped unharmed.

A vitally important, and lifesaving, side effect of the Riverside County SWAT team's planning process became apparent only after the incident had ended. During the follow-up questioning, the girlfriend of the hostage taker told the police that, after shooting his twelve-year-old son, the man had put the shotgun up to the head of his nine-year-old son with the intention of shooting him. The assault-and-rescue team's dynamic entry through the window and the detonation of the flashbang device, however, startled the man, and when the gun went off, it missed the child and instead went through a wall.

It is because of this startling effect that police SWAT teams use flashbang devices whenever possible when making a dynamic entry. The few exceptions to their use would be if the SWAT team feels their effect could be detrimental to someone in poor health, or if the area they are to be used in is so small that the explosion of the flashbang could injure an innocent party.

The chilling reality of the Riverside County incident, however, is that, if the police hadn't got the information about the placement of furniture in front of the door and consequently changed their tactical plan, there would have been several seconds' delay in the detonation of the flashbang while the officers pushed the furniture out of the way. This delay would have eliminated the element of surprise, particularly since the man expected them to come through the door anyway. The man would then have undoubtedly succeeded in shooting and possibly killing his nine-year-old son. Because planners were able to quickly modify their plan to account for the new information they had received, the SWAT team was able to make an immediate, dynamic, surprise entry through the window, and consequently to save the young boy's life.

Intelligence, which to police SWAT teams means any information relevant to and useful in resolving the incident they have been called to, and which is exactly what the information received by the Riverside County SWAT team was, is probably the most important ingredient in any successful SWAT operation. The more intelligence a SWAT team can obtain on the suspects, on the hostages, on the armaments available to the suspects, on the fortifications inside the incident scene, on the layout of the incident scene, and on anything else relevant to the incident, the better the chances are of formulating a workable plan, of using this plan to successfully carry out the safe rescue of any hostages, and of resolving the incident.

"Good intelligence is the crux of solving any SWAT incident,"

said retired FBI agent and former SWAT team commander Wayland Archer in a telephone interview (January 24, 1995). "You
don't want to go ahead without it."

A SWAT team that attempts to resolve an incident without
first gathering all of the good intelligence available about it is
flying blind. Good intelligence means information that is not only
relevant to the present situation but also useful in resolving it. On
the other hand, it is also possible for police SWAT teams to gather
bad intelligence, which is information that is no longer true or
never was. In addition, police SWAT teams sometimes gather
neutral intelligence, which is information that, while true, is not
relevant to resolving the incident. A SWAT team leader must sift
through these pieces of information and use only good intelligence when making tactical plans.

There are many types of good intelligence SWAT teams need
to gather about a SWAT incident if they want to resolve it peacefully. They need to know why a suspect has committed whatever
act it is that has brought the SWAT team, the suspect's propensity
for violence, the number of hostages, the area they are being held
in, the safest entry route into a SWAT incident site, and any other
information that will assist the SWAT command post personnel in
developing a tactical plan that will maximize everyone's safety.

In addition to assisting in the tactical planning, good intelligence can also make a large difference in the success or failure of
the hostage negotiators. The more information the negotiators can
gather on the hostage taker and the reasons *why* he or she has
resorted to hostage taking, the easier it is for them to establish
rapport. People who take hostages usually feel they have been
pushed into doing it as a last resort, and they do it because they
believe it is the only way they can get other people to pay attention
to them or to their problem. They are desperate individuals, and
negotiators must use every resource and piece of information
available in order to persuade them to surrender peacefully. A
fully informed hostage negotiator can often build rapport by talking knowledgeably about the hostage taker's problems, and by
empathizing with the pressures the hostage taker feels brought

the incident on. This skillful and careful talking, by itself, this giving of a sympathetic, knowledgeable ear, many times brings about a peaceful surrender. But this can be done successfully only if the negotiator both has and makes expert use of the good intelligence gathered on the hostage taker.

This intelligence used at SWAT incidents, both by the planners and the hostage negotiators, is aggressively gathered by SWAT officers from many sources, such as family members of the perpetrator, fellow employees, neighbors, and even bystanders. Also, SWAT officers at the command post immediately begin gathering historical intelligence from such sources as a criminal record that shows a history of violence, records of stays in mental hospitals, job termination paperwork, files of the department of motor vehicles, counselors, parole and probation officers, and police officers who have previously dealt with the perpetrator.

In addition to seeking out historical intelligence, much present-time intelligence, as we have seen, is gathered by the SWAT snipers, who are always set up right away, usually very close to the center of the action. Snipers often observe a hostage taker's attempts to fortify a location or observe what his or her response is to the presence of the police. Important present-time intelligence is also gathered by hostage negotiators through their conversations with the hostage takers or hostages. Such information is often lifesaving, as we saw with the negotiators in the Riverside County incident above. Just by speaking with the hostage taker, negotiators often obtain crucial intelligence on the person's temperament and resolve.

Intelligence also comes from just looking around. "We almost always first do a 'leader's recon,'" said Indianapolis Police Department Lieutenant Stephen Robertson. "The leader goes out and gets an 'eyes-on' assessment of the situation."

This "eyes-on" assessment gives the SWAT team leader an opportunity to see an incident site personally, which is always preferable to having it described by other SWAT officers. No matter how good their description, it can never be as complete as a personal look. In addition, a SWAT team leader often has a different point of view when surveying a SWAT incident site. While a SWAT officer is looking at the dangers involved and the best way to gain access to the site, the SWAT team leader, in addition to these items, also looks at the logistics of mounting an assault, at the number of officers needed to maintain security at the site, and at other things that affect supervisory concerns.

Good intelligence, in addition to the sources already mentioned earlier, also comes from the uniformed patrol officers at the scene of the SWAT incident. SWAT team members are seldom present when the incident begins, and often, many events important for the SWAT team to know about have been witnessed by uniformed patrol officers originally dispatched to the scene. Therefore, one of the first intelligence sources looked to by the SWAT team is the initially responding uniformed patrol officers. What did they see when they first arrived? What did the perpetrator say and do? What was his or her mood?

As the SWAT team members begin accumulating all the bits and pieces of information about a person from as many different sources as they can find, the resultant picture is often unwieldy and unorganized. A number of SWAT teams solve this problem by using standardized SWAT forms that organize pertinent information on all of the people involved in a SWAT incident. A suspect profile form, for example, has spaces available for such information as name, age, physical description, clothing, weapons available, medical history, psychiatric history, military or police experience (for familiarity with firearms and tactics), drug or alcohol use, criminal record, propensity for violence, medications used, and any other information that is relevant to the present situation. Command post personnel also fill out a form for each hostage with much of the same information, and with a picture if possible so no hostage will be mistaken for the perpetrator in the event an armed assault by the police becomes necessary. These forms are then kept in the command post, and anyone just coming to the scene can get a quick rundown of the intelligence available on the people involved.

There are times, however, when even the most thoroughly

gathered and organized intelligence, put into the most carefully conceived tactical plan, can be thrown off by something for which the SWAT team is unprepared. Either the perpetrator does something completely unexpected, or, just as likely, some completely unexpected event occurs that throws even the best prepared and researched tactical plan askew. These unexpected events occur all too often during SWAT incidents and are a vital safety concern whose possibility can never be overlooked by the SWAT team leaders and members. The following incident demonstrates very clearly just how the unexpected can occur and the possible consequences of not being prepared for it.

On July 15, 1987, Hugh Johnston read in the Atlanta, Georgia, morning newspaper about a sports car for sale. When he went to see the car, he liked it and bought it. Later that day, Hugh pulled the car up to the Artlite Office and Supply Company on the northeast side of Atlanta; left his dog, named Too, in the car; and went inside. Walking around the store, Hugh began picking up items for purchase and placing them at the cash register, then going back for more. For some unknown reason, Hugh suddenly became agitated and began talking to himself very loudly, finally making such a scene that the other customers became frightened and began leaving the store. A psychologist who happened to be shopping in the store approached Hugh and attempted to see if he could help him. Hugh, however, apparently didn't want to share anything personal with the psychologist and instead began attacking him with the walking cane he used.

Seeing this, store employees naturally called the police, but by the time the officers arrived, Hugh had already left and driven away with his dog. But Hugh was not done for the day. Apparently still upset about something, Hugh soon became involved in several hit-and-run accidents. The driver involved in Hugh's last hit-and-run accident, though, followed Hugh and chased him. Hugh sped home, then jumped out of the car and ran into his house, apparently forgetting and leaving his dog behind.

The motorist, not ready to give up, went to a nearby house,

asked to use the telephone, and called the police. An officer responded to the call, and while he was talking with the victim of the hit-and-run accident, Too suddenly jumped out of the back of Hugh's new car and walked across the front lawn of Hugh's house. The hit-and-run victim pointed out the dog and said that it had been in the car with the hit-and-run driver. The officer whistled to the dog, and Too came running over to him. The officer picked up Too and put him in his police vehicle.

Hugh had obviously been watching what was going on because, as soon as the officer put the dog in his police car, Hugh ripped open the front door of his house and began shooting at him. The officer and the hit-and-run victim immediately dove for cover, and the officer radioed for assistance.

Anytime a police officer radios for help under these circumstances, dozens of police officers immediately respond, as they did in this case. The arriving officers, finding they had a barricaded subject, began setting up perimeters and tried to contact Hugh through a loudspeaker. Hugh, however, answered with more gunfire, and so the officers called for the SWAT team and began evacuating the nearby houses.

When the SWAT team arrived, they set up a command post in a nearby house and, while positioning snipers and replacing uniformed officers on the inner perimeter, began gathering intelligence on Hugh and why he had suddenly become so upset. At the same time the SWAT team was doing this, however, Hugh was calling the police dispatcher and demanding that the police clear out of his neighborhood. According to the dispatcher, Hugh seemed completely out of touch with reality, insisting to the dispatcher that he was "the supreme commander of all times." But along with demanding that the officers clear out of the neighborhood, Hugh also demanded that the police give him back his dog.

The intelligence gathered in the first few minutes of the incident indicated that Hugh's mother might possibly be trapped inside the house with him. For this reason, the police stayed back and didn't try to approach him. However, the police soon located a friend of Hugh's and brought him to the command post. The friend told the command post personnel that Hugh's mother wasn't in the house but was currently out of town. He also revealed that Hugh was gay and had recently discovered he was HIV positive. As a result, the friend believed, Hugh had been acting both depressed and strange lately. Hugh's friend then gave the SWAT team the telephone numbers of two separate lines Hugh had going into the house.

From the intelligence gathered so far on Hugh, the command post personnel began to fear that they might have a potential "suicide-by-cop" individual. A suicide-by-cop is a person who wants to commit suicide but lacks the nerve or resolve to do it himself or herself. A suicide-by-cop hopes to be able to force the police to assist in the suicide by making them kill him or her. Unfortunately, suicide-by-cop incidents are not that uncommon.

Using the telephone numbers supplied by Hugh's friend, one of the negotiators called Hugh and attempted to talk with him, hoping to be able to determine his motives. The negotiator only received screaming threats from Hugh of what he would do if they didn't give his dog back to him. The command post personnel quickly realized that this incident was not going to be resolved peacefully unless they could get Hugh to talk rationally with the negotiator. The dog, they knew, was the key.

Since Hugh refused to speak with the negotiator over the telephone, several officers, including one of the negotiators, positioned themselves on a porch next door to Hugh's house. Then, on the other side of Hugh's house, a SWAT officer brought Hugh's dog, Too, and put him into Hugh's yard. The negotiator on the porch, using a bullhorn, called for Hugh to look out into his yard.

Hugh had apparently been watching what was going on because, when the SWAT officer placed Too in the yard, Hugh opened the door a few inches and began calling out for the dog to come to him. The dog, however, after taking several steps toward Hugh, stopped and looked back at the SWAT officer, then over at Hugh. Too did this several times as Hugh continued to call out for the dog to come to him. Finally, the dog, apparently deciding he was safer with the SWAT officer, turned and raced back to him.

That was it. That was all it apparently took to make Hugh snap completely. All at once, Hugh burst out of the front door of his house, cursing and screaming. Seeing the officers standing on the porch next door, he turned and fired two shots at them, with both shots just missing the startled officers by inches. A sniper set up across the street saw this and fired, killing Hugh.

What Hugh did is called a *breakout*, when, without warning, a person who has barricaded himself somewhere suddenly bursts out shooting. This is often an attempt to complete a "suicide-by-cop" and is always dangerous to the police officers involved, as the officers on the porch in the above incident found out. A breakout is one of those "unexpected events" that have a tendency to occur often in SWAT incidents and that are always extremely dangerous. No one in the incident above expected the dog not to want to go to Hugh, nor did they expect the consequences. The officers standing on the porch then became easy targets because they hadn't expected the unexpected to happen and weren't prepared for it. They escaped being shot and possibly killed only by luck. It is for this reason that gathering personal intelligence on the people involved in a SWAT incident, particularly intelligence on suicidal tendencies and a propensity for violence, becomes so vitally important. But it is also vitally important to act on this information. The officers in this case, since they knew Hugh had been acting strangely, was depressed, and was a possible suicide-by-cop case, should never have exposed themselves as they did by standing unprotected on the nearby porch. This was an unacceptable risk considering the intelligence they had on Hugh, and particularly since he had already demonstrated a propensity for violence by shooting at other officers.

On the other hand, people initiating SWAT incidents who have no history of violence, who have committed no crimes or at most a minor one, and who seem to be simply frustrated about some life event are usually able, unlike Hugh, to be talked out of a SWAT incident site peacefully. Conversely, people who have already committed a serious crime, who have a history of violence, and who have become hostage takers for some violent purpose are likely to have to be taken out of the site by force. These different types of people obviously require different kinds of police strategy, but only through good intelligence can a SWAT team make the best judgment possible about how to proceed.

Along with indicators of the possibility of violence, though, SWAT team members also want to know about a perpetrator's propensity toward suicide, the danger of which was demonstrated in the case of Hugh Johnston. Good, reliable intelligence is vital in this area because there are a number of known indicators that can point to the strong possibility of suicide, especially when more than one of these is present. These include when the perpetrator:

1. Makes threats of suicide.
2. Has made previous suicide attempts.
3. Is aged nineteen to fifty.
4. Is widowed, divorced, or separated.
5. Is unemployed and unskilled.
6. Has suffered a recent significant loss and has no social support system.
7. Has a history of drug or alcohol abuse.
8. Has had a psychiatric illness (schizophrenia or depression).
9. Has a chronic medical illness.
10. Expresses feelings of hopelessness.

In addition, however, to gathering this intelligence on the people involved in a SWAT incident, SWAT planners also find it important to gather intelligence about the site where the incident is occurring. For the best possibility of a successful resolution, the SWAT team planners needs to know:

1. The type of premises (offices, home, factory, etc.).
2. The number of entry points.
3. The type of doors (material, open in or out?) and locks.
4. The building's construction material.

5. Which part of the premises the suspect is believed to be in.
6. Who has keys and access to the site.
7. The geography around the site (bushes, walls, open areas, etc.).
8. Whether flammable materials are stored there.
9. What utilities the site has.
10. Whether the lights are on a timer (the SWAT team doesn't want to be surprised during an assault).
11. Whether there is an alarm system.

The SWAT team keeps this information, like information on the people involved in an incident, on a form at the command post, along with a form that tells all of the known facts about the incident, with updates as changes take place. Anyone visiting the command post can read these forms and then know all of the information available about the incident.

However, obtaining information about what the inside of a SWAT incident site looks like while the situation is actually going on, though very important, is often extremely difficult. A number of SWAT teams have attempted to plan ahead for this problem and, in doing so, have surveyed their communities, trying to decide where the most likely spots for SWAT incidents would be. When they decide on these possible sites, such as courthouses, government operations buildings, sites owned by organizations targeted by groups known to be violent, and areas that have attracted violent protests in the past, the SWAT teams begin gathering intelligence about these sites beforehand. They obtain blueprints, occupant lists, and any other information that would be helpful in resolving a SWAT incident.

But in the event an incident occurs in a building that the SWAT team is not acquainted with, to the observant officer a number of facts about the inside of a building, particularly a home, can still be determined simply by examining the outside. For example, buildings over twenty-four feet wide need a load bearing wall inside that runs in line with the peak of the roof. In homes, one wall of a hallway usually serves this purpose. Vents on the roof can indicate to an officer where the bathrooms are, while chimneys usually run into living areas. Windows can also tell officers much about a home. Large windows with transverse drapes are usually living areas, middle-sized windows are usually bedrooms, and high, small windows next to the bedroom windows are usually bathrooms. Using this information, SWAT officers can get a general idea about the layout of the inside of a home, often without ever actually being inside.

Complementing the methods described above for gathering intelligence, SWAT officers often discover considerable information about what is happening at the present moment inside a SWAT incident site through electronic means. To do this, SWAT teams use devices such as transmitters concealed inside items introduced into the site, pinhole cameras (cameras with tiny lenses that can peer through small holes in walls), laser bugs (laser beams bounced off windows that can pick up sounds), chimney microphones (listening devices slipped down chimneys), and, as demonstrated in the following two cases, electronic stethoscopes (devices that can pick up sounds through walls and other barriers).

An inmate from a Missouri prison being transported for trial to Columbia, Missouri, managed to escape. Within a few hours of his escape, the police received information that the man, now armed with a sawed-off shotgun, had barricaded himself inside a room at the Hilton Hotel in Columbia and claimed he had a hostage. The police immediately went to the hotel, and a member of the police SWAT team entered the room next door to the one in which the escaped prisoner had barricaded himself. With the use of an electronic stethoscope, the officer confirmed that the escaped prisoner was in the room, and also that he was in the room alone. The officer passed this information on to the negotiator, who then took a hard line with the escaped prisoner. Finding that the police knew he was bluffing, the escaped prisoner eventually surrendered without violence.

In another incident, also in Columbia, Missouri, the police

were called to a home where a man had barricaded himself inside. The man, who was having religion-oriented hallucinations, had set up booby traps around the house, preparing for when the police would try to come in. He had also nailed some of the doors shut and had stuffed clothing into the heating vents to prevent the introduction of tear gas. In his preparation, the man had also constructed a stronghold in his bedroom, where he planned to make his stand against the authorities.

The event occurred in a duplex, and so the police gained entry into the other side of the house. Again using an electronic stethoscope, the police confirmed that the man was in the bedroom and that there were no other people in the house. The police were then able to mount an assault on the house without having to worry about endangering innocent people, and they eventually took the man into custody.

All of this intelligence that police SWAT teams gather, important as it is, is still only a tool meant to be used to build a plan for resolving the incident. But since it's always possible for SWAT incidents to explode into violence at any moment, often not a lot of time is available for this planning. Because of this possibility of violence, the SWAT team must develop and have an emergency assault-and-rescue plan ready as quickly as possible after arriving at the scene. A SWAT team therefore strives to gather as much good intelligence as they can in a short time in order to construct an emergency plan that is as viable as they can make it. They do this because, without at least some good intelligence, any plan can turn into a hazardous undertaking.

"One of the most dangerous things a SWAT team has to do is make a hostage rescue right after arriving at the scene," said Lieutenant Larry Beadles of the Richmond (Virginia) Police Department SWAT team, referring to the extreme danger of moving into a situation with little or no good intelligence.

Unless absolutely necessary, before taking any action police SWAT teams prefer to put together a preliminary assault-and-rescue plan, based on whatever intelligence is available at the time, and then to update and refine this plan as more, and better, intelligence comes in. In addition to this plan, the SWAT team always develops alternative plans in the event the main SWAT assault-and-rescue plan becomes unfeasible. But all of these plans must be based on good intelligence and on realistic expectations of the team's capabilities.

A number of SWAT assault-and-rescue attempts over the years either have failed or have had less than the desired outcome because the assault-rescues were poorly planned or the plans were based on bad, or incorrect, intelligence. Just as bad as poorly drawn plans, though, are tactical plans that are too complicated. The cardinal rule when developing a SWAT tactical plan is the "KISS" rule: "Keep it simple, stupid!"

In order to have the best chances for success, a SWAT tactical plan must be kept simple so that it is flexible and can be changed at a moment's notice. No matter how good the intelligence is, or how good the planning is, in any SWAT incident the officers are usually pitted against a highly emotional, and often irrational, person who will do illogical and unexpected things (as Mr. Johnston did). A plan must expect the unexpected and allow for on-the-spot changes. No one can really be sure what will be encountered or what will happen at a SWAT incident site, and therefore, complicated, precise plans with no flexibility are often useless when the assault-and-rescue attempt actually begins.

A tactical assault-and-rescue plan, though, along with being flexible and simple, must also be based on an accurate assessment of the threat or danger involved. Although no plan, when one is dealing with violent, irrational, or highly frustrated people, can ever be completely free of danger, a SWAT team must still assess to the best of their ability the danger to hostages, to innocent bystanders, and to the police officers involved. Such threats must be weighed before any tactical plan is implemented, as is demonstrated by the following incident.

In Hawthorne, California, a man who claimed to be a professional killer approached officers working undercover in a storefront sting operation. Thinking he was dealing with criminals, the hitman offered the undercover officers his services. After collecting intelligence on the man, the police decided he was just what he claimed to be, a contract killer, and so they then decided to allow him to make overt acts toward completing a contract murder and then arrest him.

Because of the hazards involved, the Hawthorne Police Department assigned its SWAT team to make the apprehension. The SWAT team realized that the contract killer was obviously a very dangerous person, and so they knew that the arrest site had to be a location that would afford the least threat to innocent citizens who might happen to be nearby. The SWAT team finally decided to use an apartment building in a deserted area of the city, where most of the neighborhood had already been demolished.

In preparation for the arrest, undercover officers secretly taped a meeting with the man during which he arranged the proposed murder. The suspect told them that he would knock the victim unconscious with a baseball bat and then cut out his brains with a butcher knife. Undercover officers gave the man $3,000, a picture of the proposed victim, and the address of an apartment in the deserted apartment building.

The police planned to allow the man to travel to the apartment building in order to show his intentions, and then to have the SWAT team, which would be positioned in the inner perimeter, move in and arrest him. According to the plan, uniformed officers would set up an outer perimeter to prevent any possible escape in a vehicle, while K-9 officers would also be nearby in the event a foot chase ensued. The plan called for some SWAT officers to be hidden in a U-Haul truck, some in garages, and two officers, dressed in street department work uniforms, sitting in a dump truck parked near the apartment building.

On the day of the proposed murder, the man showed up as he had agreed to do and walked around the area for a moment, seemingly confused about the address. Then, apparently seeing the apartment building, he headed for it. As the man walked past the U-Haul truck, the SWAT officers came out of their hiding places and surrounded him, then took him into custody without incident. He was eventually convicted of conspiracy to commit murder and was sentenced to prison.

The success of the above case clearly demonstrates the value of good planning. In developing this plan, the police used a location that greatly reduced the danger to innocent bystanders and, by using a large number of police, also reduced the risk to the officers.

While the plan for the incident above was developed ahead of time, SWAT call-ups don't usually have this luxury. Most SWAT plans must be developed at the scene of the incident while the incident is occurring. Most SWAT commanders therefore know that, even though they have given their officers the best tactical plan available, based on the best intelligence they have been able to collect, the plan is still usually put together in a hurry and, for various reasons, may not work exactly as laid out. For this reason SWAT commanders keep the plans simple and flexible, and they know that they must be able to depend on their officers' ability to see when a plan is working and when it isn't. When it isn't working, SWAT commanders must also be able to depend on their officers' ability to know how to make last-minute, on-the-spot changes, modifications, and additions. The ability to do this has resolved many SWAT incidents and has saved many lives—of both civilians and officers.

5

Command Post Operations

At about 2:30 A.M., on October 8, 1986, in a rundown hotel in Cincinnati, Ohio, the desk clerk manning the PBX telephone station noticed that the telephone line for room 819 was open. Since, a half hour earlier, he had helped the man in that room, a man named Danny, place a long-distance telephone call to Winchester, Kentucky, the clerk assumed there must be an equipment problem. When he checked on the line, however, the clerk was surprised to find that the long-distance call was still going on. What really surprised and upset the clerk, though, was the short conversation he overheard.

"I'm going to blow this place sky high," Danny told the woman he was talking to in Winchester, Kentucky. "I've got thirteen sticks of dynamite wired up here, and everyone in this town will know it when I die."

The clerk naturally became concerned and called the police. The first arriving uniformed patrol officer, on being informed of what was happening, requested that a sergeant be sent to the scene. Immediately after arriving, the sergeant had the desk clerk allow him to listen in on the conversation, which was still going on. The sergeant deduced from what he heard that Danny had been convicted of sexually molesting his two daughters in Kentucky and was talking with a woman who was his court-appointed therapist, and with whom Danny had fallen in love. The sergeant heard Danny tell the psychologist that he had called her because he wanted to say good-bye, and to ask if she would please tell his daughters that he had a serious psychological problem, and that that was why he had molested them.

In light of the apparent seriousness of the incident, the sergeant called for SWAT. Within minutes, a command post was established in the hotel, and the command post personnel began gathering intelligence as the negotiators set up and prepared to get to work. At the same time, the command post had SWAT tactical officers begin evacuating other residents of the hotel and also had officers secure the area around Room 819 and ensure that Danny could not leave the room.

When contacted by a negotiator and advised that the police knew what he was planning to do, Danny's only demand was that the police get the innocent people out of the hotel before he blew the place up. He gave the police the serial numbers of the dynamite he claimed he had wired up to explode. The command post attempted but was unable to verify the serial numbers as authentic.

One of the SWAT team's negotiators, after advising the command post of what he wanted to do, got into a three-way conversation with Danny and his psychologist. He found that, when talking with the psychologist, Danny seemed very despondent, often crying, but that whenever the negotiator cut in, Danny became very hostile and threatening. It became obvious to the negotiator that Danny was showing off for the psychologist.

Once the hotel had been evacuated, the command post agreed with the hostage negotiator that the best move to make at that point was to isolate Danny from his emotional support system and make him deal and talk only with the police. The command post therefore had Danny's telephone connection with the psychologist cut off. Danny immediately became hostile and threatening, saying he was going to blow up the hotel. Earlier though, while listening in on the conversation with Danny's psychotherapist, the police negotiator had heard Danny say that he wanted her to be certain his two daughters got his life insurance money. The negotiator, therefore, assured Danny that, if he did blow up the hotel, his insurance company would not pay off, and his children would be left with nothing. After a few seconds, Danny said that, OK, rather than blow up the hotel, he would just make the SWAT team kill him. The negotiator advised Danny that this wasn't an option. They weren't going to kill him.

After hearing this, Danny didn't seem to know what to do. The negotiator saw his opening and began talking to Danny about coming out of the room. Danny hesitated, however, because he said he was afraid of going to jail. The negotiator assured Danny that the police only wanted to get him help, not to arrest him, and that, if he came out, they would send him to the hospital rather than to jail.

Thinking it over for a few moments, Danny agreed that this was what he wanted to do. However, he said he didn't trust the police to keep their word. He told the negotiator that, if he heard the promise he wouldn't go to jail on the radio station he was listening to (a local AM country-western station), he would believe the police meant to keep their promise, and he would come out.

Following a discussion among the various supervisors at the scene, the command post contacted the radio station, told them the problem, and persuaded the radio station personnel to play the following message: "It's OK, Danny. They will keep their word. Come on out."

Everyone in the command post waited for the message to be aired as the country-western music seemed to play on and on. There came some tense moments in the command post when the radio station played a song with the theme "You are lying to me," and then another with the theme "I'm leaving the world behind." Finally, however, the disc jockey came on the air and gave the message. After hearing it, Danny walked out of the room with his hands up. No explosives were found, and Danny was taken to University Hospital.

Once it begins an operation, a police SWAT team, as in Danny's case above, must have a central command that makes the crucial decisions and also coordinates the activities of the tactical officers, the negotiators, and the support staff. This direction and decision making comes from the SWAT command post. Once established, the command post serves as the headquarters for the SWAT incident commander, who is in charge of the scene. It is at the command post that decisions are made about tactical assaults, about perimeter security, and about negotiations. The command post is where the SWAT incident commander and the SWAT team leaders meet and develop their plan of action. The SWAT command post is the conduit through which information is funneled about the incident so that this intelligence can then be passed on to the people who need it. It is at the command post that the decision is made that negotiations are no longer viable and that an assault must be ordered, and it is at the command post that the decision is made to give the SWAT snipers permission to fire. Except in instances of dire emergency, where action must be taken immediately in order to save a life, the command post makes the decision about when to talk and when to use force at a SWAT incident site.

Usually, a SWAT command post is set up at a location near the scene of the incident, a location that will give the command post personnel immediate access to all officers at the scene. The command post must be close enough to the incident site so that "eyes-on" decisions can be made, but not so close that the command post personnel must constantly dodge bullets.

"We try to find a spot close, but not too close, to the incident for the command post," said Sergeant Marvin McCrary of the Columbia, Missouri, Police Department in a telephone interview (January 24, 1995). "The commander has to be able to see what's going on without worrying about getting shot."

The command post, however, does not have to be a fixed site. It can also be mobile. A number of large communities have outfitted motor homes or large vans with all of the equipment and supplies necessary for a command post. Then, with these vehicles, when a SWAT incident occurs there is no need to search the nearby area for a location with the necessary communications equipment and other facilities. An officer simply drives the mobile command post to the site and parks it in a secure, but closeby, location.

A SWAT command post, whether mobile or fixed, is a necessity at any SWAT incident scene because the SWAT incident commander and the staff (which may include a communications officer, a logistics officer, a negotiations team leader, a SWAT tactical team leader, a clerical officer, and others) must have a place that is conducive to both thinking and planning, and also from which they can immediately receive and disseminate information and orders. To keep any distractions and confusion (which are always present at any large police operation) to a minimum, the command post is usually designated as off limits to anyone without a specific reason for being there.

Police departments also quite often try to keep the news media away from the command post and instead gather them somewhere near the incident scene, usually under the control of a public information officer, who regularly briefs them about what is occurring. Police SWAT teams have learned from far too many incidents in the past that, when the news media have access to the command post and its personnel, the plans for what the SWAT team intends to do are often broadcast beforehand, many times to the person causing the SWAT incident, who is often monitoring the news coverage.

Although the SWAT command post is responsible for overseeing the actions of all officers involved in a SWAT incident, which is a major job in itself, it is also responsible for the logistics of the call-up. The command post must see that the SWAT officers have the equipment necessary to carry out their mission (firearms and ammunition, chemical weapons, breaching instruments, etc.), that all officers assigned to the site for long periods of time are fed and have access to toilet facilities, and that additional personnel are available when relief is needed. The command post must also be able to obtain whatever a hostage taker demands (within reason). In many incidents, the suspect will request something simple, such as a pizza, soft drinks, or, as in the incident above, a radio station announcement of something. Often, hostage negotiators can obtain the release of hostages for these simple items, and it is the command post's responsibility to obtain or coordinate them.

In addition to these responsibilities, the command post is responsible for ensuring the availability of other emergency personnel, such as firefighters in the event that chemical weapons start a fire, medical personnel to attend to any wounded, traffic officers to reroute vehicles around the event, and personnel to evacuate anyone close to the scene who could be endangered by an armed hostage taker or a barricaded person.

Through the thousands of incidents that SWAT teams have responded to over the last three decades, the police have found that, in order to resolve an incident successfully, the SWAT command post must follow certain steps:

1. Contain and isolate the suspect; then attempt to negotiate a surrender.
2. If unsuccessful, demand that the suspect surrender.
3. If unsuccessful, use chemical weapons to force the suspect to surrender.
4. If unsuccessful, use snipers to neutralize the suspect.
5. If unsuccessful, order a SWAT assault.

A SWAT command post must always start at Step 1 and work up to Step 5. A command post cannot authorize a jump right into Step 4 or 5 unless there is an imminent threat of death or serious injury to someone. The guiding principle is that, before using Step 4 or 5, all possibilities of resolving the incident peacefully must first be investigated and attempted. This principle stems from the following incident, which eventually became a landmark court case known as *Downs v. United States of America* (1975).

On October 4, 1971, two men hijacked an airplane in Nashville, Tennessee, and ordered it to fly to Freeport in the Bahamas. The pilot, however, told the hijackers that the plane did not contain enough fuel to make it to the Bahamas and that it would have to stop in Jacksonville, Florida, to refuel. Since this incident involved the hijacking of an interstate flight, Federal Aviation Administration (FAA) officials notified the FBI at the onset of the hijacking, and FBI agents immediately proceeded to the Jacksonville airport.

When the plane landed in Jacksonville, an air traffic controller directed it to an isolated terminal, which, in plans developed to deal with hijackings, had been designated as the area to use for any hijacked aircraft. This isolation was necessary in order to minimize the danger to innocent bystanders in the event an armed assault was necessary, to lessen the chances of an escape by the hijackers, and to be certain the hijackers would not be able to take any more hostages. Once the hijacked airplane had taxied to the designated terminal and stopped, an FBI agent in the control tower, on instructions from the FBI agent in charge of the incident at the command post, ordered the pilot to cut the plane's engines. The pilot, however, requested that a fuel truck and an engine starter be sent out to them. The FBI agent in charge of the situation, however, again ordered the engines to be cut and told the agent in the tower to tell the pilot that no fuel or starter would be sent. The pilot once more asked for fuel and a starter, telling the FBI that the hijackers had both guns and twelve and a half pounds of plastic explosives.

The FBI agent in the tower, according to the court record, told the pilot, "The decision will be no fuel for that aircraft. No starter. Run it out, any way you want it. Passengers, if you are listening— the only alternative in this aircraft is to depart the aircraft, to depart the aircraft."

Within a few minutes, the copilot left the airplane and was met by FBI agents. He told them that he had been sent out by the hijackers to negotiate for fuel. He also told the agents that there were two men aboard the aircraft armed with handguns and explosives, and that a woman passenger had earlier been hysterical but had now quieted down. The copilot said he feared that, since one of the hijackers, the leader, had been drinking he might force the plane to take off without refueling, and he said that they had less than thirty minutes of fuel left. The FBI agent in charge of the incident dismissed the copilot's concerns and said that the information about plastic explosives was "a lot of malarkey."

A few minutes after this, one of the hijackers left the airplane, also to negotiate for fuel. The FBI immediately placed him under arrest and didn't question him further about the hijacking.

When the aircraft had been on the ground for a total of fifteen minutes, the FBI agent in charge at the command post decided to take action. He first had the aircraft blocked in by cars and then ordered an agent to shoot out one of the tires. The agent fired several rounds at a tire but couldn't deflate it. The FBI agent in charge then approached the aircraft, identified himself, and ordered everyone inside to get off the airplane. Two shots were heard coming from inside the aircraft, but no one got off. The FBI agent in charge then fired several shots at another tire, trying to get it to deflate, and ordered other agents to shoot at the right engine, the left engine having been shut off earlier so that the two men could leave the airplane.

Once the right engine had been silenced, moaning could be heard coming from inside the airplane. The FBI looked inside and found two people, the pilot and the woman hostage who had earlier been hysterical, both dead, and the remaining hijacker mortally wounded from a self-inflicted gunshot wound.

Brent Downs, the widow of the murdered pilot, sued the FBI for negligence and, after appealing an initial court finding in favor of the FBI, eventually prevailed and received an award of almost $270,000. In addition to finding the FBI negligent, the U.S. Court of Appeals also ordered the FBI to pay over $60,000 for the damage its agents had done to the aircraft by shooting the engine. But in terms of SWAT policy, the most significant aspect of *Downs v. United States of America* came through the guidelines the U.S. Court of Appeals laid down for handling SWAT-type incidents.

Among its findings, the court warned that "where one trained in the field of law enforcement, such as an FBI agent, is called on to make a judgment which may result in the death of innocent persons, he is required to exercise the highest degree of care commensurate with all facts within his knowledge; such care must be exercised in order to insure that undue loss of life does not occur."

What the court did in the *Downs* case was to lay down a blueprint and guideline for how SWAT-type incidents with innocent people involved must be handled. There is no place in these situations, the court said, for "Rambo" types who want to start shooting right away, without first looking for more peaceful methods of resolution. Anyone in charge of a SWAT incident, the court said, must plan and coordinate the activities at the site with extreme care, and any plans and actions must be made with the safety of innocent people as their first and foremost concern.

The court in the *Downs* case told SWAT command post personnel that, after unsuccessfully attempting to resolve an incident peacefully, they must then carefully weigh what threat the execution of any assault-and-rescue plan holds for the innocent people involved. The command post must consider their safety utmost in any such plan development and execution.

To accomplish this mandate from the courts, SWAT commanders have found that, in the execution of any assault-and-rescue plan, they must depend on strict discipline and teamwork. They have found that only by having a SWAT team which operates as a coordinated and professional unit can they consistently ensure that assault-and-rescue plans will be carried out with the least risk to innocent people. Only through having a SWAT team made up totally of well-trained and experienced officers can command post personnel ensure that, in any actions taken by SWAT team members, the safety of innocent people will be utmost in their minds.

Discipline and Teamwork

"Heads you die, tails he dies." The young Asian man gave two of the hostages an icy smile as he flipped a quarter. "First we shoot you in the leg, then in the chest, then in the head."

The forty hostages, tied up and then bound together in groups of three and four, all cringed and trembled as they waited to see who would die first. They knew the man and his three accomplices were serious—deadly serious. They had already shot two of the hostages. It was almost 9:30 P.M., and it seemed the nightmarish ordeal that had begun nearly eight hours earlier was about to reach a ghastly end.

A little after 1:30 P.M. on April 4, 1991, the Good Guys Electronics Store in the Florin Mall on the south side of Sacramento, California, had been filled with customers. As the customers picked out merchandise and employees rang up sales, no one could expect or be prepared for what was about to happen.

Suddenly, four young Asian men burst in through the front door of the store and began firing weapons into the ceiling. For a few moments, the shoppers and employees of Good Guys froze in amazement and surprise. Then, before most of the people in the showroom had had time to recover, the four men began rounding them up. The people, however, were spread out all over the store, and several managed to slip out during the confusion and call the police, reporting what they thought at the time was a robbery attempt.

Uniformed police officers responded to the call immediately and found the four gunmen still inside Good Guys holding about forty people hostage. The officers quickly sealed off all possible escape routes; then, a call went out for the Sacramento County Sheriff's Department's SWAT team, called in Sacramento the Special Enforcement Detail (SED).

Within thirty minutes, the SWAT team had set up a command post in a nearby bank. The incident commander attended to the first order of business (positioning two of the SWAT officers as snipers), while the negotiators starting their dialogue with the gunmen. After this, the command post personnel began intensive intelligence gathering, first talking to the people who had escaped, then conferring with store managers in order to get a layout of the building, and to find out if the store sold police scanners, fearing that the gunmen could use these to overhear police movement and plans. The store, fortunately, didn't sell scanners, and the building engineer provided the command post with a floor plan of the Good Guys Electronics Store.

Unfortunately, while the scanner problem didn't materialize, a problem very similar to it soon developed. The news media began arriving almost as quickly as the officers and immediately began broadcasting live coverage, showing all of the police actions at the scene. This media coverage caused considerable concern because television sets covered one complete wall of the Good Guys showroom, and all of them were turned on and broadcasting the news. A quick meeting with the media, however, resolved this crisis when the media agreed to air only what was happening at the front of the store, which had large glass windows through which the hostages and gunmen could be seen. With this problem settled, and while negotiations with the gunmen continued, the SWAT team began developing an assault-and-rescue plan.

Although the police didn't know this right away, the Good Guys incident wasn't what they first thought it, a robbery gone bad. It was instead an intentional hostage taking for the purpose of notoriety. The four young men had taken the hostages simply to attract attention. Feeling dissatisfied with their lives in America, the four men may have wanted to become media stars and had decided that taking hostages would be the way to do it. This type of hostage taking, the police usually find, is extremely dangerous for the hostages because there is little room for a negotiated settlement. (There are no perceived wrongs to be aired, no estranged spouses or loved ones to be brought to the scene, and no serious material items to be demanded.)

To make matters worse, intelligence efforts discovered that the four gunmen were members of an Asian street gang named the Oriental Boys. The police knew from several recent tragic cases that some of the Asian street gangs operating in Sacramento were extremely vicious and bloodthirsty. Several of these gangs had been specializing for the past few years in preying on Asian refugees, committing what are called *home invasions*, a crime during which the gang members break in and then torture the residents of a home until they reveal the location of their valuables.

But what really worried the police in the Good Guys incident was that the demands of the four gunmen went from unfocused to unrealistic. The demands varied from $4 million in cash to a helicopter large enough to carry fifty people, and from various firearms to 1,000-year-old ginseng root for making tea. One of the gunmen even stated that, because the four of them were unhappy with their lives in America, they wanted to fly to Southeast Asia to fight the Vietcong. Finally, however, the demands became more focused, and the gunmen settled on bulletproof vests, which the police began trading for hostages.

While the dialogue with the gunmen went back and forth, the SWAT command post personnel, uncertain that a peaceful, negotiated settlement could be reached, formulated and then put into operation an assault-and-rescue plan, just in case. By examining the floor plan and interviewing employees of the store, the SWAT team found they could enter the building undetected through a freight door and hallway that the electronics store shared with the fabric store next door. As the negotiations wore on, seven members of the SWAT team stealthily entered the building through the freight door, finding that the hallway led to the rear door of a Good

Guys storage room, which also had a door leading into the show-room where the hostages were being held. The SWAT team de-cided that this would be their entry point into the showroom. However, when the officers started to open the door into the storage room, they heard a voice on the other side shouting, "Stay away from that door!"

All of the officers froze with their weapons ready, but then a few moments later, they heard the sound of boxes being pushed around in the storeroom. One of the officers, using a stepladder, removed a ceiling panel in the hallway and then, with a pole-mounted mirror, looked down into the storage room and saw one of the gunmen supervising the blocking of the rear door of the storage room, which was equipped with a panic bar. He had apparently been shouting the warning about staying away from the door to several of the hostages, who were being forced to move large boxes in front of the door.

Within a few minutes, the noise stopped in the storeroom. The hostage taker ushered the hostages back out into the showroom and tied them up again. The SWAT team officers realized, how-ever, that, had the gunman opened the door from the storeroom to the hallway, they would have suddenly been facing an armed adversary. They knew they needed more intelligence on the place-ment and movement of the hostages and gunmen, and so they had a pinhole camera brought in and mounted on the wall of a utility room that also opened into the Good Guys showroom. A pinhole camera is a camera with a very tiny fish-eye lens. For its use, only a very small hole must be bored through a barrier, in this case a wall.

With this equipment in place, the SWAT officers removed several ceiling panels and then climbed over the hallway wall and dropped into the storeroom of the Good Guys Electronics Store. Immediately, however, the officers found they faced another prob-lem. The showroom side of the door leading from the storeroom into the Good Guys showroom was also blocked with large boxes. The SWAT team leader therefore designated two metal roll-up windows on either side of the door as optional entry points in case they could not get out through the door.

Once in position in the storeroom, the team waited for the order from the command post to begin before taking any action. However, in the event that any of the gunmen should enter the storeroom, the command post had instructed the team to shoot him with the sound-suppressed automatic weapons they carried, and then to begin an immediate emergency assault on the showroom. (Police SWAT teams often carry weapons equipped with sound suppressors. Although these don't work quite as efficiently as the "silencers" depicted in movies, they are so efficient that anyone not familiar with the sound a firearm makes with a suppressor wouldn't connect this sound with a weapon firing.)

While the SWAT team was entering and setting up in the storeroom, and then waiting for the signal to begin their assault-and-rescue, out in the showroom the four gunmen decided they needed to send someone out to emphasize their demands to the news media. Earlier, the gunmen had released several hostages unharmed in exchange for the promise of bulletproof vests but had received only one vest so far. They very likely felt they weren't being taken seriously. Finally, they selected a store employee, Sean McIntyre, as their messenger and example.

"We'll let you go if you promise to give our message to the press," one of the gunmen told McIntyre. "But we're going to have to shoot you in the leg first. Is that fair?"

McIntyre, with little choice, reluctantly agreed, and one of the gunmen shot him in the leg and then forced him to crawl out the front door. After reaching safety, he gave a short message to the press. "They want three bulletproof vests, a helicopter, and firearms. That's it. That's all they want" (Paddock 1991a, 1).

Not long after this, the gunmen decided to shoot another hostage to show how serious they were. The four men looked around, making all of the hostages cringe and look away. Suddenly, one of the male hostages began having a diabetic attack.

"Well, it looks like he's just decided who's going to be next," one of the gunmen said. He shot the ill hostage in the leg and pushed him out the door.

Although earlier the gunmen had released several hostages

unharmed, they had now shot two of the hostages and appeared ready to shoot more. The command post personnel decided that the time had come to stage a forced rescue. They gave the order for the snipers to fire when they had a clear shot and then ordered the assault-and-rescue team in the storeroom to be prepared to coordinate their entry into the showroom with the sniper shot. The command post personnel didn't want to wait until the four gunmen started killing the hostages, because it would be too late then to save many of them. What the police didn't know was that inside the store, the gunmen, when they still hadn't received any more bulletproof vests, had begun flipping coins to decide which hostage would die first.

A short time later, acting on the gunmen's continued demand for bulletproof vests, and hoping that one of the gunmen would expose himself to get them, the police dropped a vest off in front of the store. Instead, however, the gunmen attached a long tether to one of the female hostages and sent her outside to retrieve the vest. As she was doing this, it turned out that a gunman stood exposed as he held the door open for her. One of the two snipers found he had a clear, unobstructed shot, and so he took aim and squeezed the trigger. As often happens in incidents such as this, however, unexpected events occur that shatter the best-laid plans. Just as the bullet was fired, the gunman let the door close, and the bullet hit the door frame instead of the gunman, ricocheting and smashing the glass in the door. After an initial moment of shock, the gunman turned and opened fire on the hostages, walking up and down the front of the store, and shooting them again and again with a shotgun.

Immediately after the sniper fired the round, the command post gave the order for the seven SWAT officers in the storeroom to begin their entry into the showroom. The officers opened the door, shoved aside the boxes that had been piled in front of it, and then charged out into the showroom.

They didn't, however, just charge blindly into the room with their weapons firing, as is often depicted on television and in the movies. Instead, according to the predetermined plan, they entered in teams, three of them going around to the west side of the showroom with one acting as rear guard, and four of them going around to the east side and then splitting into teams of two. During their assault, the SWAT officers kept in constant radio contact with the snipers and officers stationed in front of the store, who couldn't fire because of the possibility of hitting one of the SWAT officers or hostages, but who did keep the assault-and-rescue team apprised of the gunmen's placement and movement.

The first gunman the SWAT team encountered was the one with the shotgun, who had been shooting the hostages. Spotting the SWAT team, he fired a blast at one of the officers but missed when the officer dove for the floor; the other officers quickly flanked the gunman and then killed him. Because the SWAT officers were using automatic weapons with sound suppressors, even though the other gunmen saw their accomplice fall they didn't know which direction the gunfire had come from, and one of them actually ran right into the line of fire. The officers also shot him, as they did the other two gunmen in quick order. The bloody siege was over only seconds after the SWAT officers had entered the showroom.

When the gun battle ended, the SWAT officers found three of the gunmen dead and the remaining one in critical condition. Three of the hostages had been tragically killed by bullets fired by the gunmen, eleven of the hostages had been wounded by the same gunfire, and three hostages had been slightly wounded by flying glass.

The senseless and horrifying death and injury to so many innocent victims make this incident especially tragic. Unfortunately, this also meant that the SWAT team received less than glowing admiration and thanks from both the hostages and the press. This is not uncommon. Had the sniper hit his mark, very likely none of the hostages would have been killed and the SWAT team would have received accolades from everyone. However, whenever a mission like this doesn't go perfectly and death and serious injuries result, it is difficult for those outside law enforcement to understand and accept the outcome. This lack of understanding stems from the fact that the public and the press, the police find, are often conditioned by television and movies to believe that any event such as this one should always end with the bad guys captured and all of the innocent people rescued unharmed. Unfortunately, real life is never that clear-cut and simple. There are just too many variables in an operation as complex as this one that the police can't control, particularly in cases where the perpetrators are vicious and unfeeling.

And these four young men were definitely vicious and unfeeling criminals who enjoyed preying on the weak and helpless. They demonstrated this viciousness by the delight they expressed in shooting the two hostages before releasing them, and in ceremoniously flipping coins in front of the hostages to decide who was going to die. These men had come into the store with the intention of hurting people, and they had enjoyed the terror they aroused in the hostages. As a result, the police simply could not guarantee that the gunmen wouldn't harm any of the hostages before the SWAT team could stage a rescue.

A major complaint voiced about the incident was that the police hadn't negotiated seriously enough with the four gunmen. But considering the gunmen's mentality, it is doubtful that any number of concessions by the police negotiators would have changed the eventual outcome. These four men were members of a tough street gang and had reputations to uphold. They felt bound by their reputations to terrorize the hostages. What made serious negotiating with these hostage takers extremely difficult was the fact that the four men weren't doing this for anything they could get from the negotiators. They were doing it for the notoriety. They were reportedly elated when they found they were on television and getting widespread attention. Therefore, had the police given in to their demands for any of the outlandish items they requested, such as the 1,000-year-old ginseng root or the large-capacity helicopter, this action would very likely have made the gunmen feel larger than life and would have served only to bolster their determination to continue. In addition, the police also realized they could not realistically negotiate with or appease men who had such a feeble grasp on reality that they actually believed they could fly to Southeast Asia and fight the Vietcong. But people are always able to decide after the fact, whether in a police action, a serious medical operation, or a professional football game, that the outcome could have been changed if something had been done differently. This is just human nature.

Sacramento County Sheriff Glen Craig answered these complaints at a news conference the day after the incident. "I don't know what we could have done differently," he said. "We are satisfied they would have begun shooting people within seconds of the time we took action to move in and save the hostages" (Paddock, 1991b, 1).

In truth, this was an excellently planned and executed SWAT operation. A point missed in all of the criticism was that the SWAT team had brought thirty-seven people out of the store alive—and that was a real victory, considering the reckless and vicious nature of the four hostage takers. When the police deal with extremely vicious or extremely disturbed people they know they can't always expect a perfect outcome. Such people don't always respond the way normal people do, and don't always have the same fears and inhibitions. The fact that so many people were rescued alive makes the operation at the Good Guys Electronics Store a victory.

The reason this operation was a victory, however, didn't have anything to do with luck or happenstance, as can often occur in police work. Victory came because of the superb teamwork and discipline shown by the members of the SWAT team hidden in the storeroom. The natural impulse, particularly once the adrenaline has been building up for long periods, and particularly after hearing gunfire and the hostages screaming, is simply to charge out. Just as strong is the impulse simply to charge out en masse with weapons firing. The officers, because of their discipline, didn't do this.

Some of the hostages complained afterward that they believed the SWAT team hadn't entered the store quickly enough when the shooting started. A sister of one of the murdered hostages was quoted in Paddock's *Los Angeles Times* article as saying, "If they had rushed, my brother wouldn't be dead now." This belief, considering the woman's loss, is certainly understandable, but it may or may not be correct. She was right, however, that the SWAT team didn't just rush out, firing their weapons wildly with a "spray-and-pray" mentality. They came out in predetermined teams, each team taking its previously designated route, and each team holding its fire until it had positively identified a target. To have done otherwise would very likely have resulted in some of the SWAT team members and more of the hostages being killed or wounded in the cross fire and in wild firing. On the contrary, no one in the Good Guys Electronics Store operation but the gunmen was shot by the SWAT officers, as many of the hostages as realistically possible were rescued, and none of the SWAT team members were killed or injured. This is the ultimate goal of all SWAT teams. To expect otherwise, to expect officers who are already taking great risks to needlessly and pointlessly expose themselves to deadly gunfire, as the SWAT team certainly would have if they had simply rushed out of the storeroom with no order or plan, is asking too much.

The strict discipline and teamwork displayed by the SWAT officers in the Good Guys incident can be developed only through hours and hours of often difficult training. SWAT training officers will attest that it isn't an easy task to get a group of police officers to perform with strict discipline and teamwork. As baseball coach and manager Casey Stengel once said, "It's easy to get the players. Getting them to work together, that's the hard part." But along with making SWAT teams operate in top form as a unit, this strict discipline and teamwork also has benefits for the individual team members.

Undoubtedly, the most important benefit of strict discipline and teamwork for individual SWAT team members is the suppression of fear. No matter what some officers may claim afterward, assaulting a site like the Good Guys Electronic Store, a site in which there are a number of armed suspects who have left no doubt that they are willing to shoot it out with the police, will raise fear in any officer. This is true no matter how many similar incidents he or she has been involved in. Being part of a trained and disciplined team, though, can reduce the fear level because, through intense training, the officers can trust and feel confident that they know what to do, and that the other team members are also highly trained and know what to do. Most important of all, since they are a highly disciplined team, they know they can depend on each member to look out for the other members. This intense training, teamwork, and discipline can also build a strong esprit de corps within the team. This is vital because being part of a tightly knit, disciplined team usually makes the fear of letting the other team members down larger than the fear of the adversaries (see photo below).

SWAT officers deploying from SWAT van as a team (photo by Robert L. Snow).

"Discipline is critical to the success of any mission," said Steve Gentry, former member of the U.S. Army's elite SWAT team, the Delta Force, in a telephone interview (January 24, 1995). "Everyone must be able to unquestionably count on everyone else. You must be more afraid of letting your partner down than you are of the enemy."

I used the Good Guys Electronics Store incident, however, not only to demonstrate the effect of discipline and teamwork, but also because I wanted to make a point about perceptions. There are dozens and dozens of other SWAT incidents I could have used to demonstrate the effect of good teamwork and discipline, incidents in which all of the hostages were rescued unharmed and the bad guys were captured without injury. I didn't, though, because of the false perception far too many people get from watching television police shows or police movies. In these television programs and movies, once the police arrive no one innocent is ever killed. In the real world, this is just not always possible. Occasionally, the outcome of a police operation in the real world is less than perfect.

This is particularly true in SWAT incidents where the police must deal with highly unstable and often heavily armed individuals whose thought processes and emotions are not normal. Many times, these people do not respond in the same way normal people do to threats or fear, and they often do bizarre and completely unexpected things. Therefore, the police cannot guarantee in these incidents that everything will always work out storybook-perfect. Occasionally, there are situations like the Good Guys Electronics Store incident in which, despite the best actions of the police, despite excellent teamwork and discipline, innocent people are injured or killed. That is simply a fact.

The type of teamwork and discipline that the Sacramento SWAT team displayed, however, is what allows SWAT teams to defeat groups like the four gunmen who took over the Good Guys Electronics Store. Teamwork and discipline make them a fighting force superior to almost all criminals and are essential ingredients in any successful SWAT operation. There is no room on a SWAT team for officers who want to do things their own way without considering what the other team members are doing, and no room for officers who want to rush ahead of the others and begin firing randomly. SWAT teams are successful only when they work together as a disciplined unit. When police officers *don't* work as a disciplined unit, tragic consequences can result, as the following incident demonstrates.

On June 30, 1954, more than a decade before police departments across the United States began forming SWAT teams in response to America's spiraling rise in violence, an event occurred in Indianapolis that, although in the following decades would seem commonplace, was considered extraordinary at the time. And since the police in 1954 considered the event extraordinary, so was their response to it.

Howard Ellis was a sixty-four-year-old man with a long history of mental illness who had been released from a stay in Central State (mental) Hospital just a little over a year before. In the middle of that June, his wife, Janie, would later tell reporters, he began acting strangely again. He began once more, as he had just before his last commitment, telling her that he knew he was never going to get well and that, if he ever got the chance, he was going to kill her. Also, his wife said, whenever she or anyone else was accidentally hurt, he would respond with cackling laughter.

On the morning of June 30, a typically hot, humid summer day, Janie Ellis stepped in the back door of her house at 733 Elder Avenue on the west side of Indianapolis and found Howard beating one of the five foster children she cared for. Up until that time, the only way she had had of controlling Howard, she said, was by threatening to call the mental hospital and have them come and get him. It usually worked, but on this day, she found it backfired. Howard let the foster child go when she said she was going to call the hospital, but then, he pulled out a long-bladed pocket knife and came at Janie, telling her that he wasn't going back to the hospital. He was going to kill her.

According to Janie, the two of them struggled for several

moments over the knife, and she finally managed to get away by sinking her teeth into Howard's arm and biting him hard enough so that he screamed and dropped the knife, pulling away from her. Seizing the opportunity, Janie fled out the back door of her house and across the yard to a neighbor's home. She said she realized she was leaving her five foster children with a mentally unbalanced man, but she knew that, if she stayed there, he would just kill her. She had to get some help. Using her neighbor's telephone, Janie called the mental hospital and told them what Howard had done. The doctor she spoke with advised Mrs. Ellis to call the police and have them bring Howard back to the hospital.

When Howard had been committed to the mental hospital the last time, Mrs. Ellis later told reporters, she had given away all of Howard's firearms. He was an avid hunter and a crack shot, and she said she wouldn't have been able to sleep in the house if she knew Howard had a firearm. During the time Howard had been home from the mental hospital, she had searched the house several times to be certain he hadn't hidden any new firearms anywhere. However, while Janie Ellis spoke with the police, who told her just to stay where she was and said that they would send a car out to help her, she also kept watch for Howard out the window of her neighbor's house. To her horror, she saw Howard go into the chicken coop behind their house and a few moments later walk back out carrying a rifle, a shotgun, and an armload of ammunition. For the next few minutes, Janie Ellis said, she waited and prayed she wouldn't hear gunfire coming from her house.

"My husband's gone crazy again!" Janie shouted to the two officers who at last pulled up in front of her neighbor's house. "He needs to go back to Central State. I just talked to the doctor there, and he told me to have you take him back."

Patrol officers Chris Greenwood and Robert Bates attempted to calm Janie down and assured her that they would handle things. After listening to her story, they told her to go back home and they would follow. But as the three of them walked across the yard to the Ellis house, a shotgun blast suddenly rang out, and Janie screamed and fell to the ground, a gunshot wound to her thigh oozing blood. The officers, stunned for a second, finally grabbed Janie and dragged her to safety as more shots rang out. While one of the officers gave Janie first aid, the other called police headquarters and gave an account of the situation they had on Elder Avenue.

Within minutes, sirens screamed from all directions, and dozens of city police, county sheriffs, and state troopers arrived and took up positions around the house, using whatever cover they could find. Officers hid behind bushes, behind telephone poles, behind trees. All had their guns out and aimed at the house, but no one could shoot back at Howard because they believed the foster children were still in the house. Lieutenant Paul Pearsey arrived at the scene within minutes of the call and climbed out of his police car, walking calmly up toward the house. Suddenly, a shotgun blast struck him in the left shoulder, and he fell to the ground. Several officers ran to his aid and helped him away to safety.

A few minutes after this, Officer Dora Ward crept toward the rear of the house through the shoulder-high weeds. A rifle shot from inside the house struck him in the head, blood gushing from the wound as he fell to the ground. Officer Ward struggled up to his feet and staggered out to the sidewalk in front of the house. A few seconds later, when three officers exposed themselves by rushing to his aid, shots from inside the house struck all three of them, and Officer Ward collapsed to the sidewalk, where he lay for a half hour in the hot summer sun. Several times, Howard fired at anyone who tried to help Officer Ward, even pumping another round into Ward as he lay helpless. Finally, one of two armored cars pressed into service by the police rescued Officer Ward.

After talking to bystanders and neighbors, the police eventually discovered that everyone inside the house had managed to flee before the shooting had started, and that Howard was in there alone. On this discovery, the officers ringing the house began laying down a withering barrage of fire. They used their service revolvers and shotguns, and some even used Thompson submachine guns brought out from police headquarters. The officers fired over and over, running out of ammunition several times, and each time having more brought out from police headquarters, along with tear gas and tracer rounds that they hoped would set the house afire and force Howard out.

Nothing the police did, however, seemed to have any effect on Howard, who just kept shooting and hitting any police officer foolish enough to expose himself. Officer after officer was dropped by Howard's uncanny aim. Tear gas, the police found, didn't work, while the tracer rounds simply wouldn't set the house on fire, even though the police fired dozens of them into the rickety wooden structure. The machine guns and tear gas launchers brought out from police headquarters jammed and misfired time and time again. The gas masks brought out for the officers didn't work. Even the officers inside the two armored cars that had been pressed into service were not safe. Officers firing out of the armored cars' gun ports were struck by pellets from Howard's shotgun that somehow got through the tiny openings. Howard even managed to blast out the windshield of one of the armored cars, injuring the officer driving it.

The shootout went on for two and a half hours, with over two hundred police officers firing over ten thousand rounds into the house. Yet Howard kept firing back. Hundreds of spectators crowded the streets as they watched the gun battle, often hampering police efforts. And while a number of high-ranking officials came to the scene, including the governor of Indiana, George N. Craig, who watched the gun battle from behind a bush, no one seemed to know what to do other than to continue to pour thousands and thousands of rounds into the house. Finally, however, the police realized that pumping ammunition into the house really wasn't accomplishing anything. Every time they thought they had him, Howard would just start shooting again. They were simply going to have to go into the house after him, dangerous as that would be.

The officers at the scene finally came up with a plan. Using the armored cars as cover, ten police officers approached the rear of the house and then had the two hundred officers ringing the house blast it with gunfire as the they forced open the rear door. Suddenly, the word came over the police radio to cease firing. There were officers in the house.

Once inside, three of the ten officers started forward while the remaining officers covered them. The three officers almost immediately encountered Howard, who had apparently been completely untouched by any of the rounds fired into the house. Hiding behind a heavy bookcase, Howard leaped out firing his weapons when he saw the officers, but he missed them. Shots from a Thompson submachine gun, a shotgun, and a revolver all struck Howard, but he didn't fall and he didn't die. Instead, he ducked back behind the bookcase and reloaded his shotgun, then leaped back out. Again, the officers shot him over and over. Simply refusing to die, Howard leveled his shotgun directly at the chest of one of the officers, but when he pulled the trigger, it misfired, and the three officers continued to shoot him repeatedly. Finally, with twenty-six bullets in him, Howard Ellis fell to the floor dead.

The toll of "The Battle of Elder Avenue," as it became known in Indianapolis Police Department lore, was extraordinarily heavy. Along with Howard Ellis being killed and Janie Ellis being injured, eight police officers were shot, and three officers were struck by ricocheting shotgun pellets. It took over two hundred police officers two and a half hours and over ten thousand rounds of ammunition to finally stop one man armed with only a shotgun and a rifle.

The comparison of the police operations on Elder Avenue and at Good Guys Electronics Store is striking. For two and a half hours, the police on Elder Avenue had no plan and no discipline and employed little teamwork. Officers simply ran forward and fired, and many were gunned down. Once the officers got inside the house, if Howard Ellis's shotgun hadn't misfired, an officer would very likely have been killed. The officers at Good Guys Electronics Store, on the other hand, had a plan, had teamwork, and had the discipline to stay in formation and fire only when they knew firing would have positive results. There was no rushing forward and firing as there was on Elder Avenue, and consequently, none of the officers in the Good Guys assault were injured. The difference between the shootout in the Good Guys Electronics Store, which lasted only moments once it began, and the shootout on Elder Avenue, which lasted two and a half hours, was teamwork and discipline. The result of teamwork and discipline is almost always a police victory. And even though the police finally did prevail on Elder Avenue, it is difficult to call this shootout a police victory with so many officers shot.

Fortunately, incidents such as the one on Elder Avenue in Indianapolis and at the Good Guys Electronics Store in Sacramento are relatively rare. In only a small percentage of incidents do the police have to assault a site as they did in these two cases. In most instances, police SWAT teams are able to peacefully negotiate the surrender of hostage takers and barricaded subjects. However, when the need to assault a site does arise, strict unit discipline and teamwork become paramount. When these qualities are part of a SWAT team's operation, success almost always follows.

Equipment

On the morning of May 4, 1988, Renard Jones stormed into the Fox Plaza office building on the Avenue of the Stars in Los Angeles and then immediately took the elevator up to the twenty-sixth floor. It would be a day few of the workers on that floor would ever forget.

Jones had had several personal injury lawsuits pending in the courts for over five years and had complained to several people recently that, while his attorney kept assuring him the cases would be settled soon, nothing had happened in five years. He said he was sick of all the delays.

Stepping off the elevator, Jones stomped into the law office on the twenty-sixth floor with the intention of seeing his attorney and demanding that something be done immediately on his lawsuits. However, when Jones finally located his attorney's secretary in the law office conference room and told her he wanted to see his attorney, the secretary replied that Jones's attorney was in court at the moment and unavailable. Jones either didn't believe her or didn't comprehend what she was saying and continued to insist on seeing his attorney. The secretary simply kept repeating that his attorney was not in the building, but in court.

After apparently fuming for several minutes, Jones finally yanked a long knife out of the knapsack he carried and took the secretary hostage in the conference room. Pointing the knife at her, Jones ordered the woman to sit in a corner and not move, and then, he slammed the conference room door shut and began piling furniture up in front of it, afterward yelling to the receptionist outside that he wanted to speak with his attorney right now or else he would kill the hostage. The receptionist immediately called the building security office, which then called the Los Angeles Police Department.

Uniformed police officers immediately responded to the scene and found that Jones was demanding $5,000 as an advance against his expected lawsuit settlements, with the threat that, if he didn't get the money, he would not only kill the hostage but also blow up the attorney's office with a bomb he had in his knapsack. The officers, realizing the gravity of the situation, began securing the area around the conference room and also evacuating those in nearby offices. In addition, they requested the assistance of the Los Angeles Police Department SWAT team.

As the SWAT team set up and began developing a tactical rescue plan in the event it would be needed, a hostage negotiator first spoke with Jones through the closed and barricaded door and then finally persuaded Jones to take a crisis phone left outside the door to the conference room. A crisis phone is a communications device much like two regular telephones attached by a long cord, but with some important differences. While it allows a negotiator to talk with a perpetrator, it doesn't allow anyone outside the SWAT team to have access to the line. However, it does allow a secondary negotiator, the SWAT incident commander, or another person to listen in, and it allows the conversation to be taped. Along with being used as a communications device, a crisis phone is also often used as a tactical intelligence tool because the police give the suspect a phone with only a certain length of wire. The police then know that, when the person is using the telephone, he or she must be within a certain distance from where the crisis phone was put into the site.

The negotiator soon established what he felt was good rapport with Jones by first presenting a calm, reassuring demeanor, and then by allowing Jones to tell his story and thereby vent his anger. During the dialogue, the negotiator also attempted to gain information about the bomb Jones claimed he had. When asked about the bomb, though, Jones quickly became evasive and then angry and threatening, demanding the $5,000 and now also a car. The negotiator dropped the dialogue about the bomb and again began trying to calm Jones down.

In an attempt to ease a situation that had suddenly got tense, the police delivered food to the conference room door. However, when Jones opened the door to get the food, he saw the reflection of a SWAT officer in a mirror the police had set up to monitor the hallway in front of the conference room. The sight of the heavily armed SWAT officer agitated and infuriated Jones, and he leaped back into the room and began making more threats against the hostage, accusing the police negotiator of trying to trick him. To keep down the chances of violence against the hostage, and to reestablish rapport between Jones and the negotiator, the police decided to attempt to pacify Jones, and they delivered the $5,000 he demanded by slipping the bills under the door. This action seemed to calm Jones for a bit, but before long, he became agitated again and once more began demanding a car.

Although the negotiator felt that, by delivering the money, he had reestablished a good rapport with Jones, he still could not convince Jones to surrender. Instead, Jones continued demanding a getaway car. When the police stalled on his request for a car, Jones finally put a very frightened hostage on the crisis phone.

"You ... You'd better do what he says about the car," the hostage said. "If you ... you don't, he says he'll chop me into a thou ... thousand pieces."

The negotiator finally advised the SWAT incident commander that because of Jones's refusal to surrender, his agitated state, and the repeated threat that "he had his finger on the switch" of a bomb, the negotiator could no longer guarantee the safety of the hostage. In addition, the SWAT commander had the problem that Jones was still insisting the police provide him with a car. The SWAT commander, however, could see that, if he allowed the situation to go mobile, it would only multiply the dangers. There-fore, the SWAT commander decided to try a rescue attempt. It was obvious, though, that, in order to be successful, the rescue would have to be dramatic and swift, so as to reduce the chances of Jones doing harm to the hostage, and also to reduce Jones's chance of being able to use the bomb he claimed he had. Since the door to the conference room was barricaded with furniture, and the police figured it would take at least several seconds to force the furniture away from the door, which was plenty of time to harm the hos-tage, an explosive entry was decided on.

To keep the situation calm until the rescue could be set up, the negotiator began talking to Jones about his request for a car. Jones, however, soon began demanding that, rather than any car, he wanted the hostage's car, and he wanted the police to bring it around to the front of the building and park it so he could see it from the conference room windows. The negotiator saw his chance to buy some time and agreed, telling Jones it would take a while to locate the car in the parking garage where the hostage said she had parked it. During this time, in order to draw Jones toward the windows and away from the door, the police had a helicopter from the Los Angeles Police Department Air Support Division fly close to the building. During this diversion, the police placed explosive charges on the door to the conference room.

Once everything was in position for the rescue, the police drove the hostage's car around to the front of the building and the negotiator asked Jones to look out the window and give them directions for its positioning. When Jones walked over to the window and began doing this, the SWAT rescue officers readied themselves, and then, the police detonated the explosive charge. The device worked perfectly, and the explosion blew a six-foot-by-three-foot hole in the door, more than large enough for the waiting SWAT officers to charge through, and also powerful enough to knock away the furniture barricading the door.

The explosion, magnified inside the closed conference room, apparently also knocked both Jones and the hostage off their feet, and when the police raced into the room, they found Jones lying on the floor. Jones, though, grabbed the hostage and tried to use her as a shield, the knife still in his hand. But on seeing the SWAT officers armed with automatic weapons, he immediately surrendered, and the police pulled the hostage, unharmed, away to safety. The Los Angeles Police Department Bomb Squad examined Jones's knapsack but found no explosives.

As stated in previous chapters and shown above, SWAT officers are armed with much more destructive and dangerous equipment than are regular police officers, such as the automatic weapons and explosives used during the Fox Plaza office building incident. These are dangerous devices, and this is one of the reasons SWAT teams are very selective about who they allow into their unit.

Explosive entry devices, such as the one in the case above, though only occasionally used because of their danger, come in many forms. Some of the explosives used by police SWAT teams to breach doors and walls are soft, with the consistency of clay, and can be molded into the shape of the hole wanted. Another type of breaching explosive has the consistency of caulk and is actually applied with a caulk gun. There is also an explosive product called Foamex, which is applied with an aerosol can. An especially effective, but also very dangerous, type of explosive that can be used for forced entry through steel-reinforced doors is called a *linear flex-shaped charge*. This is a type of explosive used in the construction industry to cut I-beams. The explosive charge has a lead backing that gives it a cutting effect. While working very well on strong metal doors, the explosion must be contained to protect anyone nearby from flying shrapnel.

While a breach explosion, such as the one in the Fox Plaza office building case, is a controlled explosion, meant only to breach a door or wall, any nails in a wall, hinges or locks on a door, and other hardware can, during the explosion, become deadly projectiles. It is for this reason that, to gain entry through a door, many police SWAT teams use other methods if at all possible. For example, many SWAT teams use a specially made entry device called a *hooligan tool,* which looks like a large pickax with an opposing flattened blade. The tool is used either to bash a door down or to pry it open. Also available to gain entry through a reinforced door is a device which is a double-action pump that pushes against both sides of a door frame, separating the door frame from the door and its locking mechanism. Another device, the *door breaker,* wedges on either side of the door frame and then uses this wedging as a brace for the device to ram the door open. Many police departments use a much simpler device for forcing open doors: hand-held battering rams. At one time, the Los Angeles Police Department used a motorized battering ram, but the lawsuits that resulted from the danger involved in smashing through doors and walls with such suddenness and force eventually limited its use (see photo below).

SWAT entry tools, including battering rams, hooligan tools, and shok-lock rounds (photo by Lieutenant Stephen Robertson).

Another popular device for breaching locked doors is a special shotgun shell called a *Shok-Lock round* (also known as *Avon rounds* or *Mickey rounds*). These shells, rather than containing buckshot, contain dental plaster and metal dust. The shotgun is held close to the door's locks or hinges when the round is fired. While the impact tears off hinges or locks, the round disintegrates after impact, so there is little danger to people standing on the other side. A Shok-Lock round, for example, will produce a three-inch entry hole when fired at a fifty-five-gallon drum, but it will not damage the other side of the drum.

Because police SWAT teams use such aggressive entry equipment, many criminals have begun fortifying sites with steel bars or gratings. Police SWAT teams, however, have met this challenge with devices called *breaching hooks*. These are large metal hooks that are looped over the bars or grating and are then attached to a vehicle, after which the bars or gratings (and usually the door or window they are attached to) are ripped off. There is even a device available that can pull off windows or doors which are barred on the inside.

But once the police breach a door or wall and enter a building, the really dangerous part of the mission begins. They must then face and apprehend a usually heavily armed, and almost always desperate, person or group of people. To do this as effectively and safely as possible, the police must be prepared to meet force with force. Most SWAT officers, therefore, carry at least two weapons, usually a sidearm and a submachine gun or assault rifle.

While for over a hundred years most law enforcement officers in America carried revolvers as sidearms, very few police SWAT officers carry them. Instead, most SWAT officers carry semiautomatic pistols. Although surprising to those unfamiliar with firearms, semiautomatic pistols are not more powerful than revolvers, yet SWAT officers carry them for a number of reasons, one being because they are much easier to reload than revolvers. In the heat of combat, a person's fine-motor skills, such as those needed to reload a revolver, often disappear. Reloading a semiautomatic pistol doesn't require such skills. SWAT officers also carry semi-

automatic pistols because they have much less recoil than revolvers, which makes multiple shots quicker and more accurate.
This is important because, again in the heat of combat, shots often
miss, and quick additional shots may be needed to stop a suspect.
But probably the most important reason SWAT officers carry semiautomatic pistols is that they hold many more rounds than revolvers. This is extremely important in situations where there are
multiple suspects.

In addition to a sidearm, most SWAT officers also carry some
type of automatic-fire assault rifle or submachine gun. The sight of
these weapons, it has been found, has a strong psychological effect
on suspects, as it did on Mr. Jones in the case above. The Heckler
and Koch MP5 series of submachine guns stands out by far as the
gun of choice for the majority of police SWAT teams. These
weapons are favored because they are compact, reliable, and very
accurate. SWAT teams also like them because they can be set to fire
a single shot, set to fire two or three shot bursts, or set on automatic fire. In addition, while a good submachine gun must be
capable of rapid fire, it must also be accurate in single-shot fire,
which the MP5 series is. However, as fine a weapon as the MP5 is,
it is not the only automatic-fire assault weapon used by police
SWAT teams. Some teams use the Steyr AUG, others use the Colt
M-16 or AR-15, and some use the MAC 10. During the attempted
assassination of President Reagan, television viewers very clearly
saw that the Secret Service agents protecting the president carried
Uzis.

A few police SWAT teams have their officers carry shotguns,
rather than submachine guns. These weapons are not as favored
as submachine guns are, because shotguns are not target-specific
except at very close range. Shotgun pellets have a tendency to
disperse after traveling a short distance. When a shotgun is fired at
a target from anywhere other than close range, there is a strong
possibility that those standing close to the target will be struck by
stray pellets. For teams that do carry shotguns, however, the
favored brand is the Benelli, which has good close-range accuracy
and excellent reliability. But along with the serious problem of

buckshot spread, another problem with using shotguns is their limited magazine capacity. Most hold only four or five rounds. To compensate, there is a shotgun called the *street sweeper*, which is a weapon favored by many street gangs. It is a shotgun with a revolving cylinder that holds twelve rounds.

To facilitate the use of whatever weapon the SWAT team selects for its members, a number of weapon accessories are available. One of the most commonly used is the sound suppressor (or what is known in the movies as a *silencer*). While sound suppressors look like the "silencers" often seen in movies, they aren't quite that efficient and don't totally silence a weapon. Even when subsonic ammunition is used (so there will be no sonic crack, which occurs when a bullet travels over eleven hundred feet per second), still the mechanical clattering of the bolt action as the gun loads new shells and ejects the used casings can be heard. This is particularly noticeable in rapid-fire submachine guns. However, most people aren't able to associate this noise with a gun, and often, the noise is covered by ambient sound (normal background noise in the area, or sounds specially generated to cover the noise of the gun's bolt action).

However, an important consideration for police SWAT teams that use sound suppressors is that these devices significantly reduce the velocity of a bullet and consequently its power. While a bullet fired from a suppressed gun will usually still kill or incapacitate a person, a sound suppressor seriously affects a bullet's ability to penetrate glass, doors, and so on. Sound suppressors, however, can be a real boon to police SWAT teams that must assault large, multiroomed or tall, multistoried buildings. Using them, SWAT teams can neutralize suspects in one part of the building without the suspects in another part knowing it.

Another important, and often used, accessory for police SWAT weapons is the laser-aiming device. This is simply a laser attached to a submachine gun, a sniper's rifle, or even a pistol. The laser emits a beam that becomes a dot on the target and shows exactly where the round will strike. This beam can be very intimidating when placed on a suspect. Also available is an infrared laser-aiming device, whose laser dot can be seen only by someone wearing special infrared goggles.

But not all of the specialty equipment used by police SWAT teams are explosives or deadly weapons. Many of the pieces of equipment used, as demonstrated in the following incident, are protective devices or high-tech surveillance equipment.

The residents of East Harlem in New York City have seen more than their share of crime over the years. Stabbings, shootings, and robberies are not unusual in their neighborhood. But on March 4, 1987, a crime unusual even for that neighborhood occurred. At around 3:15 P.M., Ismael Igartua, a twenty-five-year-old man on parole for robbery, began banging on the door of Apartment 4N at the Metro-North Plaza apartment building on East 101st Street. The police later theorized that Mr. Igartua was planning a drug rip-off.

Mr. Igartua found that either no one was at home in Apartment 4N or no one would answer the door. But then, when the door to Apartment 4M opened as a female visitor prepared to leave, Mr. Igartua raced over and barged inside, wildly firing the weapon he carried. During the initial moments of confusion, a woman who had been inside Apartment 4M managed to escape and notify the police. Thus began a thirty-hour ordeal, during which Mr. Igartua would hold four people hostage, including a four-year-old girl, and would fire more than two dozen shots inside the apartment, down the hallway outside the apartment, and out the apartment's windows.

Immediately responding to the call, two housing police officers arrived at the scene very soon after the incident began, and they very likely kept Mr. Igartua from escaping with the large supply of drugs he found inside Apartment 4M. On discovering that the housing officers were at the door, Mr. Igartua was reported to have grabbed the four-year-old hostage and held her in front of him as he fired his gun at the housing officers, telling them, "This is a matter of narcotics, you shouldn't be involved."

It occasionally happens, when the police arrive quickly and

block a criminal's escape, that the criminal resorts to taking hostages without any real plan or purpose, only to hold off an immediate arrest. Once this happens, the police response is to contain the incident and then find a way to persuade the hostage taker that his or her best action would be to release the hostages unharmed and give up. Although, as in the Igartua case, this approach often takes quite some time.

In this case, in addition to the two housing officers, more than one hundred other police officers soon responded and arrived at the scene of the incident, including the New York City SWAT team. The SWAT team immediately set up a command post in another apartment of the building, positioned snipers, and cordoned off the area for five blocks in all directions. During this time, a hostage negotiator contacted Mr. Igartua. However, since Mr. Igartua was now high on the drugs he had found inside Apartment 4M, and since he very likely hadn't gone there with the intention of taking hostages, his demands during the ordeal were bizarre, and his emotional state was unstable. Therefore, the police knew they were going to need more information about what was happening inside the apartment.

This is a classic problem for police SWAT teams facing a hostage incident in which the hostage taker is unstable or irrational, or under the influence of drugs or alcohol. The police know they cannot rely on what they are being told by the hostage taker, who may be lying, hallucinating, or simply unaware of what is actually happening. The police, however, dealt effectively with this problem in the Igartua hostage incident through the use of electronic listening devices that could pick up sounds through both the walls and the pipes running into the apartment. The information gathered through these devices allowed the New York City SWAT team to know what the people were saying and doing inside Apartment 4M.

Another problem that presented itself in the Igartua incident, and that quite often presents itself in other SWAT incidents, is how to move officers safely over large, open areas, where they are likely to be exposed to hostile gunfire, such as across parking lots or along sidewalks. In the Igartua incident, the problem was how to transverse a seventy-five-foot-long hallway, down which there was little cover and down which Mr. Igartua had already fired his gun several times. The SWAT team accomplished this by using another specialized piece of equipment. They used a device called a *portable ballistic barrier shield*, which is a bullet-proof barrier about the size of one side of a telephone booth. The shield completely conceals an officer behind it, yet it is portable, so the officer using it can wheel it to a location. It also contains a bullet-proof view port, through which the officer can see what is happening in front of the shield.

"I was in that hallway in 1987 in New York," said retired New York City police officer Al Baker in an article in *The Tactical Edge*. "I was among those spared gunshot wounds by the shield. During those tense thirty hours, many of my colleagues were similarly protected."

During the thirty hours of the Igartua hostage incident, the negotiations many times went rocky. Several times, when he apparently didn't feel he was getting his way, Mr. Igartua tied up and then untied the hostages, threatened the lives of the hostages, and even held the four-year-old hostage in front of a window, either as a shield or as a threat. One time, he told the negotiator that he was going to shoot one of the hostages and then counted down from five and fired his weapon, after which one of the hostages began screaming. It was soon discovered, however, through the electronic listening devices that he hadn't actually shot anyone.

Also making the negotiations rocky was the problem that, during the incident, Mr. Igartua was taking a large amount of drugs. At one point, through the use of the electronic listening devices, the police heard him tell someone in the apartment to pass him another bag because he wanted to get real good and doped up. Throughout the ordeal Mr. Igartua demanded baking soda from the police as a prerequisite to ending the incident, but the police refused, fearing he wanted to make crack cocaine, which they worried would make him even more violent and irrational.

"His mood was like a roller coaster," said Chief Robert J. Johnson, Jr., of the New York City Police Department (Ravo 1987, B1). The specialized pieces of equipment used by the New York City Police Department SWAT team eventually made the difference in resolving the incident. Although the police, through the ballistic shield, were able to get close enough to the apartment to stage an emergency entry if needed, they were spared having to undertake this hazardous operation because the electronic listening devices allowed them to overhear what was happening and being said inside the apartment. Through the electronic listening devices, they knew no one was actually being harmed when Mr. Igartua had the hostages scream. Finally, after thirty hours of talking to him, after sending in a videotape on which Mr. Igartua's girlfriend pleaded with him to surrender, after finally being able to convince him that he had nothing to gain by continuing the incident, and after just basically wearing him down, the police got Mr. Igartua at last to come out and surrender.

This incident, like so many others resolved in the past several decades by police SWAT teams, was resolved peacefully because the police handled the incident professionally. They used procedures that have been shown many times to be successful in persuading even highly erratic hostage takers like Mr. Igartua to surrender without harming anyone.

But even the best SWAT teams in the world, following the best procedures, are still often at the mercy and whims of highly erratic and usually highly unstable individuals who have taken hostages or barricaded themselves somewhere because of some perceived wrong. To be successful, a SWAT team needs every edge it can get, and there are hundreds and hundreds of specialized pieces of equipment available that will give police SWAT teams this extra edge.

For example, two years before the Igartua hostage incident, the New York City SWAT team had been called to the basement of a Manhattan apartment building where a man had barricaded himself and fired a half dozen shots at the police. After a period of negotiation, the man finally told the SWAT team he wanted to give up and then threw out two guns and stepped into the hallway. What the police didn't know was that the man had hidden in his waistband a third gun, which he later admitted he meant to use on the police.

However, rather than having the SWAT team come down the hallway to confront the man, the police first sent a mechanical robot with a high-intensity light that startled the man and distracted him long enough for the officers to rush down the hallway and take him into custody without injury. Like the portable ballistic shield in the Igartua incident, the robot in this situation very likely saved several police officers from serious injury or death.

A large number of other devices can be used by SWAT officers to make their jobs safer and more efficient. For example, in addition to the rolling ballistic shield used in the Igartua incident, police SWAT teams also often use smaller ballistic shields that are carried in much the same way as the shield of a Roman soldier. These are used by officers who must advance into very dangerous places. However, while giving protection against most gunfire, they will not stop all bullets. In 1990, in Virginia, for example, a SWAT officer was killed when a bullet fired from a high-powered military rifle penetrated the ballistic shield he carried.

Another piece of protective equipment used by SWAT officers is soft body armor. This is a lightweight woven material that will stop most—but again, not all—bullets. Soft body armor works through its fibers absorbing and then dissipating a bullet's energy. Most SWAT officers also wear ballistic helmets and protective eyewear (see photo on page 113).

In the hope that this protective material won't be needed, however, SWAT teams usually try to gain as much intelligence as possible on any hostage taker or barricaded subject. In addition to the electronic equipment used in the Igartua case, there are dozens of other pieces of high-tech intelligence-gathering equipment available. For example, there is a small video camera on a telescoping arm that allows officers to safely see around corners, in windows, and into rooms with open doors. These are so small that

SWAT equipment, including automatic weapon, ballistic helmet, and ballistic shields (photo by Lieutenant Stephen Robertson).

they can be inserted through a two-inch hole. There are also electronic stethoscopes that can be attached to walls, windows, doors, or, as in the Igartua case, pipes, and there is also a spiked stethoscope that can be driven through insulated walls. One of the newer listening devices is the *Laser Bug*. This is a laser beam that, when bounced off a window, picks up the modulations of the glass, which can be converted to sound.

Thanks to modern microtechnology, tiny transmitters can often be smuggled into a SWAT incident site hidden inside other objects. For tactical purposes, it is better if two transmitters can be placed inside an incident site. Then, it is possible to pinpoint a suspect's location by determining which transmitter has the strongest signal. If, however, it becomes impossible to smuggle the transmitters inside, there are tube microphones that can be inserted through keyholes, under doors, down chimneys, or through air vents. There are also pinhole microphones and pinhole video cameras, which need only a very small hole to operate through.

Being able to see what is happening at all times is particularly important at a SWAT incident. While at one time darkness worked to the advantage of the perpetrators at SWAT incidents, this is no longer so. Most SWAT teams now use night vision technology. These devices allow the wearer to see in darkness, using any small amount of light available, such as starlight, which is intensified many times. In total darkness, the equipment uses infrared light, which it converts to visible light. These devices can be used either as goggles or as sighting devices for weapons.

Besides being able to see a suspect at a SWAT incident site, the police must also be able to communicate with the suspect while at the same time cutting off his or her ability to communicate with anyone else (since communicating with others, including the press, often encourages a suspect to resist surrendering). This can be accomplished with a hostage or crisis phone. These come in several models. With one, the police cut the telephone service to a house or building and then tap the crisis phone into the line. The SWAT team can then talk to the suspect and even let a third party talk to him, but the conversation is controlled by the SWAT team, not the suspect or the third party. These phones also allow for the conversations to be taped and for people in the SWAT command post to listen in.

At locations that have no phone service, police SWAT teams many times use a "throw phone" (called this since the device is often thrown to a suspect because of the danger of approaching too closely). The police used this type of crisis phone in the incident at the Fox Plaza office building.

While all of this equipment is useful and often very helpful in bringing about successful resolutions to SWAT incidents, SWAT training officers become nervous when they see their officers becoming too dependent on equipment, at the expense of good, sound tactics. While good, sound tactics almost always generate positive results, even the best equipment can malfunction, misfire, or, as in the following incident, simply not produce the effect expected.

On an August afternoon in 1986, a man hurried into the Anaheim, California, Police Department and told the police that his forty-four-year-old son, Frank, had just purchased a .22-caliber rifle and three hundred rounds of ammunition. His son, the father said, had a long history of mental illness and had told him that he intended to take the rifle down to the courthouse and kill as many people as possible. At that moment, though, the man said, rather than being at the courthouse, Frank was at home holding his mother hostage.

A police dispatcher notified the uniformed officers patrolling near the home, and they immediately responded, first setting up security perimeters around the location to contain the situation, and then making contact with Frank over the telephone. Despite orders from the police, however, Frank refused to leave the house and also refused to allow his mother to leave. The uniformed officers requested the Anaheim Police Department SWAT team.

Once the SWAT team had arrived and taken control of the situation, a hostage negotiator called Frank on the telephone and established a dialogue with him. After several hours of talking to Frank, the negotiator finally convinced him to release his mother unharmed. But just a few minutes after Frank had released his mother, with everyone at the scene believing his surrender was imminent, Frank came out onto the front porch, fired several rounds with the .22-caliber rifle at a nearby parked car, and then stepped back into the house.

The dialogue over the telephone started again, but when after several more hours of talking the negotiator still couldn't convince Frank to surrender, the SWAT commander decided to become more aggressive, and SWAT officers began firing tear gas shells into the house. Over the next fifteen hours, they fired over forty tear-gas projectiles into the house. The gas inside the home became so thick that officers close to the house had to wear gas masks to keep from being overcome by the escaping cloud. The gas, however, even though extremely thick, had no apparent effect on Frank. This is something often seen by the police when dealing with the mentally ill or with people high on drugs. They are many times impervious to the effects of chemical irritants, no matter how strong. This is something to think about for any person who carries a container of tear gas, expecting it to be excellent protection. The truth is that it doesn't always work (see photo below).

When morning finally came, Frank asked for some cigarettes, and the negotiator had two cigarettes delivered to the front porch. The officers noticed immediately that, when Frank stepped out to pick up the cigarettes, he left his rifle inside. Several more times, Frank requested cigarettes, and each time, the police delivered them, but each time, they placed them a little farther away from the front door, and each time, Frank came out unarmed to pick them up.

Since it was apparent that chemical agents were useless against Frank, the SWAT team devised another plan. On the next delivery of cigarettes, if Frank came out unarmed, a takedown by

Tear gas projectile launchers used by police SWAT team (photo by Robert L. Snow).

SWAT officers would be attempted. At the same time as the take-down, other officers would enter the back of the house, which would be easy since Frank had shot off the rear door while firing at the police. These officers would snatch the .22-caliber rifle and outflank Frank from the rear.

When Frank again requested cigarettes, the command post told all officers to get into position. The police delivered the cigarettes, and once again, Frank stepped out onto the porch unarmed. When he knelt down to pick up the cigarettes, an officer armed with a 37-mm gas gun loaded with a short-range muzzle-blast cartridge rushed up and fired at Frank from about four feet away. The shell struck Frank in the chest, knocking him off his feet, and though not overly affected by the chemical irritant, Frank was momentarily blinded by the explosion of the chemical agent dust. Officers positioned nearby rushed forward and took him into custody without further injury.

The job of a police SWAT team is to resolve any incident with as little injury and loss of life as possible. In the preceding situation, for example, the officers could have justifiably shot and killed Frank since he had shot at them, but they instead chose a nonlethal means to apprehend him. For SWAT teams that want this non-lethal option, many pieces of nonlethal weaponry are available.

While the police in Anaheim used a makeshift nonlethal weapon to apprehend Frank by striking him in the chest with a 37-mm tear-gas round, there are rounds specially designed to strike and stun an aggressive suspect. There is, for example, a device called a *stingball*, which is a grenade containing small rubber balls that both sting and stun a suspect. Additionally, there are shotgun shells that contain rubber pellets, as well as shotgun shells that contain fabric bags filled with lead shot. There is also what is called a *rubber impact cartridge*, which is a shell made of preformed rubber that, when fired, expands to an X shape, which gives it more impact. Being hit by any of these nonlethal shells, say people who have been hit by them, is similar to being struck by a line-drive baseball. In rare cases, though, they can be fatal.

But of course, as in the case of Frank above, when wanting to first try nonlethal methods to resolve an incident, the police often use tear gas or some other chemical irritant such as the new OC (oleoresin capsicum), a chemical that contains an extract of cayenne pepper. These are usually, but not always (as Frank demonstrated in his indifference to the tear gas), effective. According to the National Institute of Justice (1988), "Moreover, mentally disturbed and highly emotional subjects, or those in an aggressive mood induced by drugs or alcohol, are known to be relatively unaffected by tear producers or to become even more excited by them" (p. 7).

While the police must always consider the possibility of suffocating a person by using too much tear gas or other chemical irritant (the amount necessary to do this depending on the size of the area in which they are used and the ventilation available), this is actually a very small possibility, since the irritating effects of chemical weapons usually drive an affected party out into the fresh air. The minimum amount needed to affect a person, on the other hand, depends on that individual's own personal reaction to the chemical irritants. And while there are occasional cases like Frank's above, the police find that chemical weapons are usually very effective.

In many cases, however, chemical weapons are not an option (because of other parties being present, because of closeby sites that can be affected, etc.), and nonlethal shells are not practical (because the suspect is behind cover, behind hostages, etc.). In these cases, the police, in order to apprehend a suspect without killing him or her, must be able to distract the suspect long enough to safely rush him or her. For this purpose, police SWAT teams often use diversionary devices. These are devices that will either distract a suspect's attention or stun and disorient the suspect long enough for the SWAT team to enter and stabilize the situation.

SWAT officers can, for example, use smoke grenades both to distract a suspect and to hide a SWAT team's advance. Along with these, SWAT teams can also use diversionary tactics, such as breaking windows in several locations at once so that the suspect will not know which way the officers are coming in. The most common diversion used by police SWAT teams, however, is the "flashbang." These devices were first used tactically by the Israeli commandos during their daring rescue of hostages at Entebbe, Uganda. A flashbang is a device that explodes with a tremendously loud bang and a brilliant flash of light, but that does little damage. The combination of the brilliant flash and the loud bang overloads a suspect's sensory organs and consequently stuns and disorients him or her.

The effects of a flashbang usually last from six to eight seconds, which is often all the time needed to rush and overpower a person. But since the effects of this device (which include confusion, disorientation, and bewilderment) are involuntary, several devices can be used, one after another, to lengthen the effective time if necessary.

There are certain drawbacks to using flashbangs, however. Although they are usually constructed of cardboard, so that they cause no dangerous fragmentation, objects close to them when they explode can become lethal flying objects, and the explosion of a flashbang is quite powerful at close range. When a French police SWAT team stormed a hijacked Air France flight in Marseille, France, in 1994, one of the officers lost his hand when a flashbang exploded as he was holding it. Also, since flashbangs ignite at about 2,700 degrees Celsius, they can start fires. And so, even though very effective, and usually considered nonlethal, flashbangs can be dangerous to both officers and suspects, as the following incident illustrates.

In San Francisco in 1990, a man, who had been stalking a woman for eight years, who had been arrested three times for harassing her, and who had just been released from jail two weeks earlier after being convicted of prowling her property, broke into the woman's house. When the woman came home from work, he surprised her with a gun and tied her up. However, before they could leave the house, the victim's mother telephoned, immediately sensed something was wrong, and called the police.

Quickly arriving officers caught the stalker bringing the woman, still bound, out of the house. When he saw the police, the stalker let the woman go and ran to a nearby garage. Yet he didn't go inside right away but hid nearby. It was cold outside that night, and the stalker finally went into the garage to warm up and was surprised by SWAT officers waiting for him. When he went for his weapon, the SWAT team threw a flashbang, and though stunning the stalker, the concussion also injured two of the officers. The police arrested the stalker without further problems, but two officers went to the hospital with injuries caused by the force of the explosion.

Flashbangs can also have fatal effects. In 1989, a Florida jury acquitted a man of killing a police officer after the SWAT team had tossed three flashbangs into the man's house. The court had the police detonate a flashbang in the parking lot so that the jury could see what the effects were, and the jury then said they believed the man was very likely so terrorized after the police tossed the flashbangs into his house that he didn't know who he was shooting at. In another case, this one in Los Angeles, the family of a forty-three-year-old woman killed when she apparently fell on a flashbang tossed into her home during a narcotics raid sued the city for $10 million.

But in addition to these dangers, flashbangs also cause problems by creating large amounts of smoke, which inhibit breathing, lessen vision, and usually set off smoke alarms, which lessen the ability to hear at SWAT incidents. Also, flashbangs may not cause the distraction hoped for.

"We had a possible suicide, and we thought that a flashbang would distract him long enough for us to rush him," said Sergeant Marvin McCrary of the Columbia, Missouri, Police Department. "But when it went off, he didn't even flinch. He just fired a couple times at the police and then killed himself."

Despite all of these drawbacks, however, flashbangs are a potent nonlethal device that, if used properly, often resolves SWAT incidents with little or no injury or loss of life.

As can be seen by all of the devices I have discussed in this and preceding chapters, there is a huge amount of equipment available to police SWAT teams. The only limitation is finding the money to buy the equipment. Some of the equipment is very expensive. But even if a police department has a large enough budget, equipment alone is not the total answer. No equipment—and for that matter, no tactics—will be effective if the officers using them are not properly trained, as we shall see.

Training

It had been a typical Wednesday evening at Henry's Pub on Durant Avenue. Located only a block from the University of California campus at Berkeley, the bar that evening held close to sixty customers. The clientele, mostly students, had filled the tables and booths in the popular nightspot all evening, sharing drinks with classmates and talking about the semester that had just begun. The drinkers paid no attention to the raven-haired man who came in with a friend just a little after midnight. Minutes later, though, when the bar announced the last call for drinks, the man suddenly pulled a Smith and Wesson .44 Magnum handgun from the briefcase he had brought with him. Without warning, he began randomly shooting the bar patrons.

As the shots rang out and people began to scream and fall from the bullets, a stampede started immediately out the north door of the pub to Durant Avenue and out the east door into the Durant Hotel lobby, which occupied part of the same building as the pub. Thirty of the sixty-seven customers and employees known to be in the establishment managed to escape within the first few moments after the shooting; seven of the patrons had been shot, one fatally. The thirty-seven people who didn't escape, however, would curse their fate because they then began a seven-hour hostage ordeal that would involve more shooting, threats of death, and forced unnatural sexual encounters with each other. They began what many would later call "a nightmare come true."

The hostage taker, Mehrdad Dashti, a thirty-year-old Iranian student at the University of California, had earlier that evening told a friend he wanted to go someplace where there would be lots of blond women. The friend apparently had no idea what Dashti planned for that night since the friend willingly went with him to Henry's Pub, yet escaped with the first rush of people and then became the main source of intelligence for the police about Dashti.

When the gunfire began, a police officer who happened to be close to the pub heard it and thought it was probably firecrackers. But when he went to check and saw the people screaming and bleeding as they fled the bar, he knew he needed help and called in on his radio to report what was happening. A call from the police radio dispatcher went out immediately, both for more uniformed officers and for the City of Berkeley's SWAT team, called in Berkeley the Barricaded Subject Hostage Negotiation Team (BSHNT).

The SWAT officers began acknowledging the call and heading for Durant Avenue from all over the city. At the same time, a number of the uniformed patrol officers who had been nearby immediately responded and began establishing an outer perimeter around the scene. Other uniformed officers began taking up inner-perimeter containment positions around the bar.

As the SWAT officers began arriving, the incident commander set up several of them in sniper positions and then deployed the others to replace the uniformed officers on the inner perimeter. Additional arriving SWAT members began collecting intelligence by interviewing the bar patrons who had escaped and by talking with Dashti's friend. To assist with management of the scene, a city employee drove Berkeley's Mobile Command Substation (a large motor home outfitted with all the equipment needed by a SWAT command post) to the location and parked it a block north of the incident. This became the incident command post, and from there, the SWAT incident commander directed the SWAT team's actions.

Just ten minutes or so after the incident began, a male and female hostage suddenly walked out of the pub. The police on the scene suspected their leaving might be a ruse by Dashti to escape, and they immediately stopped and challenged the couple. But while the police were talking to the couple, Dashti fired a shot at them from inside the pub, slightly wounding a police officer and sending everyone scurrying for cover. The couple, it turned out, had been legitimate hostages, and thirty-five people were now still hostage inside Henry's Pub.

Following this incident, except for occasional random firing by Dashti into the ceiling, after which he would order the hostages to scream as if shot (though the police weren't fooled), the intentional shooting stopped and the situation began to stabilize, as these types of incidents usually do. What ordinarily happens in this type of incident is that the police negotiators begin a conversation with the hostage taker, listen to the demands, let the hostage taker vent his or her anger, establish rapport, and then, through negotiation, persuade the hostage taker to release the hostages and surrender. Most of the hostage situations faced by police SWAT teams are settled through negotiation. This one, however, wouldn't be.

Dashti, as it turned out, was not an ordinary hostage taker. For one thing, he refused to talk directly to the police negotiators; instead, he talked through a hostage he positioned at the front door of the bar. And even later, when the police established telephone contact with the pub, Dashti continued to talk only through a hostage, who relayed what he said to the police. But it was his bizarre behavior toward the female hostages during the ordeal that made him definitely not an ordinary hostage taker.

After the incident, his actions inside the pub that night would be explained in part when the police found in his apartment copies of letters he had sent to prominent people, including the president of the United States, the chief justice of the U.S. Supreme Court, and the mayor of San Francisco (whose city sits across the bay from Berkeley). In these letters, Dashti complained of hearing voices and of the government experimenting on his mind. He demanded that the states of California, Nevada, and Oregon be given to him as payment for his "mental telepathy" work for the federal government. The police would also find records in Dashti's apartment which showed that the county health department had diagnosed him as a paranoid schizophrenic.

But despite all this later evidence of an unbalanced mind, Dashti had enough of a grip on reality and enough awareness during the hostage incident to take exceptional safety precautions against a police assault. Besides refusing to speak with the police, he also positioned hostages in front of all the doors and windows in order to discourage a forced entry by the police. And even though the main door to Henry's Pub had been heavily damaged during the initial stampede to get out, and this damage gave the officers stationed outside a partial view of the inside of the bar, Dashti never exposed himself to them.

While the police would not receive documented information about Dashti's disturbed mind until after the incident had ended, once the negotiation phase began the demands he issued, demands both bizarre and completely unrealistic, made the police immediately begin to worry about Dashti's mental state. He demanded, for example, $16 trillion for "mental telepathy" services to the government. He also made other equally outrageous demands, such as insisting that the San Francisco police chief appear on television with his pants down. In their intelligence gathering, the SWAT team found, however, that Dashti and his mental state were not totally unknown to them. He had been investigated recently, they discovered, for cashing stolen checks, and during questioning, he had reportedly told the police that the government had been doing experiments on his mind and that he heard voices.

It didn't take long for the SWAT incident commander to realize that, in addition to being in a poor negotiating position, the SWAT team's tactical position, because of Dashti's security arrangements, wasn't much better. But regardless of their tactical position, the SWAT commander knew that a refined assault plan—a blueprint for entering and rescuing the hostages which would replace the emergency rescue plan devised immediately after the team had set up around the incident—had to be developed because the negotiators were getting nowhere. As this plan was being formulated, officers on the west side of the scene requested permission to shoot out the streetlights because they were compromising these officers' position. The command post gave permission but found that shooting out the streetlights upset Dashti, who had a hostage shout out the main door, "Hey, what are you doing?" A little while afterward, a female hostage managed to escape out the kitchen door when Dashti sent her to the kitchen to look for the switch that would turn off the lights inside the pub. Dashti apparently feared that the darkness outside would now make him a better target. She advised the team that Dashti was watching the live television news coverage of the incident, which was relaying everything the police were doing. She also said that he had become very agitated when the television announcer said one of Dashti's shooting victims had died.

Requesting but receiving little cooperation from the press, the SWAT team continued with their plan development, relying mostly on their training, since the Henry's Pub situation was the biggest incident the Berkeley SWAT team had ever faced. Soon though, the SWAT team had devised a detailed assault-and-rescue plan they felt had an excellent chance of success. The assault-and-rescue team, to reinforce their training and to detect any weak points in the plan, practiced the assault in facilities furnished by the University of California police. Once the SWAT team had made the necessary minor adjustments to the plan and felt it was as workable as they could make it, they presented the plan to the incident commander, who approved it but hoped they wouldn't need it (these types of incidents often end abruptly, with the hostage taker suddenly surrendering, committing suicide, or coming out shooting).

To be ready when and if called, the assault-and-rescue team moved into close proximity to their assault positions. Because the plan called for both speed and surprise, the team declined the use of heavy, hard body armor and helmets, and because of the weapons Dashti was reported to have, which included the .44 Magnum revolver, a 9-mm semiautomatic pistol, and a fully automatic .380-caliber pistol, they decided to use .45-caliber pistols and Heckler & Koch MP5's.

Inside the bar during the hours of attempted negotiations and during the hours of assault-and-rescue plan development, Dashti's moods swung back and forth from high to low. At times, wearing only a loin cloth, he would scream, "When is it going to end? How long? How long?"

But also during this time, in addition to the bizarre demands he made of the police negotiators, Dashti began exploiting his own dark and bizarre sexual obsessions. After haranguing all of the blond women hostages as sluts, he then, under the threat of death, forced them to strip naked from the waist down and had the male hostages sexually molest them with items he had brought with him. According to witnesses, he also ranted for hours about being turned down for a government loan and about the government's performing experiments on his mind, but mostly he ranted about how all blond American women were sluts. He accused American women of showing too much leg, of wearing tight skirts, and of leading men like him on. They deserved to be punished, he said. Interestingly, Dashti had reportedly been involved with a blond student.

Although, during most of the incident, the police were unaware of this forced sexual molestation, and of Dashti having been diagnosed as a paranoid schizophrenic, they did know from Dashti's demands that he was very emotionally and mentally unbalanced. And since he wouldn't talk to the police negotiators directly, but only through a hostage, it became impossible for them to convince him to surrender. An assault on the pub finally appeared to be the only viable solution. The assault-and-rescue team knew Dashti's basic location in the bar because, every time the hostage at the door would relay a question to Dashti, the hostage would look toward the northwest.

While the assault-and-rescue team was getting into position in order to be ready when the command came for them to proceed, another female hostage managed to escape through the kitchen door. After listening to her description of Dashti's mental state and actions, and after the negotiation team decided it had reached an impasse, the incident commander decided that an assault, even though extremely dangerous to both the hostages and the officers, was needed, and soon. The incident had now gone on for seven hours, and it was nearing time for the college community to begin waking up, which would only add to the problems at the scene. And so, the SWAT incident commander gave the assault-and-rescue plan the green light.

The plan that had been developed, practiced, and refined would use a five-officer assault-and-rescue team and a two-officer diversion team. The two officers would stage a diversion in the kitchen just south of the bar area, and at the same time, the five-officer team would enter the pub through the hotel lobby doors.

At the signal to prepare for the assault, the two officers slipped into the hotel lobby and took up their positions just outside the kitchen, which had doors (in addition to the one the female hostages had escaped through) that led to both the hotel lobby and the pub where Dashti was. The assault-and-rescue team then positioned themselves on the sidewalk just outside the hotel lobby entrance. When the command to go was given, SWAT officers detonated two flashbang devices in the kitchen area, and at the same time, the five-officer assault-and-rescue team entered the hotel lobby and raced for the pub. Once inside the bar area, the team split, as they had practiced so many times during that night's training, into groups of three and two and then moved in westward paths parallel through the bar toward where they surmised Dashti was. One of the officers stopped and positioned himself at the bar to act as a cover officer, while the others proceeded forward, shouting, "Police! Get down!"

Because of intense media coverage, which detailed every move the police made, Dashti had been expecting an assault, and in addition to positioning hostages in front of all the doors and windows, he had also moved furniture around him as protection. At the explosion of the flashbangs in the kitchen area, however, Dashti jumped up and fired two shots at the kitchen door. He then started heading toward a group of hostages sitting in a booth nearby. The assault-and-rescue team saw this move and, also seeing Dashti's weapon out and ready, opened fire with their own weapons, hitting him twenty-four times and killing him.

It was over. After more than seven hours, the ordeal ended in less than nine seconds after the flashbang detonation.

Although some questioned afterward why the police waited seven hours before assaulting the bar, the operation, once it had begun, was a complete success. While the police fired twenty-four shots at Dashti, and some of these passed through him, the officers, because of being properly trained, had positioned themselves so that no hostages were harmed by the bullets during the assault. The only casualty of the assault was Dashti. The operation went smoothly because the officers who took part in it had received intensive training, both on a regular basis at their monthly training sessions and during the impromptu training they had received that night while practicing the assault. Regular training for situations like the Henry's Pub incident becomes extremely important during an actual assault because this training takes the fear of the unknown out of the incident. The Berkeley Police Department SWAT officers knew, through their training and practice, exactly what they were supposed to do, and they did it with remarkable skill—and in less than nine seconds.

However, the reason the police had waited so long before assaulting the bar and rescuing the hostages is difficult to explain to anyone not involved in resolving SWAT incidents, and it would be particularly hard to explain to anyone who was inside Henry's Pub that night. But Dashti was not a typical hostage taker (typical hostage takers often take hostages on the spur of the moment, with no thought about what they are doing). Dashti was obviously well aware of what he was doing and of the tactics police SWAT teams use in hostage situations. He demonstrated this awareness by the way he positioned hostages in front of all the possible entry points, by the way he barricaded himself far back in the bar, and by his refusal to speak directly to the police negotiators. These actions meant he was prepared for and expecting a police assault. Therefore, the element of surprise, which is so often the key to successful SWAT operations, was not there, at least not in the first few hours of the incident. In addition, because of Dashti's security precautions, the use of chemical weapons was not feasible, nor was the use of a police sniper. The only choices during the first hours of the incident were to continue the negotiations, which the police did, or to conduct an immediate police assault, which would very likely have resulted in many injuries and possible death to innocent hostages.

It has been found in SWAT incidents that the majority of injuries and deaths to both police officers and hostages occur during assaults and hostage-rescue attempts. And just as important, the police have found through experience that the majority of situations like the Henry's Pub incident can be, if given enough time, negotiated to a successful conclusion. For this reason, if no one is being injured (the police did not become aware of the sexual molestation until late in the incident), SWAT incident commanders like to give their hostage negotiations as much time as they need to resolve the incident. But when they can't, and an assault is the only answer, that is when the intensive training SWAT officers undergo begins to pay dividends.

"Good training is the key to the success of any team," said Steve Gentry, a former member of the Army's top-secret SWAT team, the Delta Force. "Train well and you'll perform well."

Keeping this training up to date, though, is often a problem. With the exception of those officers on SWAT teams in very large police departments, most police SWAT team members serve only on call and hold other jobs in the police department, such as patrol officer or detective. They respond and act as SWAT team members only when an emergency requires the SWAT team to be called up. While this arrangement makes good economic sense for police departments that only occasionally need a SWAT team, it also presents the problem that, while the team may have received excellent initial training, much of this knowledge may be forgotten, and many of the tactics may become rusty between call-ups. In addition, most general police work (which these officers do between call-ups) requires independent action by police officers, and only very seldom do they do anything as a team. Therefore, the on-call SWAT officer often has difficulty making the transition from being an independent unit to becoming a team member.

The only way to prevent this difficulty and to keep knowledge, skills, and team ability high is through regular training. This means regular training as a team, performing tasks that will be required of the SWAT officers acting as a disciplined unit. Of the many SWAT teams I gathered information from for this book, about half, I found, required eight hours a month of SWAT team training, and the remainder required twelve to sixteen hours. This regular training, SWAT commanders know, is what keeps the fine edge on the team during the often long spaces between call-ups. It also assures all members that they can depend on each other, because it has been found that, when things go bad, when plans go to hell, people fall back on what they have been trained to do. On the other hand, without regular training, a police SWAT team will not work as a disciplined unit, the members will be unsure of their responsibilities, and failure is almost ensured.

"A poorly trained SWAT team is a disaster just waiting to happen," said Lieutenant Larry Beadles, who is the head of both the Training Academy and the SWAT team in Richmond, Virginia.

Also, SWAT team training, if it is to be beneficial to the officers, must be done during all times of the day and in all types of weather. Many SWAT training officers also insist that the training, if it is to be realistic, must take place in the full SWAT uniform and with all of the gear the members regularly carry. There is not much point to the training, they feel, if the officers train only on easy things and do everything the easy way. Rather, SWAT training officers usually attempt to train for the worst possible scenarios, because they will, and often do, occur. And because the worst-case scenario often happens, all officers must be trained on all weapons, including chemical weapons. A SWAT officer never knows when he or she will have to take over another officer's job.

But even beyond this, to be efficient and worthwhile, many SWAT training officers believe that training should be even tougher than the worst-case scenario, and that the training must incorporate even more stress than can be expected in any SWAT incident. Instructors increase the thoroughness and the stress of training by making the unexpected happen, such as equipment malfunctioning and plans going bad. As Coach Vince Lombardi said, "Practice should be hell so that games are fun."

A number of police departments, to make their training realistic, use actual SWAT incidents that have occurred in various parts of the country as scenarios, which are played out with each member performing his or her part. The training thus becomes particularly valuable to the SWAT officers because they know that what they are experiencing actually happened to a police SWAT team somewhere. Such training changes from just getting some interesting information into obtaining crucial data that may save their own or someone else's life someday. It is also helpful to use real-life SWAT incidents as the basis for training because the SWAT team can then critique another police department's performance, see where and why problems developed, and pick up pointers from the other SWAT team's success or failure.

Some SWAT team trainers even go so far as to recruit actors from local college drama classes or from community theaters to play parts in these scenarios. The use of actors adds realism to a scenario because, since all of the officers know each other, if an officer tries to act the part of a psychotic criminal or a frightened hostage, it is difficult for the other officers to feel that the scenario has real-life relevance. Also, it has been found that police officers, since they lack acting experience, have a tendency to overact their parts. Drama students and actors usually don't, and in preparation for one of these scenarios, the SWAT team trainer often has the actors watch videotapes of real hostage incidents and videotaped interviews with real hostages and hostage takers.

A person might question, though, just how seriously SWAT officers would take this training, since they know it is just acting. They take it with deadly seriousness. The SWAT officers know that they are being observed and evaluated by both their trainers and their fellow officers, and that their status as members of an elite team is at stake. Thus, the officers are under tremendous emotional stress to perform well, and to look good in front of the other officers. The fear of failure adds the stress that training officers are looking for. To add even more stress, since high stress is a part of most SWAT incidents, training officers often instruct the actors to do things that frustrate the SWAT officers' actions, as often happens in real-life SWAT incidents. The officers, then, when they see that their actions are not producing the effects they expected, must, while under high emotional stress, find another means to successfully resolve the incident.

When I was in charge of the Indianapolis Police Department's Training Academy, we used a system similar to this to train our officers in the best methods of handling domestic disturbances (family fights). As in SWAT training, we often had the actors try to purposely frustrate the officers, which happens often in real-life domestic disturbances. We quickly learned, though, that, because the officers became so emotionally involved in trying to resolve the incident successfully, we needed to have a training officer always standing closeby. The officers would occasionally become so frustrated (even though they knew the training was just play acting) that an altercation, and sometimes a fistfight, would erupt.

Continuing with this trend toward realism in training, many police SWAT teams build what are called CQB (close-quarter-battle) houses, fun houses, or live-fire houses. These are structures that resemble typical homes or business establishments but are built so that SWAT officers can use them to practice room and building entry, threat neutralization, and hostage rescue. Some police departments have built elaborate structures with rooms of many different sizes, with furniture, and some even with mannequins to simulate hostages and hostage takers (see photo on page 135). Unlike in real homes, however, the walls of these houses

Mannequins for CQB house (photo by Lieutenant Stephen Robertson).

must be made of some solid material, such as automobile tires filled with sand, railroad ties, or wood with gravel packed between the walls. They are built this way so that officers can fire live rounds inside the house without any danger of the rounds passing through a wall and hitting someone. The ability to fire live rounds during training is important because officers must become used to the weapon recoil and to the sound of the gunfire. In addition, it is important for officers to see how well they shoot when rushing into a room and when they are under stress. Only pretending to shoot or firing blanks won't accomplish this.

For police departments that can't afford or don't have the facilities for a CQB house, the option of paint ball shooting is available. (Paint balls are just that: little balls of paint that are shot from guns and clearly mark the spot they strike.) This training is particularly valuable when SWAT officers are learning room entry techniques and hostage rescue. Officers find out very quickly just how easy it is to be shot by a perpetrator when they rush into a room without a plan or without sound room-entry tactics.

In addition to letting officers see just how easy it is to be shot when they are careless, a paint ball striking an unprotected part of the body, as anyone who has ever been hit by one will testify, stings and leaves a welt where the person is hit. This stinging, however, can be a good experience because, the first few times it happens, an officer usually freezes, which could be deadly in a real-life incident. But after several times of being stung, the officer learns that he or she can go ahead and complete the mission even when hit. This can be a lifesaver if the officer is ever really shot while making a tactical room entry or during a building assault.

Tactical room entry is a SWAT technique that requires considerable training and practice so that officers can do it safely and successfully. Whenever officers enter a room at a SWAT incident site, they know they are apt to be entering the perpetrator's territory and are also likely to be exposing themselves to gunfire from the perpetrator. Therefore, the officers' lives depend on knowing how to enter a room quickly and properly. Officers must know how to enter a room as a team, and how to enter a room without running into each other, without being caught in cross fire, and without being shot by the perpetrator (SWAT officers never, except in the most dire emergencies, enter rooms by themselves). Paint ball use is excellent as realistic training for room entry techniques because being hit by a paint ball immediately points out any problems the officers are having.

In the interest of realistic training, a number of SWAT training officers have been successful in obtaining permission to use as training sites buildings scheduled for demolition. These locations can be of immense value because the officers can practice forced entry without worrying about damaging the building. SWAT officers can also practice and experience flashbang explosions, which is very important because, if SWAT officers don't experience what happens during a flashbang explosion, they can't be prepared for it and will be just as affected by a flashbang as the perpetrator.

One of the most important reasons for having this intense, realistic training is that, at SWAT incidents, the police are usually dealing with a highly emotional and very likely unstable person. The thinking processes of these individuals are usually jumbled, and therefore, SWAT teams can expect the unexpected to happen. Experience has shown that, the more trained, disciplined, and tightly knit a team is, the better the members react when confronted by the unexpected. It has also been shown that, when confronted with the unexpected, teams fall back on their training, and if trained well, they perform well (see photos on pages 137–139).

"Training can make the difference between life and death in any tactical situation," said Officer Kris Brandt, a trainer for the New York City Police Department's Emergency Services Unit, in a telephone interview (January 24, 1995). "I'm living proof of that.

SWAT officers being trained on how to handle confrontations with armed adversaries (photo by Lieutenant Stephen Robertson).

SWAT sniper training (photo by Lieutenant Stephen Robertson).

When things go really bad, officers fall back on what they were trained to do. I was in a shootout, and it all happened so fast I only had time to do what I was trained to do, and it saved me."

Along with realistic training in areas such as close-quarter shooting, hand-to-hand combat (often a confrontation takes place in such tight quarters that shooting is not possible, and officers are taught methods for a quick takedown and disarming of suspects, usually by instructors versed in the martial arts), room entry, chemical weapons, and other tactical matters, SWAT officers must also be trained in human psychology, particularly abnormal psychology. The team members must understand the motivations of the people they will be facing. They must understand as much as possible the thought processes of unstable people in highly emotional and stressful situations, and they must have some idea of how the people they deal with will react.

SWAT officers being taught how to shoot even if knocked to the ground. (photo by Lieutenant Stephen Robertson).

This psychological training is given in many police departments by mental health professionals who deal regularly with the kind of individuals who become involved in SWAT-type incidents. In Indianapolis, for example, a group of psychiatrists and clinical psychologists who are well acquainted with this type of individual, and who also work as on-scene advisers at SWAT incidents, handle the training for SWAT officers. What SWAT officers are taught by this group is that many of the people they will come in contact with are suffering from such problems as paranoia, an antisocial personality, an inadequate personality, or may possibly be simply undergoing some sort of extreme personal stress. Each type of person requires a different approach from a police SWAT team. For instance, when dealing with a person suffering from paranoia, SWAT teams are advised to downplay any show of force, since a show of force often feeds and accentuates the person's paranoia. Other mental disorders or personality problems call for other tactics.

But all of this SWAT training, important as it is, should not be just for SWAT team members. Police departments have found that other members of the department can also benefit from SWAT training, and that the SWAT team can benefit from having these other members trained. For example, many police departments train their uniformed patrol supervisors in SWAT procedures. This training is important because uniformed supervisors are often at and in charge of a SWAT incident for some time before the SWAT team arrives in large enough numbers to take over. Therefore, the uniformed supervisor needs to know what he or she should do to safely and properly contain and stabilize the situation until the SWAT team arrives. Police departments have also found it beneficial to train their dispatchers so that they will know what to say, what to ask, and how to act when they receive a hostage or barricaded-person call. Finally, it is also vital to instruct the command staff of a police department in SWAT procedures. The SWAT officers hope that the command staff's receiving this instruction will foster a better understanding of why the SWAT team is doing or not doing something at an incident site. This sort of understanding makes the command staff less inclined to pressure the team to hurry and wrap the situation up. For various reasons, usually political, this kind of pressure unfortunately happens at SWAT incidents. This "hurry up," though, often forces a SWAT team to take unnecessarily dangerous risks, dangerous both for them and for the hostages.

Since most municipal police departments in the United States are independent of each other, each sets its own chain of command for SWAT incidents. However, even in those cities with a tight chain of command, where no one but SWAT command officers can make decisions about what to do once the SWAT team deploys, other command-rank officers can still wield considerable power just because of their rank and status. It is for this reason that command staff training is so vital.

Along with the police department members trained above, many departments also require that their hostage negotiators attend SWAT training and that SWAT officers attend hostage negotiations training. Although performing different tasks, these officers work very closely at a SWAT call-up. By attending each other's training, they can learn to understand what each of them does and why they do it, and with this understanding, they can assist each other in their jobs at a SWAT incident.

In addition to all of the training I have discussed in this chapter, a number of police SWAT teams manage to keep sharp between call-ups, manage to learn new SWAT techniques, and manage to keep abreast of what other police SWAT teams are doing by taking part in one of the many SWAT competitions held around the country every year. These competitions, usually local or regional, pit one police SWAT team against another and allow each team to show off its abilities. SWAT team competitions also allow important peer review of performance and immediately let a police department know if its training has accomplished what it's supposed to.

But sometimes, even a police SWAT team's being well trained and keeping this training constantly updated by regular refresher training sessions is not enough. Occasionally, a situation occurs that forces a SWAT team to learn how to perform a new procedure never tried before, or to learn how to operate equipment never used before, as the following incident demonstrates.

The Ku Klux Klan (KKK) announced in the summer of 1993 that it planned to hold a recruitment rally at the State Capitol Building in Indianapolis on October 16, 1993. This organization has a long history of being involved in acts of violence against members of minority groups. But regardless of their philosophy of racial hatred, they still have the constitutional right of peaceful assembly. Therefore, even though most police officers find the KKK repugnant, they are required by their oath of office to protect its members and any bystanders from violence during a peaceful assembly.

Since this proposed recruitment rally was to be held on government property and therefore required that permits be applied for and approved ahead of time, the KKK had to give considerable advance notice of its intended gathering. As a result, the police had time to plan for the physical security of all involved, including the KKK participants, counterprotestors, and the just plain curious, who were expected to number in the thousands. While the rally was to be held on government property that falls under the joint jurisdiction of the Indiana State Police and the Capitol Police Force, the problems expected at the event were too large for these agencies to handle alone, and so they requested assistance from the Indianapolis Police Department.

Through a study of KKK rallies in other communities, the Indianapolis Police Department knew that gunfire had often occurred at these rallies, both by KKK supporters and by counterdemonstrators. The police department also received some very disturbing intelligence reports about a counterdemonstration group that had purchased both handguns and assault weapons, these latter firearms capable of firing heavy-penetration bullets. In addition, the police department received intelligence reports that another group, which was also expected to make trouble at the event, had rented rooms in a hotel that overlooked the rally area. The police, therefore, were gravely concerned about the very real threat of gunfire, both on the ground and from snipers.

With these concerns in mind, the Indianapolis Police Department SWAT team knew it needed a plan for rescuing both citizens and police officers should they become trapped and come under fire. Although the SWAT team already had a bullet-proof vehicle available that could be used for such a rescue, and its bullet-proofing would stop most bullets, it wouldn't stop bullets from some of the high-powered firearms reported to be in the hands of the counterdemonstrators. Therefore, the Indianapolis Police Department SWAT team decided that more substantial vehicles were needed (see photo on page 143).

Luckily for the Indianapolis Police Department SWAT team, the Ropkey Armor Museum is located in Indianapolis. This is a

Indianapolis Police Department SWAT van and armored car (photo by Lieutenant Stephen Robertson).

museum that contains the nation's largest collection of operable armored vehicles. After receiving a telephone call from the head of the Indianapolis Police Department SWAT team, the owner of the museum, Fred Ropkey, readily agreed to assist and gave the SWAT team leaders a tour of his collection, which includes both American and foreign armored vehicles. Often renting to movie companies, Mr. Ropkey has in his collection the tank used by James Garner in the movie *Tank* and the armored car used in the movie *The Blues Brothers*.

The SWAT team finally decided on a Cadillac-Gage V-100 armored car that had been used in Vietnam, a Russian BTR-40 armored car, and a Russian BTR-52 armored car (the two Russian vehicles had been captured by the Israelis from the Syrians). Unfortunately, none of the SWAT officers knew how to operate the vehicles, especially the Russian vehicles, and also didn't know how to maneuver them safely in large crowds.

To solve this problem, the staff of the Ropkey Armor Museum held a seminar for the SWAT officers, training them to drive and safely operate the vehicles in crowds, particularly the Russian vehicles. Because of the unfamiliar controls, operating the Russian drive system is not as easy as one might suppose, and it took some intensive training before the SWAT officers felt comfortable operating the vehicles.

By the day of the rally, though, the SWAT team members felt both ready and confident that they could safely operate these armored vehicles. At the rally, the armored vehicles, along with several hundred police officers from four departments, made an impressive show of force. As a result, the rally came off with no gunfire, very little violence, and only a few arrests. The armored vehicles were not needed, but the training, like most training, enabled the officers to be ready if the call came.

The intense and regular training I have discussed in this chapter is crucial for any police SWAT team that wants to succeed. SWAT teams that train regularly and rigorously almost always perform well when called on. Training is the backbone that supports every successful SWAT operation.

9

Perimeters and Security

At around 2:00 P.M. on April 13, 1991, nineteen-year-old Michael Lee Henry, a man with a long history of mental problems, entered the Fred Meyer shopping mall in Portland, Oregon, carrying a loaded .357 Magnum revolver in his waistband. He would tell a number of people that day that he had come there to make the police kill him.

Once inside the mall, Henry stepped into the lobby of the Pacific First Bank, finding it empty except for two female tellers, one of whom was obviously pregnant. He immediately walked up to the pregnant teller's window and pulled the revolver, which he had earlier stolen from a friend, out of his waistband and pointed it at her.

"Give me all of your cash!" he demanded.

After the obviously frightened teller had scooped the money out of the drawer and handed it to him, Henry leaped over the counter.

"Into the back room!" he ordered, waving his weapon toward a room behind the teller's area that served as an office and the vault. Once he had ushered the two women into the back room and had shut and locked the door, Henry threw the money onto the floor.

"That's not what I came here for," Henry said to the two women when they looked puzzled. "I didn't come here to rob you. I came here to make the police kill me." He then told the two women about how he had been sexually molested as a child, and about how "the system" had failed him. He told them he was doing what he was doing that day in order to get back at "the system."

Henry then instructed one of the women to call 911 and tell the police what was happening there. While the teller was on the line to the police dispatcher, giving them Henry's description, Henry found a button and asked the other teller if it was the alarm button. When she nodded, he began pushing it.

At the same time the teller was talking with the police dispatcher and Henry was pressing the holdup alarm, a uniformed police officer was standing in the Fred Meyer shopping-mall security office processing a shoplifting arrest. When he heard the broadcast of a holdup at the Pacific First Bank, along with a description of Henry, he hurried from the security office to the bank to check it out.

Inside the bank lobby, the officer found several customers waiting for service, but no tellers and no one there matching the description given of Henry. It didn't take the officer long, however, to figure out what was happening, and he quickly ushered the customers out of the bank, then notified the dispatcher that they had a possible hostage situation and requested the Portland Police Department SWAT team, called in Portland the Special Emergency Reaction Team (SERT).

In response to the officer's call, other uniformed patrol officers began arriving right away. They immediately set up an inner and outer perimeter and also began evacuating customers from the stores that were between the inner and outer perimeter, moving nearly three hundred people out of the danger area. They then waited for the arrival of SWAT.

As the first SWAT team members began arriving, they started immediately gathering intelligence on the situation. While doing this, they also formulated an emergency rescue plan in the event they had to do something right away. When more SWAT officers arrived, they began replacing the uniformed patrol officers at the inner-perimeter positions. The SWAT officers, advised by the police dispatcher that Henry had called back and said he wouldn't be taken alive, armed themselves with Heckler & Koch MP5's and Colt M-16's, and one SWAT officer who would play an important role in the incident carried a .308 sniper rifle.

As is standard procedure for these types of incidents, a hostage negotiator contacted Henry by telephone and began attempting to establish a dialogue with him, but with little success. The police department's lack of results came mostly, however, from being unable several times to get through to Henry. The police department was experiencing problems getting the telephone line that went into the back room tied down. Tying a line down means having the telephone company make that line available only to the hostage negotiator, while cutting off service to and from anyone else. The Portland Police Department hostage negotiator needed to do this because, already, news agencies were calling the bank and tying up the telephone lines, saying they wanted to talk to Henry and get "his story."

Nearly an hour into the incident, though, Henry's story had become one of confusion and dwindling courage. While he had told the two tellers, the 911 dispatcher, and the news media about his sexual molestation as a child, about how the system had failed him, and about his intention of making the police kill him, he now couldn't seem to go through with his plan. For almost an hour, he simply sat in the back room of the bank with the two tellers. Finally, Henry told the police negotiator, who had at last got through to him, that he was sending out a hostage so she could go to the bathroom, but that he would kill the other hostage (the pregnant one) if the first one didn't return within five minutes.

Once the hostage walked out of the back room, inner-perimeter SWAT officers directed her to go to the left, and then a member of the SWAT rescue team escorted her out of the danger area. Although after using the bathroom the hostage wanted to return to the back room rather than endanger the remaining hostage, the police dissuaded her and instead took her to the command post in a nearby deli in order to obtain information from her about Henry.

After speaking with the released hostage, and after reviewing the other intelligence gathered on Henry, the SWAT incident commander decided Henry's mental state was such that the police department could not guarantee the safety of the remaining hostage. He therefore authorized that, if the opportunity presented itself, Henry should be killed. Preparing for this possibility, a SWAT rescue team positioned itself close to the bank, standing ready to spirit the remaining hostage away to safety in the event an opportunity to shoot Henry presented itself to one of the inner-perimeter SWAT officers.

Inside the back room, meanwhile, Henry was becoming angrier and angrier when the first hostage didn't return. In frustration, he finally fired a shot from the .357 Magnum revolver into the wall. Immediately after he did it, however, Henry seemed to realize what he had done, and he grabbed the pregnant woman and backed up into a corner of the room, using her as a shield.

Hearing the gunfire, the SWAT rescue team believed Henry had shot the remaining hostage, and they began an assault on the back room. However, when they got to the door and were preparing to force it open, the remaining hostage called out that she was OK. The team stopped and then decided to resume their earlier standby position. From this time on, however, though the police didn't know it until afterward, Henry kept the pregnant hostage between him and the door.

About this time, the telephone company finally managed to get the line going into the back room of the bank tied down, and once the situation had stabilized, the hostage negotiator began talking again to Henry, asking him what he wanted. Henry told the negotiator he wanted certain items delivered to him: a pizza, some soda, a CD player, and three CDs, including Bon Jovi's *Going Down in a Blaze of Glory* and Traveling Wilbury's *End of the Line*.

Although justifiably concerned about the implications of the titles he had requested, the police nevertheless gathered these items and placed them on a wheeled cart. They pushed the cart to the door to the back room, close but still far enough away so that Henry would have to expose himself in reaching for it. The police also placed the items high on the cart so that Henry would have to stretch up for them and, in doing so, perhaps allow a member of the SWAT team to get off a shot at him.

When the police negotiator called and told Henry that the items had been delivered, Henry walked over to the peephole in the door and looked out, seeing the cart with the pizza and the CDs. "Come on," he said to the pregnant hostage, "I don't want to die on an empty stomach." He opened the door slowly, then stooped down and crept out the door, pulling the hostage along with him.

In the shoe store across from the bank, the SWAT officer with the sniper rifle, who was part of the inner-perimeter team, watched as Henry let go of the hostage's arm and then darted over behind the teller's counter in order to get close to the cart. Although Henry bent low, the officer could still see the top of Henry's hat protruding above the counter, and so the officer aimed the sniper rifle a few inches below that and squeezed off a round. However, as often happens in situations like this, the unexpected occurred. The bullet, while well placed, hit a vertical support in the counter and deflected, only wounding rather than killing Henry.

Although Henry had told many people that day of his intention to die, his resolve to do so had apparently all but dissolved. In obvious panic, he raced back toward the rear room, grabbing the hostage on the way and dragging her with him through the door. Once back inside the rear room, Henry immediately darted into a closet just to the right of the door and then simply stood there, holding onto the hostage's arm, trembling and cursing.

The SWAT rescue team, seeing that the shot had not done its job, reacted immediately and raced for the back room. Henry, they saw, had panicked so badly he had forgotten to shut the door to the room.

"I've ... I've got a hostage in here!" Henry screamed. "I'll kill her if you come in here! You hear me? I'll kill her!"

The rescue team stopped at the door and tossed a flashbang

into the room, then rushed in. Through the smoke and brilliant flash, the rescue team saw Henry and the hostage huddled in the closet. The way Henry held the hostage precluded an immediate shot, since the bullet might pass through him and strike the hostage. So the team immediately shifted position. As they did this, the hostage dropped to the floor and began crawling out of the way. A member of the rescue team grabbed her and rushed her out the door to safety as three members of the SWAT team fired a total of eighteen shots, all of them hitting Henry. He was instantly killed.

The incident at the Pacific First Bank was over, and Henry had attained his original goal of being killed by the police. More important, the hostage and her unborn child had escaped from the ordeal unharmed. The assault, from the time the flashbang detonated until Henry died, lasted only four seconds.

Even though Henry had started out bold and confident, the lack of resolve he showed once the actual confrontation with the police began is not uncommon. While suicidal people who want the police to kill them may at first seem brave and entirely unafraid of death, this very often isn't the case when the time to die actually comes. On the other hand, there are those individuals who are genuinely determined to die, and who will do whatever they have to in order to be killed by the police. While these types of suicidal people (including both those who decide they actually do and those who decide they actually don't want to die) may appear at first glance to be a threat only to themselves since they profess to want to die, very often this isn't the case. Many innocent victims are killed every year by people wanting to commit "suicide by cop." These innocent people are killed because a perpetrator who decides he or she really doesn't want to die after all often panics when the time to die comes and will do anything to keep from being killed, including killing the hostages or trying to use them as a shield, as Henry did in the incident above. On the other hand, in many cases, innocent people are killed by a perpetrator who, very determined to die, often feels he or she must do something drastic, such as shoot at the police or at someone standing nearby (often a hostage), in order to force the police to kill him or her. Both of these types of suicidal people, far from being harmless, are extraordinarily dangerous.

Along with "suicide-by-cop" incidents, many of the other situations SWAT teams are called out for every year, being extremely dangerous, often threaten and endanger innocent bystanders. The perpetrator may, for example, be a sniper who is looking for some unsuspecting person to kill, as happened in the 1966 Texas Tower incident in Austin (Chapter 1). Or perpetrators may be mentally unbalanced and will kill anyone they get the opportunity to for reasons known only to them. They may also be terrorists who have absolutely no problem or qualms about killing a police officer, a hostage, or an innocent bystander in order to publicize their cause. This is why establishing perimeters around an incident, as was done in the preceding case, is so very important. The perimeters enclose the area of danger and keep innocent people out of the range of killers. Along with this goal, the establishment of perimeters often saves lives by helping facilitate the resolution of SWAT incidents.

One of the keys to successfully resolving any SWAT incident is for the police to seize as much control from the perpetrator as possible. As long as perpetrators feel they are in control, the ability of the police to convince them to surrender is seriously hampered. When the police establish tight perimeters around an incident site, perpetrators quickly see that their ability to move or control the area is very limited, and they begin losing much of their feeling of power, making them a great deal more susceptible to the suggestion of an honorable surrender. In addition, by rapidly seizing control through establishing perimeters, officers can often derail a hostage taker's plan of escaping the area with the hostages, an event that can be especially dangerous to the hostages.

Two perimeters are set up at any SWAT incident. (While the term *perimeter* sounds solid and formal, and perimeters do occasionally consist of wood barricades, police vehicles, and other physical barriers, just as often a perimeter is simply a number of police officers ringing the site.) The first of these two perimeters is the inner perimeter. This is the boundary around the area of highest danger. The reason for this boundary is to contain the incident and, in doing so, to keep the danger confined to as small an area as possible. A tight inner perimeter prevents a hostage taker from taking any more hostages or an armed, barricaded person from harming anyone nearby, and it also does not allow the incident to spread or move. Mobile incidents, since they can end up anywhere, including public places where they would endanger countless innocent bystanders, are much more dangerous than confined ones. Quickly establishing a tight inner perimeter can keep the incident from becoming mobile.

The inner perimeter is usually set up initially by uniformed police officers, who are almost always the first to arrive at any SWAT incident. However, once the SWAT team members begin arriving at the scene, these uniformed officers are replaced on the inner perimeter by SWAT officers. This replacement serves several purposes. First, inside the inner perimeter is an area of extreme danger, and SWAT team members are better armed, better outfitted with protective equipment, and better trained for safely controlling this area. And second, the uniformed officers are usually pulled off their patrol areas to respond to the incident, and they are often needed back on patrol in order to answer calls for service. They are also often needed for other details at a SWAT incident scene, such as maintaining the outer perimeter.

The outer perimeter is the boundary beyond which the danger is minimal. This boundary is usually maintained throughout the incident by uniformed police officers. It is the boundary behind which all spectators, who naturally gravitate in huge numbers to these types of incidents, must be kept and, depending on the policy of the police department, the line behind which members of the news media are kept. This is also where the support items, such as ambulances, fire trucks, and additional officers, are kept until needed. Maintaining this boundary also keeps innocent bystanders from unknowingly wandering into the danger area.

"You have to set up perimeters right away," said former FBI

SWAT commander Cal Black. "You can't let people without any business there just wander in and out."

Since uniformed police officers are almost always the first officers to arrive at the scene of any SWAT incident, they often, through their action or inaction, determine the eventual outcome of the incident. In any barricaded-person or hostage situation, it has been found that the first thirty minutes are extremely dangerous. It is during this time that the barricaded subject or hostage taker is the most anxious and excited, that the situation is most hectic, and that the likelihood of gunfire, injuries, and death is considerable. But seldom during this initial thirty minutes are the SWAT team officers or the hostage negotiators in place. Usually, during this time, the uniformed patrol officers and uniformed patrol supervisors are still in charge of the scene. This is why, as I said in Chapter 8, many police departments train all uniformed patrol supervisors—and some even their uniformed patrol officers— in the proper procedures at any SWAT incident, but particularly about the need to set up perimeters immediately. It is much easier for SWAT officers and hostage negotiators to work with a controlled incident than it is to work with one that has no boundaries and is uncontrolled. This control can be maintained only by establishing perimeters.

Another very important function for these perimeters, besides containing the incident, is to provide security for citizens who happen to be within the boundaries of a SWAT incident and either cannot be evacuated for some reason or don't realize they are in an area of danger. Police officers must look out for the safety not only of those directly involved in a SWAT incident, but of everyone nearby, as is shown in the following incident.

In January 1990, the police in Charlottesville, Virginia, received information from a confidential informant that a man was recruiting people to assist him in robbing the Terrace Theater in Charlottesville. The man, according to the informant, planned to enter the theater after the last show that night, confront the manager, force him to open the safe, and then kill him. The informant supplied the police with the name of the suspect, along with the names of two men who had agreed to help him, and also gave the police descriptions of the vehicles the three men planned to use.

Because of the high risk to innocent moviegoers that this situation presented, the Charlottesville SWAT team was notified. Members of the SWAT team drove to the theater to look it over and to talk with the manager. After receiving assurances of cooperation from the manager, and after gathering initial intelligence, the SWAT team devised a plan in which the suspects would be allowed to enter the theater, where SWAT officers would be positioned to make the arrest. At the same time, a tight inner perimeter would be set up just outside the theater to keep the suspects from escaping, and to prevent injury to any innocent bystanders. Uniformed officers would also set up an outer perimeter farther away from the theater just in case the suspects might escape the inner perimeter or the situation might call for the uniformed officers to come inside the theater and assist.

On the night of the robbery, at about 10:30 P.M., waiting SWAT officers spotted two of the suspects as they drove onto the parking lot of the Seminole Theater, which was located just north of the Terrace Theater. Rather than stopping, though, the suspects drove to a food store in the same shopping center that the theaters were located in, where they met the third suspect. The suspects then drove around the shopping center parking lot for a bit, apparently casing it for escape routes, and finally drove to the theater parking lot and sat and watched the theater for a while.

The final movie of the evening ended at a little past 11:30 P.M., and at this time, the Terrace Theater began emptying. According to the plan, the manager would allow the theater employees to go home as soon as possible, and then, he would go to the projection room, where he would be safe. Two of the SWAT officers would wait in the manager's office for the suspects. As the moviegoers streamed out of the theater into the cold night air, officers hidden around the outside of the theater watched as two of the suspects got out of their vehicle and walked around to the back of the theater.

Finally, the two suspects, one of them seen carrying a hand-gun and the other a sawed-off shotgun, pulled masks down over their faces and entered the theater. The command post notified all officers, and a tight, but unseen, inner perimeter went up around the theater, including officers who kept a watch on the suspect still waiting in the parking lot. While no one passing by the theater that night would have suspected that a police operation was under way, the perimeter would have, if necessary, kept them out of danger.

Once inside the theater, one of the suspects stayed near the door, while the other headed for the manager's office. In the office, two SWAT officers confronted the suspect, identified themselves, and ordered him to surrender. Instead of surrendering, however, the suspect dropped into a crouch and aimed the sawed-off shot-gun at the officers. The SWAT officers fired their weapons, hitting the suspect once in the neck with a shotgun slug and twice in the body with .45-caliber bullets, killing him. The other suspect, con-fronted by a third SWAT officer, threw his weapon away and dropped to the floor. The suspect waiting outside in the vehicle also surrendered without resistance when he suddenly found himself surrounded by heavily armed officers.

SWAT officers successfully resolved this incident at the Ter-race Theater in Charlottesville and the incident at the Pacific First Bank in Portland by entering an area of extreme danger and then confronting armed and desperate people. But before SWAT offi-cers can undertake such an operation, except in the most drastic situations, they must first consider how their actions will affect the safety of others, including not only just those directly involved in the incident, but also those who may simply happen to be closeby. Police SWAT teams do this—and consequently resolve dangerous situations peacefully—through the establishment of perimeters, thus making the incident site as safe and secure as possible under the circumstances.

Hostages and Hostage Negotiations

Recently, in Eufaula, Alabama, a community of 12,000 residents on the Chattahoochee River, the police received a call unusual for this sleepy little town. A resident, Jimmy Harris, had reportedly just shot a man, then barricaded himself inside his home, holding hostage his two children, aged three and five. What the police didn't know was that Mr. Harris was also wanted at that time in California for attempted murder.

The Alabama Bureau of Investigation and members of the Alabama State Police joined the local police in setting up perimeters around Mr. Harris's mobile home. And then, in order for the hostage negotiators to establish communication with Mr. Harris, a representative from Bell-South Telecommunications came to the scene, climbed a nearby telephone pole, and wired a line from the police command post into the mobile home. At that point, the hostage negotiators went to work.

However, the first thing the negotiators found when they attempted to contact Mr. Harris was that he was already on the telephone talking to his mother in California. The police feared that this conversation, in which his mother was encouraging him, might motivate him to resist surrendering. And so, the man from the telephone company went back up the pole and cut off Mr. Harris's telephone service to everyone except the hostage negotiators.

For the next sixty-two hours, negotiators talked with Mr. Harris, doing what is often the most important, and usually the most trying and frustrating, job at a SWAT call up: hostage negotiations. They first attempted to calm Mr. Harris, then listened and allowed him to vent his feelings, and finally, attempted to persuade him to release his hostages and surrender peacefully. To do this, the negotiators knew they had to convince him, first, that he had no chance at all of getting away and, second, that, as a father, he should show concern and compassion for his children and release them.

Persuading hostage takers to surrender peacefully is seldom an easy task since most of them are in a very excitable state and are not thinking clearly. Although most finally come to realize they have done something very foolish, they still want to be able to get out of the situation with dignity. A negotiator must convince the hostage taker that this is possible. This task is seldom quick or easy, and serving as a hostage negotiator can be a highly stressful, draining job that takes a special type of person.

In the incident in Eufaula, after almost three days of holding out, and after sixty hours of talking on and off with the hostage negotiators, Mr. Harris eventually became convinced that the negotiators were right, and he agreed to come out and surrender. He said, however, that he first had to get his children ready. But then suddenly, as often happens in SWAT situations, the unexpected occurred. The phone line went dead.

The man from the telephone company quickly began checking the line to see what had happened, while inside the mobile home Mr. Harris lost control and began screaming threats. He had dealt with the police often enough to believe that the disconnection was just a diversion to distract him so that the police could storm his house—a very hazardous, and often fatal, development for hostage takers. As Mr. Harris ranted, it seemed that all of the patient work done by the hostage negotiators over the past days would fall apart. The telephone company representative, though, soon found that the line had been disconnected inside the home. The police called out on a bullhorn to Mr. Harris to check his connections inside. He did and found that one of his small children had apparently disconnected the telephone from the wall.

But even with this reassurance, Mr. Harris had been so shaken by the event that it took two more hours of talking with a negotiator to calm him down. The negotiator, however, did his job and did it well, calming and finally persuading Mr. Harris to trust him and come out. At last, after two hours, Mr. Harris, once more composed and convinced the negotiator was right, walked out of the house and surrendered to the police, his two young children unharmed.

The police resolved this hostage incident with complete success not through an armed assault but through the actions of a hostage negotiator. Although few people know this, the police peacefully resolve a majority of the SWAT incidents that occur in the United States every year, like the one above in Eufaula, through the use of negotiators. Few people know this because, since no one is injured or killed in such incidents, they are seldom reported anywhere beyond the local news. A professionally trained and experienced hostage negotiator, however, can be one of the greatest assets a police SWAT team has. A good hostage negotiator can make an armed assault on the hostage site—an extremely hazardous undertaking—completely unnecessary. And while a hostage negotiator's victory at any hostage incident isn't as flashy or often as newsworthy as an armed SWAT assault, it is no less a victory, and it is much, much safer for everyone involved.

While I have already discussed in Chapter 2 the traits and qualifications necessary for a good SWAT officer, these are not the same traits and qualifications necessary for a good hostage negotiator. When we look at a good hostage negotiator, quite a different picture emerges.

The very first qualification necessary for a good hostage negotiator is that he or she not be a command-level officer. One of the ways that negotiators buy time, which can often be crucial at a SWAT incident, is by saying they must get approval for some demand from a higher authority. If the chief of police is the negotiator, he or she will have a bit of trouble making that argument sound logical. The rule is: Negotiators don't command and commanders don't negotiate.

The next trait necessary for a good hostage negotiator is the ability to listen. Chief Justice John Marshall once said, "To listen well is as powerful a means of communication and influence as to talk well." This is very true of hostage negotiators. Often, the hostage incident itself came about because the hostage taker could not get anyone to listen to him. It is the hostage negotiator's job to contact and talk with the hostage taker, to keep him or her talking, and to establish rapport if possible. More important, a good negotiator listens and lets the hostage taker vent his or her anger and frustration, which in itself can often defuse the situation. Many times, hostage takers resort to such desperate acts because they feel they have a problem no one cares or wants to hear about. Just having the sympathetic ear of the negotiator as they talk about their problem can reduce the stress and anxiety felt by hostage takers and often make them much more susceptible to the suggestion of an honorable, dignified surrender.

A good hostage negotiator must also, however, be able to talk. He or she must be able to talk with people of any socioeconomic class and must be able to convince people with logical arguments that what he or she proposes is the best and most reasonable solution. A good hostage negotiator must be able to negotiate without arguing, must be able to direct the negotiations toward the avenues necessary for the safe release of the hostages, and, very important, must be able to distract a hostage taker who begins showing anger or aggression toward the hostages. But most important of all, a good hostage negotiator must be able to find a way for the hostage taker to end the incident peacefully and still save face.

"A good hostage negotiator must be sensitive, astute to people's motivations, and have really good social skills," said Jeff

Savitsky, J.D., Ph.D., president of the Institute for Public Safety Personnel, Inc., a company that serves as a consultant to police department SWAT teams, in a telephone interview (January 20, 1995). "They must also be highly tolerant to stress and always certain they will eventually win."

Other desirable traits of a good hostage negotiator are the ability to empathize without becoming emotional, and the ability to play whatever role, be it parent, friend, or spiritual adviser, that is needed to resolve an incident. A good negotiator must also be knowledgeable about the psychology of hostage takers and, most important, must be perceptive to any subtle changes in the mood and thinking of a hostage taker.

Regardless of the hostage taker's mental state, it has been found through many incidents that it is much safer for everyone involved if the negotiator can reduce the hostage taker's stress and anxiety level. Negotiators do this in many ways, such as by down playing or minimizing the seriousness of any crime the hostage taker has committed, and by never acknowledging the death of anyone involved in the incident. To keep the hostage taker's stress level down, successful hostage negotiators seldom allow others, particularly family members, to take part in the negotiation process. Often, these are the very people that brought on the incident, and a negotiator can never be certain what the hostage taker's response to them will be.

On the other hand, hostage negotiators occasionally feel the need to increase the pressure on a hostage taker, particularly a hostage taker who appears too relaxed and comfortable with the hostage incident. The SWAT team can increase pressure in many ways, for example, by cutting off the utilities to a site, such as the lights, water, telephone service, and air-conditioning. Of course, this action must be taken carefully, with a good idea of the hostage taker's mental state and how he or she will respond to the added stress.

However, regardless of a hostage taker's mental state and stress level, most of the negotiations with hostage takers are done not face-to-face, but over a telephone or some other communication device. If at all possible, communications occur on a secure telephone line that allows the hostage taker to talk only with the police, and that doesn't allow others to listen in or contact the hostage taker. Negotiators often employ the "hostage phone" or "throw phone," a device used in several incidents discussed in earlier chapters, or they have the phone service into a site diverted and restricted only to the hostage negotiators, as was done in the incident in Eufaula. The reason that face-to-face negotiations are not used if at all possible is that they can be extremely dangerous. It is always possible that the hostage taker is actually a "suicide-by-cop" candidate who knows that, if he or she kills the hostage negotiator, the SWAT team will certainly have to kill him or her.

What do hostage negotiators talk about when they begin negotiating? "I always start out by asking what's going on," said police hostage negotiator Shirley Purvitis in a telephone interview (January 20, 1995). "Then, I let the hostage taker decide what we'll talk about."

"When I first start out I always ask if everybody's okay," said police hostage negotiator Judd Green in a telephone interview (January 20, 1995). "And then, to prevent any panic on the part of the hostage taker, I always assure him that nothing will happen that he doesn't know about."

The hostage negotiator, after setting up contact by telephone or some other electronic device, and after letting the hostage taker vent, must listen to the hostage taker's demands and decide what can and cannot be done. There are certain items that, through some very unfortunate incidents, have been shown to be totally nonnegotiable, such as weapons, drugs, and additional hostages. Other items, though, are negotiable, such as food, cigarettes, and the opportunity to make a statement to the news media. Yet still, no demand, even one made for a nonnegotiable item, is ever dismissed out-of-hand without first being talked about.

"A good hostage negotiator never simply dismisses an impossible or even ridiculous demand," said Sergeant Don Wright, a police hostage negotiator who has successfully resolved many hostage situations, in a telephone interview (January 20, 1995).

"Instead, a good hostage negotiator always looks for alternatives or compromises."

A tenet of most good hostage negotiators is that, for each item given to the hostage taker, there is a price; for everything given, something must be given back. Hostage takers have been known to trade hostages for as little as a ham sandwich. In January 1990, for example, a San Antonio man holding five children hostage with a shotgun traded two of the children for cigarettes.

Readers may wonder why, rather than having to trade hostages for items such as food, cigarettes, and so on, the hostage takers wouldn't instead simply threaten to kill or harm the hostages if the items are not delivered. The reason most hostage takers aren't successful in doing this is that, at the first contact, hostage negotiators make it very clear, either implicitly or explicitly, that negotiations will continue only as long as no harm comes to the hostages, and that any harm to the hostages will bring an end to the negotiations and will very likely cause an assault on the hostage takers, which is extremely dangerous for them. The same reasoning applies to accepting deadlines for action from hostage takers. When hostage takers set deadlines, they are usually ignored by the negotiators unless it is believed that the hostage takers may actually do harm to the hostages, in which case the building or area is likely to be stormed.

Through the experiences of negotiators who have successfully resolved many hostage situations, it has been shown that, while a negotiator's verbal and listening skills are essential, hostage negotiators have an even more potent weapon: time. The passage of time has been shown to have many beneficial effects at a hostage incident. It often reduces the stress and anxiety felt by hostage takers, gives them an opportunity to think rationally, and lessens their initial expectations. To facilitate this, hostage negotiators stall for time in many ways. They may discuss in detail everything the hostage taker says, ask open-ended questions, let the hostage taker speak and vent his or her anger and frustration as much as he or she wants, paraphrase and repeat everything the hostage taker says, and, as discussed above, tell the hostage taker that it will require some time for any demand to be approved by a higher authority.

"Time is what saves lives in hostage situations," said police hostage negotiator Judd Green. "After enough time, rational thought returns, and the hostage taker can see the real situation."

Letting as much time as possible pass is a tactic that works for a number of psychological and physiological reasons. When hostage situations are new, the hostage takers are often running on pure adrenaline, their demands are firm, and they seem fully in control. As the time wears on and the negotiations continue over the hours, both the energy and the resolve of hostage takers start to wane, and they finally begin to see the futility and hopelessness of their situation. While the hostage negotiators have usually been working in shifts and relieving each other (most large SWAT teams have a half dozen or more negotiators), the hostage takers, usually too nervous to rest, are often worn down and exhausted by the hours of constant stress and danger. After enough time, they are usually ready to give up if they can do it and still save face.

But of course, all of this passing time can also wear on the SWAT officers manning the perimeters, and on the assault-and-rescue team waiting for the order to go. And after enough time passes, the officers may become restless, and then sloppy and lax in their security. Despite this effect, a number of signs are indicators that the negotiations are going well and should continue regardless of how long they take, and regardless of how restless the officers become. These signs include no one being injured or killed while the negotiations take place, the threatening language of the hostage taker decreasing, hostages being released, the hostage taker revealing personal information to the negotiator, and deadlines set by the hostage taker passing without incident. What all of these signs mean is that a peaceful resolution is likely.

It is vital, however, that, in order for the hostage negotiator to resolve a hostage incident peacefully, he or she establish trust with the hostage taker. It is therefore also vital that, while the negotiations are under way, the hostage negotiator be kept aware of the

SWAT team's actions. Otherwise, the negotiator's credibility with the hostage taker may be damaged severely when something happens, such as a movement of officers, and the negotiator can't explain it. A hostage negotiator also needs as much intelligence as possible about the hostage taker and what led up to the incident. Having this information, the negotiator knows what to talk about with the hostage taker, is well versed on the situation when he or she does begin to talk, and, using this information, can lengthen and extend the negotiations.

While lengthening and extending the negotiation process—and, in doing so, letting the passing of time wear down the hostage taker's resolve—has been shown time after time to be a successful tactic, interestingly it is often the police themselves who exert pressure to hurry things up. Often, a senior command officer (usually without any SWAT experience) pressures the SWAT commander "to wrap this thing up," even though the longer the incident goes on, the more likely it is that it will be resolved peacefully. Command officers usually exert this kind of pressure for several reasons. They may be looking at the expense in personnel and equipment of maintaining the SWAT incident, or they may be buckling under the pressure they are receiving from even higher-ups. They may also be considering the inconvenience the incident is causing in local traffic flow and to displaced (evacuated) homeowners. For all these reasons, command officers often push for a quick, forceful, and usually tactical resolution.

Along with these non-SWAT command officers, the SWAT officers at the scene themselves, who have become fatigued and bored as the incident wears on, may pressure the SWAT team commander to do something. And occasionally, particularly in communities that have not experienced a hostage incident before, the news media pressure the police to do something "before airtime." Therefore, a question that often comes up is just how long the negotiations should be allowed to continue. The answer is: as long as it takes. The New York City Police Department found in a study of hostage incidents that 85 percent of the injuries and deaths to hostages occur during an assault by the SWAT team. A

Rand Corporation study found that the two most dangerous times for hostages are during the initial hostage taking and during an attempted forced rescue. As long as no one is being harmed while the negotiations are going on, and the negotiator feels he or she is making progress, there is absolutely no need to order an assault, which is inherently dangerous to both the hostages and the police.

While hostage negotiators usually attempt to extend the negotiations in order to wear down the resolve of the hostage takers, during the time these lengthy negotiations are going on an interesting psychological phenomenon often occurs between the hostages and the hostage takers. Called the *Stockholm syndrome*, this phenomenon is named after a hostage incident that took place in 1973 at the Sveriges Kreditbank in Stockholm, Sweden. During the incident, it was found that, as the time wore on, the hostages became very emotionally attached to the hostage takers (a female hostage later even became engaged to one of the hostage takers). It was also discovered that, as the hours passed, the hostages began fearing the police more than the hostage takers, and one of the hostages, in a telephone call to the Swedish prime minister, claimed that their abductors were not holding them hostage, but protecting them from the police.

This syndrome, which appears to be an unconscious, long-term reaction, is caused by a combination of factors and has been seen many times since in hostage situations. The case of Patty Hearst is probably the most celebrated. (Hearst was kidnapped and held hostage by a group of terrorists. Because of the effects of the Stockholm syndrome, she eventually joined the terrorist group, and took part in a bank robbery.) During a hostage situation, a hostage's life is in the hands of the hostage taker, and hostages are often so thankful that they aren't killed that they begin feeling indebted to the hostage takers and therefore develop a close personal and emotional relationship with them. Interestingly, hostages have been known to continue this emotional attachment long after the incident has been resolved and the danger is over. Former hostages often visit the hostage takers in prison and even set up defense funds for them. Many authorities believe that the

Stockholm syndrome is like a knee-jerk reflex, a reaction beyond the control of the people involved.

"The Stockholm syndrome can be a major problem with the hostages," said police hostage negotiator Shirley Purvitis. "It can be a problem because before long you can end up with two people you have to negotiate with."

Certain factors must be present before the Stockholm syndrome will develop. There must, for example, be positive contact between the hostages and the hostage takers, and while this positive contact may be simply the absence of expected negative contacts, such as beatings, rape, torture, or murder, any negative contacts that do occur can block the development of the syndrome. The hostages and hostage takers must also have more than just minimal contact and must both face danger and be under stress together. In addition, they must see each other as human beings with feelings, needs, and problems. The Stockholm syndrome, incidentally, also works in reverse: hostage takers often develop close, personal relationships with their hostages.

In most hostage situations, the authorities are glad to see the Stockholm syndrome developing, since hostage takers are usually reluctant to harm hostages they have developed a close relationship with. This effect was demonstrated during the South Moluccan hostage situation in the Netherlands a number of years ago, where a hostage who had been selected for execution was spared because he and the hostage takers had got to know each other and had unconsciously allowed the Stockholm syndrome to develop.

Of course, the Stockholm syndrome, while usually positive from the police point of view, may also occasionally be detrimental, since the hostages often become antagonistic toward, and distrustful of, the police, who they feel are unnecessarily endangering both their and the hostage takers' lives. A study of former hostages posed the following question: "If rescuing police shouted for you to get down on the floor, but one of the hostage takers ordered you to stand, what would you do?" The overwhelming answer was that they would obey the hostage taker (Strentz, pp. 20–21).

In addition to this mistrust of the authorities, any intelligence information given by hostages who have been held long enough for the Stockholm syndrome to develop must be carefully analyzed and used judiciously, even information from hostages who have been set free. Often, hostages give information, sometimes false, that they believe will help the hostage taker. And because of the effects of the Stockholm syndrome, any movement by the SWAT team must be hidden not just from the hostage takers, but also from the hostages. Therefore, a negotiator who senses the Stockholm syndrome developing must warn the SWAT assault-and-rescue team so they will be prepared for illogical responses from the hostages during a rescue. Interestingly, not even the hostage negotiator is immune from the Stockholm syndrome, and for this reason, there is usually a secondary negotiator, who watches for any of its effects.

The Stockholm syndrome does not occur in all hostage situations, however. In a number of hostage incidents, for example, the hostages have developed the Stockholm syndrome for only some of the hostage takers, the ones who treated them decently, but not for all of them, and in a number of hostage incidents, the syndrome has not occurred at all. Any negative contacts between the hostages and the hostage takers can block the development of the syndrome, and the more negative contacts there are, the less likely it is that the syndrome will develop. In some extreme cases, though, the hostages, even though injured by the hostage takers, have rationalized that the hostage takers had no choice but to injure them and have developed the syndrome anyway.

Often, to ensure the safety of the hostages, negotiators will try to induce the Stockholm syndrome by asking the hostage takers to check on the medical condition of the hostages, by asking them to find out whether the hostages need something, and by asking them anything else that will make them see the hostages as people, not objects. But of course, if successful, the police must be prepared for the later hostility of the hostages, which was very openly displayed in the Stockholm incident and has been in many hostage incidents since.

Regardless of any negative effects of the Stockholm syndrome, whenever a hostage negotiator is successful everyone walks away from the site unharmed. This is the ultimate goal of all police SWAT teams: to end every event as the one in Eufaula was ended, with no one being harmed. And while at one time many people might have shrugged and said that a situation like the one in Eufaula really wasn't that dangerous, since a parent would never harm his or her own children, this just isn't so.

The 1994 Susan Smith case in Union, South Carolina, the mother who admitted pushing her car into a lake with her two small children still strapped inside, has probably dispelled this belief about parenthood for most Americans. But tragic and almost unbelievable as this case was, Smith certainly wasn't the first parent ever to kill her own children for personal motives. Very often, a hostage incident involves a person holding his or her own family members hostage, usually the spouse and/or children, and far too often these incidents end in tragedy.

In Mastic, New York, in 1989, for example, Jimmy Hyrams ran his wife and seven-year-old daughter out of their home and then took hostage his eighteen-year-old daughter, Lisa, with whom he had argued earlier about her decision to live with her boyfriend. When the incident ended seven hours later, Jimmy had murdered Lisa and had also shot one of the responding police officers before killing himself. Unfortunately, murdering a family member is not that rare an occurrence.

In an attempt to stop these kinds of tragedies, it is the hostage negotiator's job to contact the hostage taker and attempt to resolve the incident, not with force, but with words, and to do it by appealing to the hostage taker's compassion, logic, and, if necessary, desire for self-preservation. And while at one time, in many police departments, hostage negotiators were a separate unit that the SWAT team would bring in only as needed, many police departments have found that hostage negotiators often play a key role in the peaceful resolution of SWAT incidents and have made them a part of the SWAT team.

Along with attempting to persuade a hostage taker to surrender peacefully, hostage negotiators also play a vital role in the intelligence collection at SWAT incidents. Through talking with the hostage taker, the negotiator can often gauge his or her temperament and likelihood of harming the hostages. One of the first things a hostage negotiator does on opening communication with a hostage taker is to attempt to measure and evaluate the person's emotional and mental stability, and to try to decide why the incident occurred. Using this assessment, the hostage negotiator can then advise the SWAT team whether it should storm the hostage site right away or allow him or her to attempt to persuade the hostage taker to surrender peacefully.

However, a special concern develops when it appears, on this initial assessment, that the hostage taker is under the influence of drugs. The first thing the hostage negotiator must determine is what drug and what dosage was taken. This information is important because, for example, stimulant takers often suffer from paranoia, and seeing the SWAT tactical team will only exaggerate this effect. On the other hand, hostage takers on hallucinogens may be completely unpredictable. The most important consideration is that a hostage taker under the influence of a drug usually has disordered thinking, so that meaningful negotiations become very difficult, though not impossible.

In some cases, even though hostage negotiators may have wanted to try to resolve—and felt at first that they had a good chance of resolving—the incident peacefully, they find after talking with the hostage taker that they can't resolve the incident and also realize that they can't ensure the safety of the hostages. In this case, the SWAT team commander is likely to order an assault and rescue. But even in these cases, the negotiator still plays a vital role. Since prolonged negotiations often lead the hostage taker into a routine, the negotiator may be able to tell the assault-and-rescue team where the hostage taker is at the moment. Or the negotiator may be able to persuade the hostage taker, through some subterfuge, to move to a certain area at the hostage site. This can assist the SWAT team in making the assault and rescue safer and more effective.

Another crucial function of a hostage negotiator, even after the SWAT commander has decided to undertake an assault and rescue, is to buy time for the SWAT team. Even if the hostage negotiator sees no way of talking the hostage taker into surrendering, while hostage takers are talking they are not hurting anyone, and while they're talking the SWAT assault-and-rescue team can be setting up, preparing, and rehearsing a tactical assault and rescue. But of course, even this approach is not always possible. Sometimes, the hostage taker is simply a person bent on violence, who means to strike soon. In this case, the SWAT team needs to move right away. To be alert to this possibility, the hostage negotiator must know the signs of possible violence and must be ready to report them to the command post personnel.

What are some of the signs of possible violence by a hostage taker? The first and best predictor of violence is a past history of violence. This is particularly so if the hostage taker has been violent to the hostage in the past. People who have hurt someone in the past are likely to hurt that person again in the future. Another indicator of a likely violent outcome is that the hostage taker has obviously put a lot of thought into the hostage taking. This means that the hostage taking was not an impulsive, spur-of-the-moment thing, but a planned act, often carried out in order to get back at someone, many times through violence.

The police have also found particularly dangerous those hostage takers who refuse to negotiate, those with whom the negotiator is unable to establish rapport, and those who have no social support system. The last type of people, those without a social support system, feel they are facing a crisis in their life alone and, out of the frustration of not having anyone sympathetic to them, will often strike out in violence. Other risk factors for violence, hostage negotiators have found, include hostage takers who are urban males, aged fifteen to twenty-five, who have a childhood history of physical abuse, subnormal intelligence, a psychiatric disorder, and a history of substance abuse. Along with these risk factors, however, there are also behavioral signs of possible violence that the hostage negotiator can perceive, including increased motor activity (the subject who cannot sit still) and the hostage taker who speaks with a loud voice. But undoubtedly, the most dangerous hostage takers are the suicidal hostage takers.

Suicidal hostage takers are dangerous because, while they usually want to die, they often don't have the courage to do it themselves and want the police to do it for them, as in the Pacific First Bank incident discussed in Chapter 9. These people are particularly dangerous to their hostages because, in order to get the police to kill them, they often do something drastic, such as shoot a hostage. In Rochester, New York, for example, William Griffin killed a worker at his house, killed his mother, and then tried to kill his stepfather. After this, he went to the Security Trust Bank in Rochester and took a number of people hostage. When the police arrived, he demanded that they kill him. They of course couldn't, so he ordered one of the hostages to leave the bank and then shot and killed her as she stepped out the door. After this, Mr. Griffin walked over and stood in front of a window and a SWAT sniper granted him his wish.

These people are also dangerous because, while they may want to commit suicide, before they do they often want to kill the people they feel are responsible for causing their need to kill themselves. In December 1987, David A. Burke had just been fired from Pacific Southwest Air (PSA). The man who had fired him soon afterward booked a seat on PSA Flight 1771, which Burke also booked a seat on, hijacked, and then caused to crash near Paso Robles, California. Burke killed not only himself and his ex-boss but also 42 innocent people on the airplane.

There are a number of signs hostage negotiators look for that point to the possibility that a hostage taker is suicidal. Often, a suicidal person will, when talking with the negotiator, make a verbal will. Another important indication is a hostage taker's revelation that he or she has settled all debts and given away all of his or her property before beginning the incident. Another sign is when the person sets a deadline for his or her own demise. One final sign, the very clearest indication of a possible suicide, is when the person has just killed a significant other.

A situation very similar to being taken hostage by a suicidal hostage taker, but much more dangerous to the people involved, is an event known as a *pseudohostage incident*. In these incidents, a hostage is taken, but not for the purpose of forcing a change in some intolerable life situation or for the purpose of bringing attention to some perceived wrong. The purpose is murder. These are actually just homicides masked as hostage incidents. The hostage taker has no intention of releasing the hostage.

A clue that an incident may be a pseudohostage situation comes when the negotiator talks with the hostage taker and finds there are no real demands, or else completely outrageous demands that the hostage taker knows can't be met. Often, the police find in pseudohostage incidents that the hostage taker has already murdered the hostage before the police arrive and simply pretends during the incident that the hostage is still alive, as occurred in Lexington, Kentucky, in 1990. In this case, Mike Purcell held off the police for seventeen hours by convincing them that his wife, Jeanie, who he claimed to be holding hostage, was alive and well, even pretending to talk with her several times while on the phone with the negotiators. When the police finally forcibly entered the home, they found Mike dead of a self-inflicted gunshot wound, and they found that Jeanie had been dead since the incident began. What makes these pseudohostage incidents different from the Burke hijacking of PSA Flight 1771 is that pseudohostage incidents usually involve those with whom the hostage taker has had some kind of romantic or family attachment. These are extremely dangerous situations, and if the police believe they are facing one, it is often better to try a tactical resolution immediately.

Almost as dangerous for the hostages as pseudohostage incidents are situations in which individuals are taken captive by desperate people caught up in hopelessly desperate situations from which there is no escape. These hostage takers often want to change things that simply cannot be changed and are in such a desperate situation that they feel they have nothing to lose by killing a hostage. Negotiating the safe release of hostages in these types of incidents requires hostage negotiators with exceptional ability and patience, as the following incident demonstrates.

Lucasville, Ohio, a town of just over fifteen hundred people, lies about seventy-five miles south of the state capital of Columbus. The town's single claim to fame is that it is the site of Ohio's maximum-security prison, the Southern Ohio Correctional Facility, where the toughest and most ruthless of Ohio's criminals are confined.

At 3:15 P.M. on April 11, 1993, a group of inmates at the Lucasville prison had just finished their outdoor recreation and were being escorted back into L Block (the inmates at Lucasville prison are housed in one of three areas: J, K, or L Block). Suddenly, a fight broke out between two of the inmates. It began to spread, and when several correctional officers tried to intervene, they were attacked, and their body alarms were activated. Prison officials, responding to the alarms, rushed all available correction officers to the L Block recreation yard. Before long, however, prison officials realized that the disturbance had got so large they didn't have sufficient personnel to stop it. The order went out to isolate L Block, which it appeared the inmates meant to take over, and to lock down J and K Blocks.

As this was being done, prison officials called for assistance from the state's prison security system and the Ohio Highway Patrol. While waiting for this assistance to arrive, prison officials successfully isolated L Block but found they had 12 correctional officers unaccounted for and very likely being held hostage by the 450 inmates who had now taken over L Block.

The first hostage negotiator to arrive received a quick account of what had happened and then made contact with the inmates and began a dialogue. The negotiations, however, began on a rocky basis because the inmates were on an emotional high, and the negotiator could hear the sounds of shouting and property destruction in the background (it would cost over $28 million dollars to repair the damage done during the takeover of L Block). Nevertheless, the dialogue continued, and by the evening of April 11, the negotiator had persuaded the inmates to release four correctional officers who had been seriously injured during the prison takeover.

Because of the physical and emotional strain on the first arriving negotiator, who didn't want to be relieved and kept the dialogue going for twenty-three hours straight, the negotiations were divided among two teams of negotiators. Soon, though, the police negotiators began to see a serious problem developing. The inmates involved in the dialogue with the negotiators were not acting as a team. A police negotiator would work for hours and accomplish what he thought was a workable scenario for ending the takeover, but then a new inmate would get on the telephone and change everything the police negotiator had set up. Finally, the police negotiators began suggesting that everything agreed on be referred to an inmate "committee." This seemed to make the inmates more cohesive in the negotiations, and they eventually issued a list of nineteen demands. These included the firing of Warden Arthur Tate and most of the prison's unit supervisors, the hiring of more black correctional officers, better jobs for black inmates, a relaxation of the strict prison rules, and constant news media coverage of the negotiations.

A problem often found during hostage negotiations is perceptions. While the police negotiators at Lucasville felt that the negotiations were going as well as could be expected considering the circumstances, and that a solution for ending the takeover might not be far away, the inmates apparently thought otherwise. The prisoners in L Block rigged up a loudspeaker system and announced over it that they were not satisfied with the negotiations.

"I'm telling you that you got problems," said a voice over the loudspeaker. "They can give us what we ask for. It's well within our rights. Then you will have someone back. Why don't they want to do this?"

On Wednesday, April 14, 1993, the inmates hung a bed sheet out of a window that said they would kill a hostage if their demands were not met. A prison spokesperson, though, downplayed the event as "a standard threat they've been issuing." However, on that day, Ohio governor George Voinovich sent five hundred members of the National Guard to Lucasville to assist the police.

On April 15, 1993, tragedy struck at the Lucasville standoff. On that day, the inmates tossed a body out into the L Block recreation yard. Since prison officials had already recovered over a half dozen murdered inmates, all of them beaten to death, they assumed it was another murdered inmate. On retrieving the body, however, they found it to be one of the hostages, correctional officer Robert Vallandingham, who had been strangled to death.

A hostage released soon after this reported that officer Vallandingham's murder was in response to the prison spokesperson's comment about the inmates' death threat being just "a standard threat." The inmates, according to the hostage, felt that this comment was a belittlement of their demands.

"He died after that woman said, 'Oh, they have been making death threats since Sunday,'" claimed released hostage James A. Demons. "As if our lives were a joke" (Aubrey, 1993, A3).

At this point, with the lives of the other hostages now in extreme danger, a tactical assault to rescue the remaining hostages seemed appropriate. It would very likely have been ordered at this time in most other hostage incidents, and the possibility of an assault had been considered from the first moment that SWAT arrived at the Lucasville prison. But this was a unique situation in which the success of such a move remained in serious doubt. While in the typical hostage incident a single or several hostage takers are holding the hostages in one location, the hostages in this case, it was believed, were being held by various groups of inmates in different locations in L Block, which was made up of eight dormitories, each with eighty cells. In addition, inside L Block were numerous offices, day rooms, staff restrooms, locker rooms, and a gymnasium. Without knowledge of exactly where all of the hostages were being held, a tactical assault would meet with almost certain failure. Therefore, SWAT and prison officials decided to see if the negotiators could still accomplish a peaceful surrender.

One of the negotiators contacted the inmates again and convinced them that, after the murder of correctional officer Vallandingham, something positive had to happen if the negotiations were to continue with any sense of purpose. That afternoon, an inmate representative walked out of L Block, bringing with him one of the hostages. The inmate and the hostage met with police negotiators at a table in the L Block recreation yard. The inmates had insisted before the meeting that it be broadcast live on radio, which it was. At the conclusion of the meeting, the hostage was released. The next day, a similar meeting won the release of another hostage, but this time, the inmates insisted that the meeting be broadcast live by WBNS television in Columbus, Ohio, which it was.

Several of the inmates' demands made during the live radio and television coverage included an amnesty for the rioting, a cessation of the forced integration of cells, more telephone calls and visitors, better pay for inmate jobs, that Black Muslims be allowed to wear prayer caps, and that the prison tuberculosis testing (which is forbidden by Black Muslims) be stopped. Commenting at the meeting on the nine inmates who had been murdered during the takeover, a representative of the barricaded prisoners said, "Those boys was killed because they was snitches" (Kinney, 1993, A3).

For the next five days, even though no more hostages were released, the police negotiators continued working to end the incident and win the safe release of the hostages. While the negotiations had ups and downs and hit snags, the police negotiators didn't give up. On April 19, 1993, however, the standoff at Lucasville suddenly took a backseat in the news media to another standoff. On that day, the FBI decided to end the standoff in Waco, Texas, with David Koresh and the Branch Davidians. As the FBI began pumping tear gas into the Branch Davidian complex in Waco, a huge fire broke out that killed almost all of the people holed up there. Whether this event had any influence on the inmates' resolution to continue the holdout at Lucasville is unknown, but that same day, the inmates hung a bed sheet out a window saying that they were willing to end the standoff, but that they wanted to talk with an attorney first.

At a meeting to finalize the surrender, a police negotiator, an attorney retained for the inmates, a representative of the FBI (to ensure that the inmates' civil rights would be protected), and a colonel of the Ohio Highway Patrol (to ensure the safety of the inmates after they surrendered) met with inmate representatives of the Aryan Nation, the Black Gangster Disciples, and the Black Muslims. The police negotiator carried a handheld radio, through which he had contact with the prison warden. Earlier, Warden Tate had given the inmates' attorney an approved list of twenty-one terms of surrender worked out by the negotiators, which included no retaliation (but did not preclude the possibility of prosecution or discipline), a promise to consult with prisoners about tuberculosis testing, and a review of certain prison rules. The inmates insisted that the surrender be covered by the news media, which it was.

On the evening of April 21, 1993, the eleven straight days of negotiation paid off as all of the inmates surrendered to waiting Ohio Highway Patrol officers. Soon after this, the remaining five hostages came out of L Block, several with bandages on their heads, but all walking under their own power.

Like the Good Guys Electronics Store incident discussed in Chapter 6, this incident did not end storybook perfect. When dealing with vicious and dangerous criminals, which the inmates of Lucasville Prison certainly were, no such ending can ever be guaranteed. But like the Good Guys Electronics Store incident, the real success story in this case was that the negotiators were able to bring eleven of the twelve correctional officers out alive.

Yet, while correctional officers and employees at other institutions, such as mental hospitals and halfway houses, realize they always stand the chance of being taken hostage by desperate and dangerous individuals, occasionally even unsuspecting private citizens can be taken hostage in their own homes by desperate criminals. These citizens must then also depend on police hostage negotiators to win their freedom, as the following incident demonstrates.

In June 1993, a man wearing a dark ski mask and brandishing a silver handgun held up the Nevada State Bank on Spring Mountain Road in Las Vegas. After shoving several bundles of money into a bag, the robber fled. However, just outside the door of the bank, a dye bomb slipped in with the money exploded and drew the attention of a passing off-duty police officer and two officers from the State Gaming Control Board, who were staking out the bank parking lot for an unrelated investigation. The three officers, alerted to the holdup, began chasing the bank robber, who ran for his getaway car. The getaway driver, however, on seeing the police pursuing his partner, panicked and sped away, leaving his partner behind.

The bank robber, seeing his getaway car take off, looked around, jumped over a block wall, and then carjacked a Chrysler LeBaron from a motorist. Meanwhile, a helicopter responding to the bank's holdup alarm joined the chase and followed the bank robber in the stolen car to a house where the getaway driver had also gone, the home of a friend of the getaway driver. In the house were three children, ages fifteen, eleven, and six.

The police SWAT team raced to the scene and set up perimeters while hostage negotiators called the house. Within a short time, the hostage negotiator was able to get the children out of the house unharmed and was also able to persuade the getaway driver to come out and surrender. When the bank robber refused to come out, however, the police first fired tear gas into the house and then finally sent in a K-9 dog, which found the robber hiding in the attic.

No matter where hostage-taking incidents occur—in a home, in a business, or in a penal institution—it has become the standard practice of police SWAT teams, because of their outstanding record of success, to first allow hostage negotiators to attempt to resolve the incident. It is much safer for everyone involved if the situation can be ended with words rather than bullets. When hostage negotiators are successful, the event ends happily for everyone.

Site Assault

On February 9, 1994, a man brandishing a .45-caliber pistol robbed the K-Mart on Bonanza Road in Las Vegas, Nevada, and then immediately afterward attempted to hold up the Sonic fast-food restaurant nearby. What the robber didn't know was that, not only had the police been alerted to his crimes, but that a private citizen was following him and keeping the police posted on his location through the use of a cellular telephone. The robber, fleeing the attempted robbery at the Sonic fast-food restaurant, next tried, also unsuccessfully, to carjack a vehicle and then, at last, finding the police suddenly and very unexpectedly closing in on him, panicked and began jumping fences and running through the neighborhood.

On Prescott Street, the robber, desperately looking for a place to hide, ran to the back of a house, broke out the glass, and then opened a patio door. Inside, he found a woman and three small children, ages six, four, and two. The police, still close behind him, immediately set up perimeters around the house and called for SWAT. For the next five hours, as the police kept the gunman contained in the house, a hostage negotiator tried to persuade him to surrender and release the hostages. The man refused and instead demanded that the police provide him with a car and also allow him to take one of the hostages along as insurance.

The police refused his demand, fearing for the life of anyone he took along, since the hostage taker had reportedly been smoking rock cocaine all day. The negotiator did convince the robber to allow him to speak with the woman hostage in order to be assured that she and the children were all right. Once he did this, the negotiator then went back to talking with the hostage taker, continuing to try to persuade him to surrender and release the hostages.

As occasionally happens in hostage incidents, however, the negotiator in this case could not persuade the hostage taker to release any of the hostages or to surrender. And in this incident, there was the added danger of the hostage taker's unpredictability because of his narcotics use. All of these factors made the SWAT incident commander decide that an assault and rescue was necessary.

But before the SWAT team could start this assault and rescue, they got a break when the woman hostage, speaking once again with the negotiator, whispered that the man appeared to be falling asleep. And so, using keys to the home provided by the fiancé of the woman hostage, the police SWAT team slipped inside and found the man lying on a bed with one of the children held up next to him, his gun sitting nearby. The police quickly overpowered the man and rescued all of the hostages unharmed.

Unfortunately, all SWAT site assaults and rescues are not as easy as the one in Las Vegas. Most are much more complicated, dangerous, and fraught with unexpected complications. For example, in December 1987, the police in Escondido, California, were called three times to the home of Robert Taschner, a U.S. Army veteran and a diagnosed schizophrenic. The neighbors each time had complained about Taschner's firing weapons out the windows of his townhouse. On the first of the three calls, the police arrested Taschner (who was, surprisingly, soon released on his own recognizance) and confiscated a large number of firearms in addition to a high-power spotting scope that was set up and pointed at the junior high school across the street. Taschner, however, apparently had access to more weapons.

On the third call, when the police knocked on the door of Taschner's townhouse, he refused to answer the door or come out, but he did talk with the police over the telephone. As the police spoke with Taschner, they found that the longer he spoke, the more irrational his statements became. And the longer the police talked with Taschner, the more dangerous they realized he was. Alarmed by the call, the officers decided they needed the SWAT team and negotiators to assist them in bringing Taschner out of the townhouse. Also, because of the irrational content of his conversation, the police began evacuating nearby residents, fearing that Taschner might at any moment completely lose his grip on reality and begin firing his weapons.

As the SWAT team arrived and scouted the area in case an assault would be needed to take Taschner into custody, the negotiator became more and more frustrated. Taschner would scream and rant and constantly unplug and then plug in the telephone, while demanding that the police provide him with a "rocket ship to the moon." The SWAT incident commander, seeing that the negotiator was having no luck in his attempt to talk rationally with Taschner, decided that, because of Taschner's past history of violence (he had an arrest record that included a charge of battery and a charge of assault with a deadly weapon) and his recent inclination to want to shoot from his upstairs windows, an assault on the townhouse for the purpose of making an arrest was called for. The SWAT team developed an assault plan and then practiced it in an identical townhouse nearby.

Once the SWAT team felt the plan was as workable as they could make it, and the SWAT incident commander had approved the plan, the assault team moved into position. After receiving the order to go, they first fired tear gas shells through the windows of Taschner's house; then two officers forced open the front door and tossed in a flashbang. Taschner, however, was waiting inside for them with an assault rifle. Dropping to a prone position, Taschner shot the two officers, who quickly retreated, both with serious injuries. At this development, the SWAT incident commander decided to pull back and reinstitute negotiations.

While the negotiator again attempted to talk with Taschner, the SWAT team developed a second tactical plan. Explosive breaching devices would be used on the shared walls of the townhouses on either side of Taschner's townhouse. These would provide entry ports into Taschner's home. While this was being done, other officers would shoot in more tear gas and lay down intense suppressive fire.

However, as often happens in such SWAT incidents, events didn't go as planned. After everyone was in position and given the go-ahead, one of the explosive charges didn't detonate because a wire had pulled loose, while the other charge only partly breached the wall, making a hole, but not a hole large enough for an officer to get through. The police found afterward that the walls between the townhouses were double-offset-studded and double-insulated, which means there were essentially two walls.

Finding that their attempt to breach the walls had failed, and knowing that through the failed attempt they had exposed their position in the adjoining townhouse, SWAT officers laid down a heavy suppressive fire through the wall and then tossed a tear gas canister in through the small hole that the explosive device had made; the canister, unfortunately, started a fire. Before long, flames engulfed Taschner's townhouse, smoke billowing out of the windows. Taschner, apparently panicking, began firing wildly out one of the upstairs windows before finally fleeing the burning structure. A SWAT officer close to the front door to Taschner's townhouse saw Taschner come out, and the officer fired a half dozen shots at him with a Heckler & Koch MP5, but Taschner continued to run. When Taschner turned the first corner and saw the negotiators, he fired a few rounds at them and then kept running.

Turning another corner, Taschner saw two police officers, one of them a K-9 officer with his dog. While running toward them, he fired at the officers, striking one officer in the hand. But then,

Taschner's weapon suddenly malfunctioned, and the K-9 dog attacked him. As Taschner fought with the dog, the K-9 officer shot him several times with a .45-caliber pistol. Still, Taschner wouldn't fall, and so an officer with a shotgun shot him several more times, finally putting Taschner on the ground. But Taschner just wouldn't stay down; he attempted to get back up while reaching for another weapon that he carried in his waistband. An officer then shot him in the head with a .45-caliber pistol, killing him. ·

While the above incident in Escondido, unlike the one in Las Vegas, didn't involve hostages and so involved no one in immediate danger, it still held a definite threat. Obviously, the police couldn't simply drive away and allow Taschner to continue firing his weapons from his home. The situation became particularly dangerous when the police found that Taschner's schizophrenia was becoming more and more acute (it was later found that he had been refusing to take his medication). And since negotiations for a peaceful surrender had failed, an assault on the incident site became the only viable option.

A SWAT site assault, however, no matter what its reason, is always an extremely dangerous and hazardous undertaking. It is during an assault that the majority of injuries and deaths to officers and citizens occur at SWAT incidents. And so, to lessen the danger level as much as possible, police SWAT teams have developed assault plans and techniques that have been found through experience to be the safest and most successful. But no matter what plan or technique is used, experience has shown that three things are necessary to bring about a successful site assault: surprise, shock, and violence of action (which reduces resistance).

Before any SWAT site assault can begin, except in the most dire emergencies, a plan must be developed that covers all aspects of the assault, including all possible contingencies. The plan must follow the "KISS rule" discussed earlier ("Keep it simple, stupid!") and must be flexible in case unexpected events occur, which inevitably will happen. Also, for the best chances of success, experience has shown it to be imperative that all officers know all aspects of the plan. No one can ever be certain what will happen, or who will have to take over another officer's job. Everyone involved, therefore, no matter what his or her job, should know where to take hostages, where to take arrested subjects, what exits to use, and so on. This careful planning is vital because SWAT teams have found that, while a well-planned site assault is dangerous, a site assault without a plan simply invites disaster.

Also, to ensure the success of a site assault, if there is time a rehearsal of the assault is held at a location similar or identical to the incident site, as was done in the Escondido incident above. In addition, before the assault begins, the SWAT incident commander ensures the security of the inner and outer perimeters, since the suspects may be, and often are, driven out of the site by the incoming SWAT assault team. For safety reasons, the SWAT officers carrying out the site assault never chase suspects who flee a site; instead, they leave this task to other officers.

While all parts of a SWAT site assault are dangerous, experience has shown that one of the most dangerous portions is the actual approach and entry into the incident site. Sites often have "kill zones" (areas of no cover, where the suspect has a good field of view) that must be crossed before officers can reach the primary "breach point." Deciding on the safest approach into a site requires good intelligence from scouts, snipers, and people who have knowledge of the building and the surrounding grounds. The more cover and concealment these approach routes provide, the better, because it has been found through hundreds of successful SWAT operations that an assault or rescue has a much better chance of success if it is a surprise. Research by the U.S. Army's Operation Counter-Terrorist Unit has found that, when surprised, a person generally needs five seconds to regain the ability to react. Therefore, if a SWAT assault team can covertly approach and enter a site, they have an excellent chance of neutralizing the surprised hostage taker or barricaded person before he or she can react and hurt anyone.

There are many ways for a police SWAT team to get to the primary breach point undetected. One of the best ways is by performing the assault after dark (using night vision goggles). To assist in this, the SWAT command post has usually already cut off all utilities to the incident site and has darkened the area around it (in the incident at Henry's Pub in Berkeley, discussed in Chapter 8, for example, the officers shot out the streetlights around the incident site).

Another method of masking the approach of a SWAT assault team is to use a diversion. For example, having a helicopter hover or approach from a side opposite the one that the assault is coming from is a very effective technique; it was used in the Fox Plaza office-building incident discussed in Chapter 7. Helicopters are noisy, attract attention, and are perceived as a threat. While the hostage taker or barricaded person watches the helicopter the SWAT team can enter through the breach point undetected. Other diversions used by SWAT teams include flashbangs and window breakings on a side away from the assault-team breach point, the setting off of a building's alarm system, and the use of smoke grenades. In addition, a hostage negotiator can also cause a diversion by verbally distracting the suspect during the assault, by moving the suspect into a sniper's view, or by pretending to give major concessions, which will make the hostage taker believe he or she has won and then consequently let down his or her guard.

Occasionally, a SWAT team attempts a "Trojan horse" site assault, which uses a seemingly harmless activity like food delivery or medical service to mask an assault. This can be an especially effective technique, as is shown by the following incident.

A woman who lived in Apple Valley, Minnesota, had been a pen pal with a prisoner at the nearby Stillwater State Prison but broke off the correspondence when she found that her pen pal had been imprisoned for murdering his fiancée. However, shortly after this, while on a medical appointment outside the prison, the inmate managed to escape with the help of an accomplice. The escaped convict and his accomplice went directly to the former pen pal's home and took her and her two small children, aged eight and six, hostage.

For two days, the SWAT hostage negotiators attempted without success to persuade the hostage takers to release the hostages. Finally, when the hostage takers began making repeated threats that "we're going to have to kill one of the children," the police knew the time had come for an assault and rescue. To cover the site assault, the police arranged a food delivery for the hostages and the hostage takers, and while the hostage takers were distracted by the delivery, the SWAT team moved in. After gaining entry into the hostage site, SWAT officers found the escaped convict holding a knife to the throat of the six-year-old hostage. The police shot and killed the man, arrested his accomplice, and rescued the hostages unharmed.

Whether done through a diversion, a Trojan horse, or covertly, the assault teams' movement to the primary breach point is always extremely dangerous. Their approach, consequently, is watched over and covered by the SWAT snipers, who, positioned at an angle to the assault, can use suppressive fire if they find that the approach of the SWAT assault team has been compromised. To facilitate this cover, SWAT assault team members usually wear radio headsets that transmit the snipers' comments of what they see as the team advances toward the primary breach point. In addition, each member of this advancing SWAT assault team has safety responsibilities for the unit. The point officer, for example, watches the front, the rear guard watches the rear, and the other officers guard the flank to either side as they advance on the breach point. And while there is a primary breach point, there is also a secondary breach point in the event the primary one cannot be breached. In addition, the team, along with having an entry plan, must have an escape plan in case things do not go as expected, which occurs quite often. This plan makes possible an organized and structured withdrawal that will prevent further possible injury.

Once the team is safely at the breach point, different methods of entry into the incident site must be used, depending on the prevailing circumstances. If electronic surveillance of the site has been possible, for example, or released hostages or the negotiator has given information about where the hostage taker is located, the team knows whether to use a violent or a covert entry. If the suspect is directly behind the entry point, the SWAT team may decide to make entry by using an explosive device. Using explosives adds to the shock and surprise of the entry, as was demonstrated in the Fox Plaza office-building incident in Chapter 7. Or the SWAT assault team may decide just to bash the door in with a battering ram or another quick-entry device, again catching the suspect by surprise, as shown in the following incident.

In February 1993, in Arlington, Virginia, the police had to make a quick, surprise entry into a house where a man was holding hostage his estranged wife, two other women, and several children. Negotiators had attempted to persuade the hostage taker to surrender, but the man finally broke off with them and said that he was going to kill everyone in the house. The police were especially sensitive to such a threat, since three weeks earlier a hostage taker in Arlington had killed two hostages, including an infant. Knowing that innocent lives depended on their being able to surprise the hostage taker with a rapid entry, the police first used flashbangs to startle and disorient the suspect, and then, they bashed down the door. In the ensuing gun battle, the police killed the gunman and brought all of the hostages out alive.

If, however, the suspect is not close to the entry point, the SWAT team may want to use a quiet method of entry so that they can get inside, covertly approach, and then surprise the suspect. There are a number of methods for doing this. For example, most knob locks can be easily defeated simply by being twisted with a pair of channel-lock pliers. In homes with aluminum siding, the siding can be peeled back, and then, the only thing beneath is insulation and plasterboard. Also, in most homes, the police find, the rear door is usually weaker than the front door. And while the police in movies may often pick locks, this is not as easy as it appears. Picking locks is not a reliable method and takes constant practice, so it is not used by most SWAT teams. In fact, SWAT officers always check first to see if the door is even locked, and in many cases, they find it is not.

Occasionally, there is no ground-level breach point that can be approached at the SWAT incident without the SWAT team's being seen, and in these cases, the team must use an unconventional method of entering an incident site. In the case of tall buildings, some SWAT teams use a helicopter to carry SWAT officers. The helicopter, with SWAT officers riding on its skids, hovers above the building top, allowing the officers to climb off and then enter the building from the rooftop, or to enter by rappelling down the side (see photo below). Helicopters can also be used to place snipers at key positions, and to extract officers from rooftops if necessary. This method, however, is noisy. To make a more quiet entry into buildings, SWAT officers occasionally use "cherry

SWAT officer rappelling down building side (photo by Lieutenant Stephen Robertson).

pickers," which are metal baskets on the end of a long crane that can lift officers to the roof or upper windows of a building.

Most SWAT teams, however, would much rather have suspects come out than to go in after them. As we have seen, the police often use chemical weapons to force the suspects out. But the use of chemical weapons inside a structure, as was demonstrated in the Escondido incident above, can be hazardous. There is always the danger of fire, and also the danger of asphyxiation if too much gas or chemical agent is used. In addition, once chemical weapons are used, the SWAT team must wear gas masks in the event the chemical weapons don't work and they must go in, and these masks often restrict the officers' crucially needed vision. Therefore, before using chemical weapons, most SWAT teams look for some other way to persuade the suspect to come out of the SWAT incident site. If they can somehow get a suspect to come outside, where he or she is no longer barricaded and protected, then the SWAT team can often neutralize him or her much more easily and safely, as the following incident demonstrates.

In the summer of 1981, Atlanta, Georgia, was in the throes of a horrifying series of killings. Every day, it seemed, a new young victim of Atlanta's serial killer, later found to be Wayne Williams, would turn up somewhere. The police department had become used to receiving calls either about the killer or about his victims. However, on a hot Sunday morning, the Atlanta Police Department received a much more unusual call. The FBI office in the Federal Office Building at Peachtree and Baker Streets, the caller said, had been taken over by a gun-wielding man who was holding a number of FBI employees hostage.

The Atlanta Police Department SWAT team reported immediately to the scene and found, on gathering initial intelligence, that a man had come to the Federal Office Building, which is normally closed on Sunday, and knocked on the main entrance doors. Most federal buildings in the United States are guarded by the Federal Protective Service, and indeed a Federal Protective Service officer responded to the knock.

"Can I hel.ρ you?" the officer asked through the locked glass doors.

"I work here," the man answered. "I need to get inside to get some stuff done."

The Federal Protective Service officer didn't recognize the man. "I'll need to see some identification, please."

"How's this?" The man standing outside the door produced a handgun. "Now open up, or I'm going to kill you!"

The Federal Protective Service officer unlocked the door and was disarmed by the gunman, who then ordered the officer to go with him up to the FBI office on the tenth floor. Once on the tenth floor, the gunman had the officer knock on the door to the FBI office, a solid wooden door with a peephole, while he stood to one side and out of view. The person answering the knock saw only the uniformed Federal Protective Service officer standing outside and so opened the door, after which the gunman rushed inside and took all of the FBI office employees hostage (there were no FBI agents working at that time).

One of the female FBI employees became hysterical and began screaming and crying. The gunman grabbed her by the hair and dragged her to the door, telling her to get out because he didn't need that. The woman saw her opportunity and ran for safety.

The gunman then herded all of the remaining hostages into the chief clerk's office, which contained the office switchboard. He ordered one of the female hostages to call whoever was in charge of the FBI office and tell him what was happening. Shortly after this call, the husband of one of the hostages telephoned, found out what was happening, and called the Atlanta Police Department. A dispatcher from the Atlanta Police Department called back to verify what was going on and spoke with the gunman, who said he wanted to see some FBI agents and his chaplain.

As soon as the SWAT team set up, a hostage negotiator from the Atlanta Police Department (asked by the FBI to handle the negotiations) called the FBI office and began a conversation with the hostage taker. After checking on the welfare of the hostages, the negotiator asked the gunman who this chaplain was that he wanted to see. Alarm bells went off in the negotiator's mind when the hostage taker said it was the chaplain at Georgia Regional, which is a mental hospital. Even more alarm bells went off when the man told the negotiator that he had been a patient at Georgia Regional and had been diagnosed as a paranoid schizophrenic.

From the gunman's actions so far, and from his lack of clear demands or grievances, the negotiator feared they were dealing with a very unstable, and possibly suicidal, individual. Most people who take hostages have some grievance or perceived wrong they want righted or at least attention drawn to. But all this man at the Atlanta FBI office wanted was to see some FBI agents and to talk with his chaplain.

The police negotiator began feeling even more uncomfortable as he talked with the man because the hostage taker's voice would change during the conversation, almost as if another person were suddenly talking. In addition, the man began reversing the order of his words, often making nonsense sentences. In the opinion of the police negotiator, they were dealing with a very, very unstable individual, and the negotiator could not be certain at all about the continued safety of the hostages. Also, several hours into the hostage incident, the man dropped his demand to see some FBI agents but continued to demand to see and speak with his chaplain from the mental hospital. The negotiator, however, wasn't sure what effect talking with the chaplain would have, whether it would calm or enrage the hostage taker. Occasionally, hostage takers want to speak with someone significant to them just before committing suicide or some other violent act.

A hostage incident at an FBI office is, of course, big news. As soon as information about this incident went out over the wire services, news media from all over the United States began calling the office, wanting to speak with the hostage taker. Because the gunman was taking all of his calls through the office switchboard, the police were powerless to stop them. But interestingly, and certainly unusual for a hostage incident, the gunman would not speak with the news media. This fact, too, though helpful in the negotiations, concerned the police, since it appeared that the cause for the hostage taking wasn't clear even to the hostage taker. Usually, a hostage taker wants very much to speak with the news media and wants to tell them why he has been forced to take such a drastic action. But the man in the FBI office wanted no part of that. The SWAT team commander realized that, if an opportunity to end the incident by force presented itself, the SWAT team had to take it.

At one point in the negotiations, the hostage negotiator persuaded the gunman to release three of his hostages as an act of "good faith." But once this was done, the hostage taker seemed to become more agitated and upset, continuously asking where his chaplain was. This increased agitation greatly concerned the negotiator. Even more alarming, once the police had spoken with the three released hostages about the gunman's mental state, they began fearing for the lives and welfare of the remaining hostages. According to the released hostages, the man was becoming more and more unstable as the incident wore on; his voice and demeanor would change abruptly, as if another person had suddenly taken over his body; and he seemed to have become increasingly edgy and jumpy.

The SWAT incident commander knew that the negotiator couldn't be successful indefinitely with a man in this state, and that the SWAT team would have to do something soon. Up to this point, the hostage negotiations would have to have been considered successful: no one had been hurt and three hostages had been released. But still, the hostage negotiator realized, as the SWAT incident commander did, that total success probably wasn't possible. Although the negotiator had done his best, he couldn't persuade the hostage taker to surrender peacefully. Yet the hostage negotiator would still play an important part in ending this incident.

It was a call of nature that gave the police their opportunity to end the incident. The rest room on the tenth floor of the Federal Office Building was located at the end of the hallway, and to use it, the hostage taker would have to come out of the office he was holed up in. Anticipating this, the command post concealed SWAT officers in rooms along this hallway and gave these officers the green light for action if the opportunity presented itself. Then, in order to get the hostage taker to come out, the police ordered food for the hostages and the hostage taker. The negotiator suggested to the gunman that he allow the hostages to use the rest room while they waited for the food. The gunman agreed.

However, when the gunman opened the door and came out with the hostages, he held a handgun in the Federal Protective Service officer's back as he marched the line of hostages down the hallway to the rest room, so the hidden SWAT officers couldn't take any action. But on the trip back, the hostage taker became sloppy and allowed himself to become separated by several feet from the hostages. The SWAT officers saw their opportunity, leaped out of their places of concealment, and opened fire. While the police shot the gunman numerous times, the hostages escaped unharmed.

Even more important than the ease of neutralization, as in the above incident, another important reason that SWAT officers would prefer the suspects' coming out of a SWAT incident site to their going in is that, once they have entered a SWAT incident site, the officers are usually (but not always) on the suspects' turf. In most cases the suspects know the layout. They know the hiding places, and they know the best spots for an ambush. Suspects in their own homes or in a building they are familiar with almost always have the tactical advantage. And so, once inside, stealth is imperative for the SWAT team. The suspects should not know the officers are inside until it's too late.

"Because of its danger, a site assault should always be the last resort at a SWAT incident," said retired FBI agent and former SWAT team commander Wayland Archer. "The guy inside almost always knows the layout better than you."

To be able to surprise suspects inside their own homes or in a building they are familiar with, officers must move with complete silence. SWAT officers have developed a number of techniques for doing this. For example, once inside a structure, SWAT officers seldom talk. Instead, they have developed a set of hand signals that relay relevant information and orders. They also wear soft-soled shoes and usually carry sound-suppressed weapons. When going up steps, SWAT officers put most of their weight on the side of the step attached to the wall and avoid the middle of the step, where it is most likely to squeak. SWAT officers inside buildings always avoid brushing against walls, and before going inside a SWAT incident site, officers tape down any jingling items.

Once inside a SWAT incident site, the officers must assume, regardless of any intelligence to the contrary, that the suspect could be anywhere. For this reason, SWAT officers never turn a corner, enter a hallway, or climb a stairway without a plan. In any of these situations, without a plan, an officer could suddenly come under fire and find he or she has little cover. To prevent this, SWAT teams have developed specific techniques for crossing or entering one of these areas, and all require the officers to attempt to see what is in the area they want to cross or enter before actually moving. Officers do this in several ways, such as by the "quick peek" method, which is a jerk of the head into the area and then back, or they do it with a periscope or a mirror attached to a long rod. However, even after an officer is assured by a "quick peek" or another method that the area seems safe, all techniques for crossing or entering these areas require that only one officer at a time cross or enter, while the other officers cover him or her (see photo on page 197).

Along with crossing or entering these danger areas, just moving around inside a building is often hazardous for SWAT officers. Tests have shown that it takes an average marksman four to five seconds to draw a bead on a moving target. Therefore, SWAT team members give themselves three seconds to move from one position of cover to another, and they never move without being watched over by a fellow officer.

In addition to these danger areas, a number of other hazardous situations occur during a building entry and search for the a perpetrator. One is the tendency of the SWAT officers to bunch

SWAT officers never want to enter areas blind. This officer is using a Swatcam (video camera on a periscope arm) to view what is around a corner.

up while searching a building. This bunching can lead to a situation called a *fatal funnel*, in which many officers stack up together and make an easy target. In addition, SWAT officers are taught never to stop or silhouette themselves in a doorway (called in SWAT slang a *vertical coffin*) or in front of windows, and to avoid any back lighting that will make their shadow precede them.

A number of deadly experiences have shown that a highly dangerous situation inside a SWAT incident site is the searching of a closet. Suspects often hide in closets, and an officer opening the door makes a good target. Even in the event the officers know the suspect is inside the closet, they still usually can't shoot first because of the danger of there also being a hostage in the closet.

Another grave danger that SWAT officers must anticipate is booby traps, especially in locations such as bikers' houses, survivalist stockades, and other similar buildings or areas. A few of the more common booby traps found are spiked boards laid where the SWAT officers will jump or roll to when fired at; fish hook entanglements, which are many fish lines and hooks hanging down in one spot; shotgun shells inserted into drilled holes in the floor, which when walked on push the shell's primer against a nail; steps removed from darkened stairways; and heavy items set up to fall when officers pass under or by them. Because of the possibility of booby traps, SWAT training officers instruct team members that, if they find anything unusual or out of place while searching a SWAT incident site, they should never touch it.

In addition, SWAT officers have learned from many experiences never to dismiss any space as being too small or cramped for a person to get into or through. Frightened human beings can do amazing things. An incident that occurred when I was a uniformed street sergeant drove this point home to me. Very early one morning, I heard a report over the police radio of a burglar alarm going off at a bowling alley that I happened to be only a few blocks from. Racing to the spot, I found that a burglar had tried to break through a large brick-glass window with a sledge hammer. (Brick glass is a translucent block of glass used in the construction of buildings when the owner wants a window that the sunlight can come through, but that no one can see through.) I assumed that my quick arrival, however, had frightened the burglar off, since the hole through the brick glass was only about a foot in diameter and had jagged edges. Also, the window led into the kitchen area of the bowling alley, and inside, directly in front of the hole, sat a pot still on the stove, indicating to me that the burglar had not yet attempted to get through the hole. When the bowling alley owner arrived, he said he needed to go inside and block up the hole. I preceded him into the darkened bowling alley and, a few seconds later, had one of the worst scares of my police career when the owner flipped on the lights and I suddenly found myself standing less than a foot away from the burglar. He and I both screamed and jumped backward, and then, I recovered my wits and quickly placed him under arrest.

SWAT officers, however, unlike me at the bowling alley, always expect to find a perpetrator inside a SWAT incident site. But once SWAT officers are inside a site and standing outside the room the suspect is believed to be in, a new set of problems arise: how can they enter the room as safely as possible and still be able to neutralize the suspect? Just to charge in blindly invites disaster.

"Building and room entry are two of the most important things we teach here," said Officer Kris Brandt, a trainer for the New York City Police Department's Emergency Services Unit. "Doing them right means staying alive."

And so, police SWAT teams have developed a number of room entry techniques that have been shown to have the best chances of success, while providing the most safety. Before actually going into the room, the SWAT officers try, if at all possible, to find out what and who are inside and where they're positioned in the room. If the door is open, officers get this information with mirrors or periscopes, or if these are not available, they use a technique called *slicing the pie*. With this technique, an officer on either side of the door pivots around and examines the slice of the room he or she can see (see photo on page 200).

However, regardless of whether the officers can see what's inside the room, they still must enter it. A number of room entry

SWAT officers with sound-suppressed weapons preparing to make entry using flashbang devices (photo by Robert L. Snow).

techniques have therefore been developed, such as the crisscross, the button hook, the cross button, and the cross lean. Using the crisscross technique, the officers enter and go to the side of the room opposite the side of the door they were standing on. The button hook technique, on the other hand, requires the officers to hook around the door frame as they enter the room.

The strategy of all the room entry methods mentioned above is the same; only the technique used is different. They are all meant to get SWAT officers through the doorway, or the "vertical coffin," as rapidly as possible, and then to allow them to move quickly to their designated spot inside the room, from where they will secure the part of the room they are responsible for. However, all the while officers are doing this, they must assess the situation and respond to whatever threats present themselves. Officers are taught never to take up positions in the corners of rooms, as these tend to act like natural funnels and draw fire. Which one of the above room-entry techniques SWAT officers are trained to use often depends on the preference of the training officer, and on the success a SWAT team has had using the technique. There is no room-entry technique that can be said to be decidedly better than the others.

For any room entry, the first officer through the door is usually the team's best shot, as he or she is likely to be the one who first engages the suspects. While at one time officers were taught always to first neutralize the suspect who had the biggest, most deadly, weapon, this is no longer so. Now SWAT officers are taught to go after the first suspect who moves, because the movement means this suspect has recovered from shock and is reacting. Also, with the increase in the number of hostage takers and barricaded subjects wearing bulletproof vests, officers are taught to shoot two or three times to the chest and, if the suspect doesn't fall, to put one or two shots in the head.

To help increase the surprise of a SWAT team's entry into a room, a flashbang is usually thrown in first. Another technique is to throw in a large flashbang followed by a smaller one, and to enter the room between the two explosions. Often, if the SWAT officers realize that the suspect knows they're outside the door, stalling the entry for a few minutes will put the suspect under extreme stress and anxiety, which will often cause him or her to make mistakes.

Unfortunately, the stress and anxiety go both ways, as SWAT officers themselves realize that they can never be sure how the *hostages* will react. Hostages under the influence of the Stockholm syndrome have been known to jump between the officers and the suspects, to grab the officers' weapons, and to refuse to obey the commands of the officers. Even after the room has been entered, the suspects have been neutralized, and the incident has been basically resolved, the hostages must still be led out of the site. Because of the Stockholm syndrome, however, this is not always an easy task. Hostages are often uncooperative and refuse to go with the officers. Hostages under the influence of the Stockholm syndrome may also be dangerous because they may allow a "sleeper" (a hostage taker pretending to be a hostage) to become part of their group. For this reason, even successfully assaulting a SWAT incident site, neutralizing the suspects, and rescuing the hostages does not end the incident. Before the site assault can be considered successful and finished, the hostages must be taken to a secure location where they can be questioned, and the SWAT team can be certain they were all actually hostages.

Having to assault a SWAT incident site is always extremely dangerous to everyone involved, and therefore, assaults are used only when absolutely necessary. However, when there is no alternative and an assault is necessary, SWAT officers successfully carry it out by using tactics and methods that have proved themselves. While a tactical SWAT assault is always extremely hazardous, SWAT officers know that, occasionally, in order to save lives, they must risk their own.

12

Mobile Threats and Hijackings

"Okay now, listen up!" Conn Wayne Duncan told the hostage negotiator. "I've got a bomb in here that'll go off if I drop it! You understand me? If I fall, it'll blow!"

The police hostage negotiator assured Duncan as soothingly as possible that he understood; he also knew that he needed to get this information to the SWAT incident commander right away. Although Duncan had gotten himself caught up in a senselessly desperate situation, the hostage negotiator didn't think he was mentally ill or drunk. Instead, Duncan sounded very serious. Deadly serious.

A man with a history of violence and encounters with the Anchorage, Alaska, Police Department, Duncan had earlier that morning reportedly broken into a mobile home off Old Glenn Highway in Anchorage, where his ex-girlfriend, who had recently broken up with him, was staying with friends. The ex-girlfriend told the officers who responded to her call for help that she was staying with these friends because, after she had broken up with Duncan, he had tracked her down and assaulted her, and she had therefore had a felony arrest warrant issued for him. After questioning Duncan's ex-girlfriend further, the police learned that she'd awakened earlier that morning in the mobile home to find Duncan standing over her with a 9-mm pistol and a package he claimed contained a bomb. Seeming very agitated, she said, he ordered her to get dressed because she was going with him. Apparently, however, she didn't move fast enough, and Duncan fired a shot from the 9-mm pistol into the floor of the mobile home, awakening the family she was staying with: a man, his wife, and two young daughters, aged four and ten.

Understandably concerned about what was happening in his home, the man confronted Duncan and kept him occupied long enough for Duncan's ex-girlfriend to escape the mobile home and call the police, who immediately dispatched officers to her location. The ex-girlfriend told the officers that Duncan was very likely at that moment holding the four people hostage at the mobile home. The officers reported this information back to the dispatcher, and the Anchorage Police Department immediately called up their SWAT team, the Crisis Intervention Response Team (CIRT).

The summoned SWAT officers began quickly converging on the area around the mobile home, and one of the first arriving hostage negotiators contacted Duncan by telephone. Duncan told the negotiator immediately and very emphatically that he didn't intend to go back to jail and that he had a bomb to ensure he wouldn't. The hostage negotiator tried to calm Duncan by assuring him the police weren't going to do anything to provoke him. Duncan then gave his demand, which was that the police send his ex-girlfriend back into the mobile home so they could talk things over.

As the negotiators continued their dialogue with Duncan, the SWAT incident commander positioned his snipers, replaced the uniformed officers on the inner perimeter with SWAT officers, and began evacuating all of the residents nearby. The SWAT team also began gathering intelligence about Duncan. They first obtained a recent picture of him and a description of the clothing he was wearing and then got a rundown on his likelihood of using violence, which turned out to be considerable. As for Duncan's claim of having a bomb, the police knew that, though they receive many such threats each year, most turn out to be just fabrications. However, while gathering intelligence on Duncan, the chance that he had a real bomb suddenly moved from being only faintly possible to perilously likely. The police spoke with a friend of his who said that Duncan had recently built a bomb from several pounds of C4 explosive he had stolen. One of the first supervisors to arrive on the scene of the incident was a specialist in explosive ordnance disposal, and he gave his assessment of what such a bomb could do if detonated. "It'll make one hell of an explosion, and probably destroy the mobile home," he told them. The police knew that getting the hostages out was paramount.

However, Duncan told the negotiator, who was attempting to persuade him to release the hostages, that he wasn't going to release any of the hostages, and that, if they didn't send his girlfriend back into the mobile home pretty soon, he was going to blow it up.

Once the content of the negotiator's conversation with Duncan, as well as all of the intelligence information gathered on him, had been relayed to the command post personnel, they decided Duncan was very likely serious about having a bomb and also serious in his threats to detonate it. Because of this deadly potential, they decided Duncan could not be allowed to leave the area, no matter what. Even though the police had evacuated everyone from the zone of danger, and even though it would be disastrous enough if Duncan detonated the bomb inside the mobile home, this wouldn't be anything compared to the threat he'd present if they allowed him to leave the area and become mobile with the bomb. The threat to innocent people would be enormous. The decision was made to kill Duncan if he came out of the mobile home with the bomb and refused to surrender. The command post gave the snipers, who were armed with bolt-action .308 rifles and telescopic sights, the green light to shoot. Also, containment teams armed with Colt M-16 assault rifles were put into position, while an assault-and-rescue team armed with Heckler & Koch MP5's stood ready to move in as soon as needed. The SWAT incident commander hoped they wouldn't have to use deadly force, but they were prepared to. Duncan would not leave the area with the bomb.

A stratagem often used by negotiators when they want to increase the pressure on a perpetrator who is uncooperative or unreasonable is to cut off communications for a time. The command post made the decision to cut the telephone service to Duncan for a while, since they couldn't honor his demand to send his ex-girlfriend back in. Soon after the police did this, however, Duncan released the four-year-old hostage with a note demanding that the telephone be turned back on within an hour or else he would detonate the bomb.

Soon after the police restored the telephone service and negotiations resumed, Duncan also released the ten-year-old hostage, much to the surprise of the negotiators, who hadn't heard him say anything or hadn't sensed anything in his mood that would make them believe he was going to do this. A few minutes later, he also released the mother, still not telling the surprised negotiators why he was releasing the hostages. When the police spoke with the mother, though, they found out why. Apparently, when Duncan realized the police weren't going to send his ex-girlfriend back in, she told them, he had made the decision to leave the area, taking her husband along as his hostage. The order went out from the command post to kill Duncan as soon as the opportunity presented itself.

Within a few minutes, the door of the mobile home opened, and Duncan and the male hostage came out, Duncan carrying the 9-mm pistol in one hand and the package he claimed contained a bomb in the other. The snipers and containment teams immediately began watching for a clear shot. Even though Duncan wasn't using the hostage as a shield, but simply walking behind him, no clear shot presented itself until after Duncan ordered his hostage to open the driver's door of a red pickup truck parked close to the mobile home. Still apparently not concerned about using his hostage as a shield, Duncan shoved the man into the truck and instructed him to slide across the seat. As Duncan started to climb in, one of the snipers opened fire and hit him. Duncan tumbled into the truck after being shot and bounced off the steering wheel.

Seriously injured, Duncan staggered back out of the vehicle and fell face first against the truck's open door as the hostage leaped out the passenger's side and raced to safety. A member of one of the containment teams fired at Duncan with an M-16 assault rifle and struck him in the back. Duncan then fell down against the truck's running board and began clutching and pulling at the package he carried. Believing Duncan was trying to detonate the bomb, a sniper shot him again, and, at the same time, a member of a containment team also shot him through the truck door. Duncan collapsed onto the ground just as the bomb detonated. A huge explosion completely destroyed the pickup truck, moving it several feet, and sending parts of Duncan's body flying over one hundred yards.

The male hostage, who had managed to get down behind a nearby vehicle and to escape being harmed by the explosion, afterward told the police about his courageous role in this terrifying scenario. Once Duncan realized the demand to send his ex-girlfriend back in wasn't going to be granted, the man told police, Duncan said he planned to leave the area and take the hostages with him. The father insisted that he would cooperate only if Duncan released the rest of his family first. Duncan readily agreed, the man said, because he seemed positive that, since he was carrying a bomb, the police wouldn't try to stop him.

What Duncan didn't realize was that, while there are some situations in which the police may allow a SWAT incident to go mobile, there are others in which they simply cannot, no matter how volatile or dangerous the situations are. Duncan's case was one of the latter. Since the police believed he actually did have a bomb, for them to allow Duncan to go mobile would have presented a much larger danger to many more people than he presented when holed up in the mobile home. And so, the police simply made the tough decision to act, no matter what.

"If you're not prepared for it, a mobile SWAT incident can be really hazardous," said Indianapolis Police Department SWAT Tactical Commander Stephen Robertson. "By going mobile, the perpetrator's controlling the situation, and all you're doing is following him around."

There are certain situations, however, though small in number, in which the police will allow a SWAT situation to go mobile. But first a number of factors must be examined and weighed: how persistent and threatening is the perpetrator about wanting to move his location? Are any hostages likely to be harmed or killed if he is not allowed to move? Is the perpetrator now in a heavily fortified location that has a clear and commanding view of the surrounding area? If so, might it not be in the best interests of law enforcement to allow him to move to a much more vulnerable position? How many hostages does the perpetrator now have? If he has more than will fit into the vehicle he has asked for, he will very likely release some of the hostages.

"It's usually best if you don't let a SWAT incident go mobile," said former FBI SWAT commander Cal Black. "But if you do, you have to quickly evaluate where it's going and what the consequences are going to be."

While allowing a SWAT incident to go mobile is seldom advisable, when one does go mobile it occasionally has tactical benefits for the SWAT team. A very vulnerable time for hostage takers, as was demonstrated in the case above, is when they are coming out of the fortified location and moving toward the escape vehicle. A well-trained sniper can often end the incident at this point.

Even if the hostage taker does make it to an escape vehicle, the car can still be directed into a selected area, where a controlled vehicle-stop and hostage-rescue can be executed with minimal danger to bystanders. To do this, the police escort the hostage taker's vehicle much as a dignitary escort, blocking all crossroads. Interestingly, because of the feeling of importance this gives them, few hostage takers oppose the escort. Using this tactic, the police can guide the car into a suitable, selected location where an assault team is set up and ready.

Before any vehicle demanded by a hostage taker is delivered, it is often equipped with a remote kill switch that will allow the SWAT team to kill the car's engine at any exact moment and location. If this switch isn't available, explosive charges can be attached to the wheels. In addition, before a car is turned over to a hostage taker, a tracking device is also often attached. If none is immediately accessible to the police, the roof of the vehicle can be marked so that aerial surveillance is possible. If, however, the vehicle must be brought to the incident scene right away, and there is no time to do any of these things, the car can still be made easily identifiable by something as simple as breaking out a tail-light.

While incidents such as the one above in Anchorage, in which perpetrators carrying dangerous materials attempt to go mobile against police wishes, are rare, they do occur, and they can, and do, threaten even the most powerful people in the nation, including the First Family, as the following incident demonstrates.

On December 8, 1982, television viewers all over the world held their breath as they watched live coverage of a standoff at the Washington Monument in our nation's capital. A man dressed in a blue jumpsuit, his expression hidden behind the face mask of a motorcycle helmet, sat in a truck parked next to the entrance to the 555-foot monument. The truck, the man claimed, was packed with dynamite.

This terrorist incident started at a little after nine in the morning, when a man later identified as Norman David Mayer, a former maintenance man from Miami Beach and a well-known nuclear disarmament proponent, drove his truck onto the Washington Monument grounds and parked it next to the monument entrance. On the truck were painted the words "#1 Priority. Ban Nuclear Weapons."

When the authorities arrived, the driver of the truck immediately showed them a radio transmitter that he claimed would detonate a half-ton of TNT he had in the truck. After that, Mayer would no longer talk to the police. He told them he wanted an unmarried male reporter with no dependents to act as his intermediary.

Through this reporter, he made his demand, which was that a national dialogue be held on the nuclear weapons question. To clarify what he demanded, he gave the reporter a pamphlet that said, "A national dialogue on the nuclear weapons question as the first order of business on an agenda of every organization in the USA. Churches, businesses, fraternal, unions, sports, etc., no association excepted. Local, state, and national elected bodies and bureaucracies must comply. National and local media must carry these discussions daily, 51 percent of their time and space. The book *Fate of the World* to be the guide."

After reading the pamphlet, the authorities decided Mayer probably meant the book *Fate of the Earth* by Jonathan Schell, a book that told how the world would eventually be destroyed in a nuclear war. In response to the threat Mayer presented, the police immediately activated their SWAT units, while also bringing along fire trucks, ambulances, and even an armored vehicle. No one was really certain if Mayer actually had explosives in the truck, but if he did, a half ton of TNT would produce a huge explosion and do considerable damage. Explosive experts estimated that such an explosion would very likely dig a crater a hundred feet deep and shatter windows as far away as the White House. As a precaution, the Commerce and Agriculture Department offices and the Smithsonian Institution's National Museum of American History were evacuated. Even President Reagan and the First Lady were briefed as to safety measures, being advised to stay away from the Pennsylvania Avenue side of the White House as long as Mayer remained a threat.

Negotiating with Mayer was extremely difficult, since he refused to talk with the police and instead sent messages back and forth through the reporter. Still, tactical decisions and plans had to be made. Negotiators briefed the reporter on what to say and then tried to gauge Mayer's mental state by what the reporter said Mayer had told him. By what little intelligence they could glean through the reporter, the police SWAT teams decided Mayer was probably a very dangerous person.

Although Mayer became more and more agitated as the day wore on with no movement on his demands, he did allow the evacuation of nine people who hadn't been able to escape during the first minutes of the siege and had become trapped in the Washington Monument. Regardless of this goodwill gesture, the authorities made the decision, like the decision made in the incident in Anchorage, that, at all costs, Mayer would not be allowed to leave the area. They decided this because, when gathering intelligence on Mayer, the police discovered he had recently been attempting to buy explosives. In addition, the police could see that the truck appeared to be heavily loaded. The only thing more dangerous than the present situation, they decided, was a roving bomb moving through the streets of Washington, D.C. Ironically, it was decided that if a thousand pounds of TNT had to be exploded somewhere in the Washington vicinity, the open area around the Washington Monument was probably the safest place for it to occur.

And so, a little after 7:30 P.M., when the truck suddenly started moving, the drama began spiraling toward its end. Mayer first backed the truck up a few feet and then moved forward, apparently very tense and anxious, since he struck one of the flagpoles around the monument. The SWAT teams responded immediately and several police snipers shot Mayer. Mortally wounded, Mayer lost control of the truck, and it careened about two hundred yards down the slope in front of the monument before finally flipping over. As the truck lay unmoving on its side in the evening darkness, the back door now open, the tires still spinning, the world seemed to stop, and everyone at the scene held their breath. In the silence, three helicopters hovering overhead concentrated their spotlights on the truck, everyone waiting breathlessly for the tremendous explosion experts had warned that a thousand pounds of TNT would cause. When, after a time, no explosion came, police SWAT teams cautiously approached the vehicle, the officers first handcuffing the still breathing Mayer to the steering wheel, then searching the truck for explosives. Sixty-six-year-old Norman David Mayer died soon afterward. The police found no explosives in the truck.

As demonstrated by this incident and the one in Anchorage, special problems for a police SWAT team immediately begin to develop whenever a threat becomes mobile. A person holding hostages or carrying dangerous or deadly materials while moving from place to place presents a much more serious and dangerous situation than a static incident. Much of the success of police SWAT teams in resolving the incidents they are called to has come through their ability to isolate both the perpetrators and the incident and, by this isolation and control, to resolve the incident through negotiations—or an assault, if necessary. As demonstrated in both the Anchorage and the Washington incidents, the police simply cannot allow perpetrators with dangerous and deadly materials—in these cases, explosives—to become mobile. To do so would only endanger even more people than those involved in the original incident.

"We weren't about to let the van leave the monument grounds," said Marion Barry, mayor of Washington, D.C. (Komarow, 1982, A1).

"If the truck had become mobile, we would have had a moving time bomb in the city of Washington," said Chief Lynn Herring of the U.S. Park Police (Komarow, 1982, A1).

In addition to a perpetrator who wants to move from one location to another, mobile SWAT incidents can also occur when the incident itself takes place aboard a moving vehicle, such as a car, bus, train, or airplane. These situations are much more difficult to resolve than static, contained incidents because the incident location can quickly move away from where the police have brought and set up the resources necessary to resolve the situation. Even worse, if the incident moves from one jurisdiction into another, it often requires a new police agency to respond, usually with little knowledge of what has preceded the present situation. For this reason, one of the first tactics the police use in mobile situations that take place in cars, buses, trains, or airplanes is to disable the vehicle, on some occasions with better results than on others. For example, in the Downs case discussed in Chapter 5, when the FBI shot at the tires and engines of the hijacked airplane, one of the hostage takers responded by killing two hostages and then himself. While this tactic in the Downs case had tragic consequences, allowing a hijacked aircraft to leave the ground can also be extremely hazardous, as the following incidents demonstrate.

In 1974, Sam Byke shot and killed a police officer at a security checkpoint in the Baltimore-Washington International Airport. He then ran to the nearest gate and randomly boarded Delta Flight 523. In his bungling attempt to gain control of the airplane, he shot and killed the copilot and then wounded the pilot. Finding that in his rashness he had grounded himself, Byke, uncertain what to do for several moments, finally dragged an elderly woman out of the first-class section, put her in the copilot's seat, and ordered her to get the airplane off the ground.

In response to the killing of the officer at the security checkpoint, the police boarded the airplane and, in the ensuing gun battle, shot Byke, who then, finding himself about to be captured, turned his gun on himself and took his own life. In tapes he had mailed to people on the day of the attempted hijacking, Byke stated that his intention was to hijack the aircraft shortly after takeoff and then crash it into the White House. And so, if his plan hadn't gone awry with his premature murder of the police officer and the copilot, and instead he had succeeded in hijacking the aircraft once it was off the ground, he could very possibly have killed all of the passengers onboard the plane, along with causing untold damage and death on the ground where the airplane struck.

Much more recently, on December 24, 1994, terrorists hijacked an Air France flight at the Algiers airport. The flight, originally scheduled to end in Paris, landed at Marseille, France, and from this point, the French police refused to allow the aircraft to leave the ground, even though the terrorists threatened to begin killing the hostages if the airplane wasn't refueled and allowed to depart for Paris. Instead, a French police SWAT team stormed the aircraft, killed the terrorists, and rescued the hostages. By not letting the airplane leave the ground, the French police saved many, many lives. It was found afterward that the terrorists had wired the aircraft with dynamite that they intended to detonate as they flew over Paris. This hijacking would then have ended with an unbelievable toll in lives and property damage.

In most aircraft hijackings, except when the hostages are in imminent danger, police SWAT teams have found that an immediate aircraft assault is seldom the best option. Instead, it is often far better tactically to allow a little time to pass for the hijackers to become tired and less alert and thereby to increase the chances of a surprise assault. During this time, the police are not idle. Police SWAT teams have a chance to gather crucial intelligence about such things as the type of aircraft, the area around the aircraft, the hostage takers, and the hostages. SWAT teams also attempt to obtain blueprints of the aircraft in order to analyze and ascertain all possible methods of entry. If possible, the SWAT team also obtains a similar aircraft in order to practice the assault-and-rescue plan. With the use of an exact replica of the hijacked aircraft, all SWAT team members will know what their exact areas of responsibility are inside the airplane, what the zones of fire are, and how quickly they can gain control of the craft. This rehearsal also improves timing. To be effective, all SWAT team members must enter the aircraft at the same moment in one swift, sudden assault. The French police SWAT team in the hijacking case above reportedly practiced their extremely successful assault twenty times before actually doing it.

Boarding an aircraft and neutralizing the hostage takers, and at the same time rescuing the hostages unharmed, is an extremely difficult and dangerous undertaking. Aircraft assaults are particularly perilous because an airplane's wings are filled with highly flammable aviation fuel, its small windows make visibility from the outside in poor at best, and the SWAT team knows that the hijackers are likely to be waiting and watching for the SWAT entry through the main cabin doors. And so, if possible, the SWAT team attempts to use entry points other than the main passenger doors, such as through the emergency doors or the aft door.

However the entry is made, it must be quick and shocking, as was the case with the French police SWAT team's assault. A successful assault must catch the hijackers by surprise and disorient them for the few seconds it takes to neutralize them and take control of the craft. To expedite such a surprise entry, SWAT teams usually assault hijacked aircrafts during the night or early morning, or they set up diversions to mask the actual entry points of the assault team. Once the action is begun, police SWAT teams assault an airplane with sudden, blinding violence. After gaining entry into the aircraft, SWAT officers aim their weapons high, since most passengers usually scrunch down in their seats, while the hostage takers are usually standing up in a commanding position. This is also true in the cockpit, where the hijackers usually stand, while the pilot and copilot are sitting.

While the recent hijacking of the Air France flight didn't involve Americans, for anyone who believes that aircraft hijackings involving Americans are just part of 1960s and 1970s history, in 1983, Glen Tripp hijacked Northwest Orient Flight 608 at the SEA–TAC (Seattle–Tacoma) International Airport for the second time. In 1980, he announced he was hijacking Flight 608, but the police arrested him before the plane could leave the ground. Since he was then just a teenager, the court sentenced him to only a few years imprisonment. In 1983, soon after his release, and this time a bit smarter, Tripp hijacked Flight 608 once it was off the ground. Claiming he had a bomb, Tripp ordered the pilot to take him to either San Diego or Afghanistan. He settled, however, for Portland, Oregon. Once on the ground in Portland, Tripp refused to negotiate with the authorities and instead constantly threatened to blow up the airplane and kill everyone onboard. The police eventually killed him.

More recently, in February 1993, a lone gunman traveling on an Ethiopian passport hijacked a Lufthansa jetliner bound for New York City out of Frankfurt, Germany. His demands were that the plane land at Kennedy Airport and that he be given political asylum in the United States. While no one aboard the airplane was harmed during the hijacking, and the man surrendered peacefully to authorities in New York, still a very unstable, unpredictable, and dangerous person controlled the aircraft on its flight across the Atlantic Ocean to New York City.

While aircraft hijackings, of course, always receive considerable publicity, police SWAT teams find they are much more likely to have to rescue hostages from land vehicles, such as cars, vans, or buses. Therefore, police SWAT teams have worked out some very precise methods for handling these types of mobile SWAT incidents.

For handling a mobile incident involving an automobile, the police again want to cut off the perpetrator's mobility. To do so, a SWAT team uses several police vehicles to stop and then pin in the perpetrator's vehicle. This technique involves having one police car stop the vehicle's forward movement and several others immediately closing in and stopping any movement in other directions. These types of stops, however, take split-second coordination so that the perpetrator is surprised and not sure what to do until it is too late. During this brief moment of surprise, the SWAT team officers rush the car and make the apprehension and hostage rescue.

SWAT incidents that occur on buses require slightly different tactics. Buses usually have many wide windows, and any assault can be seen very clearly. As in an aircraft assault, before making a bus assault the SWAT team first attempts to gain as much intelligence as possible about the incident, along with attempting to obtain a set of plans for the bus, as well as a similar bus to practice the assault on. Also as in aircraft assaults, diversions are very important for bus assaults because of the need to attract attention away from the advancing assault team, which is usually highly visible through the bus windows.

SWAT teams have found that assault-and-rescue teams can gain entry to a bus a number of ways. The SWAT officers can enter through the emergency exit doors, through the emergency exit windows, or through the regular entry door. Door controls for buses are almost always located next to the driver's window, which is never locked because of the need to be able to open doors from the outside. Once a bus assault begins, as in all other assaults, it must be over before the hostage taker has time to react or think about what is happening. However, because of the high visibility of the interior of most buses, it has been found that the use of a sniper is often a better and safer option for ending a SWAT incident on a bus.

Most police SWAT teams also practice hostage rescues on trains, although they do not occur nearly as often as other types of mobile SWAT incidents. The entry and rescue methods are very similar to those used on a bus. SWAT teams in cities around any significant body of water also usually practice hostage rescue aboard boats and ships. Waterborne hostage rescue, though, particularly on large metal ships, is particularly tricky because perpetrators can secure areas below the deck behind heavy metal doors, because most police radios will not operate between decks, and because of the danger of ricocheting bullets, which have a tendency to slide along the metal walls. But like all other SWAT assaults and rescues, these must be swift, sudden, and dynamic.

While SWAT assaults and rescues involving mobile situations, particularly aircraft hijackings, receive considerable press coverage, these type of incidents are really not very common, or at least not as common today as they were in the 1960s and the 1970s. However, police SWAT teams know they must stay prepared to handle these types of incidents because all it would require for hijackings to increase is for one person to commit a hijacking with a new twist or variation not seen before. The intense news media coverage would then undoubtedly spawn many imitations. Therefore, police SWAT teams stay ready to be called.

13

High-Risk Warrant Service

In early 1990, a newly established drug operation in Indianapolis was off to a lucrative start. In a very short time, a group of Jamaican drug dealers had established six fixed and several mobile sites, using one of the sites only for manufacturing crack cocaine, another for taking drug orders, and the rest for customer pickup. After only a few short months, the drug ring's production was running smoothly and its sales were brisk.

But the police had other plans. Learning a few weeks earlier through confidential informants of the drug ring's existence, detectives from the Indianapolis Police Department's Narcotics Branch had made several controlled drug buys from the ring and then had obtained search warrants for the operation's sites, as well as arrest warrants for its participants. However, intelligence on the group showed that they were well armed with both automatic and semiautomatic weapons and were not averse to using these weapons if provoked or threatened. Therefore, the detectives realized they needed assistance in serving the warrants, and so they contacted the Indianapolis Police Department's SWAT team.

After receiving approval for the warrant service and working with the intelligence information provided by the narcotics detectives, SWAT officers drew up plans for a simultaneous multilocation strike: supplemented by narcotics detectives, the SWAT officers would serve the warrants at all of the drug ring's locations at the same time.

The gang's diversified sites demanded several different tactics at different locations. At one of the locations, for example, officers used the cover of a U-Haul truck and an ambulance to approach a drug site located in a second-floor apartment. Able to slip into position undetected, two of the officers began the assault by firing rubber baton rounds (rounds that look like large mushrooms) from an Arwen 37 (a grenade-launching gun) through the apartment's windows. This firing created a diversion for two other officers, who used a ladder to gain access to the apartment's balcony, and for other officers, who used a hooligan tool (a pry bar specifically designed to force open doors) on the front door. Acting in coordination, the officers forced open the front door of the apartment at the same moment the officers on the balcony, after firing a Shok-Lock round at the sliding-glass balcony door, tossed a flashbang device into the apartment through the hole made by the Shok-Lock round.

During the time of this warrant service, at another location several miles away SWAT officers used a battering ram and flashbang devices, while across town at still another drug-ring location SWAT officers serving arrest and search warrants used sledgehammers and Shok-Lock rounds. As these teams stormed the fixed sites, other SWAT officers stopped and arrested suspects operating the mobile drug-selling sites.

In only a few minutes of actual assault time, these SWAT officers, through the same planning and teamwork used in other, usually highly publicized, SWAT incidents, served warrants that closed down six fixed and several mobile drug sites. They also arrested eight individuals and confiscated various pieces of drug-manufacturing paraphernalia, many different types of weapons, and large quantities of crack cocaine. But most important, they did all of this with no one being killed or seriously injured.

If asked what a police SWAT team does most of the time, the average citizen very likely visualizes such things as the police storming an airplane to arrest hijackers and rescue hostages or perhaps sees them rushing into a business where a criminal caught in the commission of a crime by quickly arriving officers is holding a half dozen customers at gunpoint. But in actuality, these type of incidents encompass only a small part of a police SWAT team's time.

While incidents like hijackings usually generate large amounts of publicity and are often what makes most of the general public aware that their city even has a police SWAT team, the activity that actually takes up the majority of a police SWAT team's time is serving high-risk warrants, such as those in the incident above. In many communities, there is enough work doing this to keep a SWAT team operating full time.

"High-risk warrant service is the majority of what we do," said Lieutenant Stephen Robertson of the Indianapolis Police Department SWAT team.

SWAT involvement in high-risk warrant service has dramatically increased in recent times, not so much because of a large growth in the crime rate but because of a side effect of our legal system's method of confronting the country's drug crimes. In the last few years, many lawmakers have come to believe that our society's very existence is being threatened by drugs and the crime they spawn. As a result, state legislatures have been passing laws that dramatically increase the penalties for being involved in drug dealing. Consequently, criminals now know that, if they are arrested and convicted of drug dealing, they face long prison sentences, often mandatory prison sentences that cannot be reduced or suspended.

Still, many people, even though facing these lengthy, increased penalties, become involved in the drug trade because of the huge profits. Unfortunately for the police, however, these huge profits also mean that these dealers have the money to purchase high-tech assault weapons, often better weapons than the average police officer has. And because these criminals know they face long sentences if arrested and convicted of drug dealing, they have begun resisting arrest with increased vigor and deadliness, many times using these high-tech assault weapons. Police detectives, armed only with pistols or revolvers, are no match for many of today's criminals. Therefore, the danger involved in serving arrest and search warrants, particularly against drug dealers and drug locations, has become so great in many communities that the police departments now use their SWAT teams almost exclusively to serve these high-risk warrants, and particularly to serve them at fortified locations, as in the following incident.

Several months after closing down the Jamaican drug ring, the Indianapolis Police Department's Narcotics Branch received information through several of its informants about a heavily fortified house in which drugs were reportedly being both manufactured and sold. The informants said that the residents of this house had hung cane screens on the front porch to hide two recently installed steel doors, the second of which had a porthole through which prospective drug buyers would slide their money and receive drugs. Informants also reported that the windows of the house had been reinforced with steel bars and had portholes through which weapons could be fired, and that the occupants had used concrete blocks to seal off the house's other entrances. Additionally, the informants warned that the occupants were heavily armed with shotguns, .44 Magnum revolvers, and Uzi submachine guns.

The Indianapolis Police Department's Narcotics Branch, after making several controlled drug buys at the location, obtained a search warrant for the house. However, because of the danger involved in the service of this warrant, the narcotics officers asked for assistance from the SWAT team.

Once receiving the go-ahead for this warrant service, the SWAT team analyzed the intelligence information supplied by the narcotics detectives. With this analysis, the SWAT team developed an assault plan that would use a large force of heavily armed SWAT officers, supported by two powerful front-loaders (self-propelled pieces of machinery similar to bulldozers but with a wide metal scoop on the front) borrowed from the street department—there just in case they needed to make an emergency forced entry into the house.

On the day of the warrant service, the SWAT team set up at a staging site several blocks from the house and waited for the SWAT commander's signal to proceed. When it came, the SWAT officers approached the house in several teams, one from the front, one from the rear, and one team driving the two front-loaders. When the officers at the front of the house were refused entry after identifying themselves as police officers with a search warrant, the SWAT officers fired a Shok-Lock round at one of the fortified windows and then tossed a flashbang device in through the hole. At the back of the house, other SWAT officers, using a chain saw, began cutting a hole in the rear door. Seeing the SWAT officers preparing to come in both the front and the rear, plus the two front-loaders positioned and ready to rip out both sides of the wood-frame house, convinced the occupants to surrender. The operation took only minutes to execute, no one was injured, and the house was put out of business permanently.

As stated above, the use of much of a police SWAT team's time serving high-risk warrants has come about because drug dealers have so increased their affinity for violence in the last few years. However, warrants for drug dealers aren't the only warrants that SWAT teams are asked to help serve, as shown in the next incident.

Joe Dewey, the Indiana State Police investigators knew, was going to be an exceedingly dangerous person to arrest. Dewey, a forty-nine-year-old man with a long history of mental problems, reportedly suffered from unpredictable mood swings and extreme paranoia. He had told people he believed that his phone was tapped, and that a recently capped tooth had a CIA transmitter planted in it. The state troopers had just received an arrest warrant to serve on Dewey that had been issued after he pulled a gun on his brother, threatened to kill him, and then ran him off the family farm.

Talking with Dewey's family members, the State Police found that Dewey seldom left the farm, and that on the rare occasions when he did, he left it only late at night. The family told the police that Dewey always kept a firearm closeby, and that he had three handguns, three rifles, and a shotgun. They also told the police that Dewey's paranoia had become so intense in the last few years that he talked constantly about how he would fight and kill any police officers who came for him, and how he had booby-trapped several doors in his house with a shotgun.

Realizing how very dangerous this warrant was going to be to serve, the State Police investigators requested the assistance of the Indiana State Police SWAT team, called the Emergency Response Team (ERT). The SWAT team agreed to assist and, in their preparation for serving the warrant, conducted an aerial reconnaissance of the farm. After reviewing this intelligence, they decided that any assault team approaching the farm would be seen long before it got there. The farm, they found, sat far back off the road and contained many buildings (two homes, four barns, and a number of outbuildings, any of which Dewey could be in); the area around the farm had no cover, being mostly cleared land that was extremely muddy because of recent heavy rains. Dewey's family also assured the police that any assault on the farm would result in a shootout. And since Dewey was known to possess several high-powered rifles and was said to be a crack shot, the SWAT team also ruled out an aerial insertion.

The SWAT team therefore decided that the only way to serve this warrant safely was somehow to trick Dewey into leaving the farm, after which he could be intercepted and arrested. Working on this premise, the SWAT team devised a plan in which Dewey would be contacted by a hospital and told that his daughter, who lived with his ex-wife, had been injured in an accident. The caller would tell Dewey that the hospital had been unable to contact his ex-wife and that he was needed at the hospital to authorize medical treatment for his daughter.

From their reconnaissance of the farm, the police knew there were only two routes that Dewey could take going to the hospital.

An "accident" would be staged along what the police felt was the most likely route he would take, and to make the accident scene look realistic, the police would have an ambulance and a fire rescue truck there. Once Dewey stopped for the accident, SWAT members, dressed as ambulance personnel or firefighters, would approach the car to speak with him and then make the arrest. They also decided that, if Dewey took the less likely route, he would be stopped and arrested at a predetermined spot.

The SWAT team, however, knew that the site for the accident had to be carefully selected. First, it had to be an isolated spot so that, if a gunfight erupted, the possibility of injury to innocent people would be minimal. And second, it had to be a location that gave good concealment for the sniper and observer teams. After careful consideration, the SWAT team selected what it felt was the best spot on the route to the hospital.

The SWAT team's plan received the go-ahead, and late in the evening, the police set up the "accident." A doctor at the local hospital, who agreed to assist the police and would be protected that night by two state troopers just in case Dewey somehow slipped by the police and got to the hospital, called Dewey and advised him of the need to come and sign for his daughter's treatment. Dewey told the doctor that he would leave right away, but he didn't. Instead, he called his ex-wife's mother and asked her to go to the hospital instead. However, when Dewey called the doctor back and told him that his daughter's grandmother would be coming to sign for the treatment, the doctor told him that only a parent or legal guardian could sign for a child's treatment. Dewey reluctantly agreed that he would come.

However, as often happens in these types of incidents, unexpected complications occurred that disrupted the well-laid plans. When Dewey came out and got into his truck to go to the hospital, it wouldn't start, and so he went back in and called the doctor, asking if it was possible to get a ride with an ambulance or a police car that happened to be near.

The SWAT team members held a quick tactical meeting to discuss this unexpected change in the plans, and they decided that

a state police officer who happened to live near Dewey, and who
was known to him, would call and offer him a ride. The officer
would be accompanied by a SWAT officer in plain clothes. Two
more SWAT officers would also be nearby in an unmarked car,
while the rest of the SWAT team would stay close to the farm.

After calling Dewey, the state police officer and the SWAT
team member drove up the long driveway to Dewey's house, and
he came out to meet them. Immediately, they saw that Dewey was
armed. The SWAT officer got out of the car and left the front door
open, then opened the rear door as if to offer the front seat to
Dewey. However, once Dewey got close to the car, the SWAT team
member and the State Police officer jumped him and took him to
the ground. The second car sped onto the scene, and within seconds, Dewey was in custody, with no injuries to anyone. They
found Dewey was carrying two .357 Magnum revolvers and a .22-
caliber pistol.

Performing high-risk warrant service, SWAT officers find,
while a bit more dangerous, is operationally really not very different from most other SWAT operations and requires much the same
ingredients for success. For example, the key to the successful
warrant service on Joe Dewey was not the detailed planning the
police did, but the flexibility of the SWAT team's planning. Once
the original plan went awry, the officers had to immediately see
another way of gaining their objective. This is true of any SWAT
operation in which the actions of the suspects must be predetermined. The truth is that suspects seldom do what the police think
they will. And this can be extraordinarily dangerous, particularly
when dealing with heavily armed and dangerous people. This is
what makes warrant service on high-risk individuals a task SWAT
teams in many cities have taken over. Detectives with handguns
are just simply much too often outgunned, as the following incident demonstrates.

Several detectives from the Indianapolis Police Department's
Homicide Branch went to a house on the north side of the city to

serve arrest warrants on two suspects in a robbery, during which an armored-car driver had been murdered. After being refused entry into the home, one of the detectives, armed only with a handgun, attempted to force open the front door. He was immediately struck by bullets from an assault rifle fired through the door. The detective fell to the porch, mortally wounded.

Finding themselves tremendously outgunned, and unable to help their fallen comrade because of their lack of firepower and the intense gunfire coming from inside the house, the other detectives were forced to fall back and call for assistance, having to leave the dying man lying on the porch. The Indianapolis Police Department SWAT team immediately came to the scene and set up perimeters and a command post. Then, using the cover of gas shells fired into the house, SWAT officers removed the body of the now dead police officer from the porch. Once this was done, negotiators gave the occupants of the house an opportunity to come out and surrender, which one suspect did; the other refused. The SWAT team, using more gas shells, one of which started a fire inside the house, eventually stormed the residence and arrested the second suspect. In December 1994, one of the suspects was executed at Indiana's maximum-security prison in Michigan City for the murder of the police officer. The other suspect is now awaiting execution.

As this incident demonstrates, while the high-profile SWAT incidents that receive most of the media coverage, such as hostage or barricaded incidents, appear very dangerous (and certainly are), they usually don't present nearly the danger level that warrant service often does. The reason is that most hostage and barricaded incidents involve emotionally distraught people who are using whatever weapon happens to be at hand. The perpetrator is seldom a professional criminal, and many of the perpetrators involved in hostage or barricaded incidents, once calmed down by the negotiators, can be talked into surrendering peacefully. Warrant service, on the other hand, can be much more dangerous because most of the people SWAT teams are asked to serve warrants on are heavily armed career criminals, who are usually very knowledgeable about the seriousness of their crime, and about the likely outcome of being arrested, which makes them much more prone to violence.

SWAT officers have found that the danger level of most high-profile SWAT incidents, such as hostage or barricaded situations, can be reduced by various means, and so SWAT teams use these same means to reduce the danger level of warrant service. One of their methods is planning. And though SWAT officers thoroughly plan a warrant service, as they would an assault and rescue, they keep the plan flexible for any contingencies that can, and usually do, crop up. To make warrant service as low-risk as possible, the officers involved must know what to do not only when things go as planned, but when the unexpected happens or when things don't go as planned. And as shown in the case of Joe Dewey, these unexpected things do happen.

Also, before any warrant-service planning can begin, like the planning for most other SWAT operations, as much intelligence as possible must be collected about the warrant service location, its fortifications, the suspects to be arrested, their armament, and their propensity to resist arrest with violence. But unlike in most other SWAT operations, much of this information comes from confidential informants, usually criminals themselves who have been inside the site. However, no police officer with any experience ever trusts a confidential informant, particularly in a situation where bad information could result in the loss of life. Therefore, all of the information obtained from confidential informants must be verified with surveillance of the target location and suspects. A considerable amount of this information, police officers know, can be verified simply by talking with people who live in the neighborhood. In addition, by passing inconspicuously through the neighborhood, SWAT officers can assess the best access routes to the location, any possible escape routes from it, and the location's proximity to high-risk areas, such as schools, playgrounds, and hospitals.

This intelligence, once gathered, is used to decide the best way to gain the objective, which is usually entry into a site. But in some cases involving warrant service, rather than a dynamic, forced entry, preceded by some type of diversion, a ruse is a much safer, and more effective, method of entry into a site. A ruse may work better because streetwise criminals often know that they can expect a diversion before a forced entry. A ruse, if it works, is better because the entry point into the location is opened voluntarily, the officers can approach the location without worrying about concealment, and the person answering the door can be apprehended quickly and safely, as demonstrated in the next incident below.

The police in Bellingham, Washington, received both search and arrest warrants for a marijuana-growing operation in which the suspects were reported to be heavily armed and dangerous. After surveillance and intelligence gathering, the police SWAT team decided that a ruse was likely to be the best and safest way to gain entry into the site. And so, using a county dump truck, the SWAT officers, dressed as laborers, pretended to be from the county road department. The officers knocked on the door of the house where the warrant was to be served and said that they had been digging down the road and had cut a gas line. They told the man who answered the door (whom one of the arrest warrants was for) that they were warning people with gas appliances to shut off the pilot lights. The man was so taken in by this ruse that, even after the police grabbed and handcuffed him, he reportedly said, "But I don't have any gas appliances."

If, rather than a ruse, a forced, dynamic entry is decided on, and the operation involves the service of warrants at an extremely hazardous site, involves very dangerous individuals, or is likely to result in heavy news-media interest, many SWAT teams like to rehearse the warrant service, as they do hostage rescues. Doing this can detect any weak points in the plan. Also, for safe warrant service, the "KISS rule" applies to all operations. Under the stress that accompanies high-risk warrant service, overly complex duties and responsibilities are likely to be forgotten or confused anyway, and so a simple operation is the most likely to succeed. Another important element in successful warrant service is surprise. As in most SWAT operations, suspects who don't know the police are coming don't have time to prepare for them, don't have time to get their weapons ready, and don't have time to destroy the evidence the police are coming after. Along with surprise comes the need for speed. These two elements work hand in hand. The suspects must be surprised and then placed under police control before they have time to react and do anything aggressive.

A major difference, however, quickly arises between regular SWAT operations, such as hostage and barricaded incidents, and warrant service when the actual entry into a location begins. Particularly in narcotics warrant service, to make their entry as dynamic and overwhelming as possible, SWAT teams often use the swarm or saturation method. This technique involves the immediate flooding of the inside of a location with police officers. Doing this gives the officers immediate control of the inside of the location, discourages thoughts of resistance, and prevents the destruction of any evidence. The idea behind the technique is to immediately dominate the site with officers and firepower. This tactic, however, has a certain inherent danger level should any shooting break out, since the officers could very easily be caught in cross fire.

When this instant dominance is not necessary, some SWAT teams will use the *snake method*, in which the officers enter a location one after another. Using this method, the officers are not so spread out as in the *swarm method*, and hence not as likely to be caught in cross fire.

Unfortunately, regardless of the flexibility of the planning, the amount of intelligence gathered, or the teamwork and methods used, serving warrants is often an extremely volatile and dangerous operation for police SWAT teams. Because of the people and situations involved, serving high-risk warrants is fraught with danger to both police officers and suspects, as the following incidents demonstrate.

In Los Angeles in 1987, an international law attorney suspected of taking part in a large drug ring fired a handgun at officers serving an arrest warrant on him. During the exchange of gunfire, the attorney shot an officer in the wrist (though not seriously injuring him) and was then himself killed in the ensuing gun battle.

In Prince William County, Virginia, in 1990, both a police officer and a suspect died after the police went to a residence to serve an arrest warrant arising out of an earlier shooting of a police officer. Although the officer used a ballistic shield, a bullet from an AK-47 assault rifle penetrated the shield and struck the officer in the head. The police then shot and killed the suspect.

In Racine, Wisconsin, in 1991, the police SWAT team went to a home to serve a search warrant for drugs. Once inside the house, the police were confronted by a man with a bomb in each pocket and one in his hand. The police shot and killed the man when he began to detonate the bombs.

In West Valley City, Utah, in 1991, the police SWAT team attempted to serve a warrant on a man who had been implicated in at least one drive-by shooting. The house the man lived in had been fortified with security doors, motion detectors, and a rottweiler attack dog. When the officers forced entry into the home, the man fired a .45-caliber handgun at the officers, striking one officer in the chest (the officer was wearing body armor, which saved his life) and one officer in the thigh. The officers returned fire and killed the suspect.

In Colorado Springs, Colorado, in 1992, SWAT officers serving a search warrant for drugs at a mobile home found themselves suddenly under fire from an assault rifle. One officer, even though wearing body armor (which will not stop many assault rifle bullets), died when a bullet penetrated the armor. The police shot and critically injured the suspect. A large quantity of drugs was found in the home.

As is evident in the news almost every day, violence in America is both flourishing and growing, and much of this violence is related to the illegal drug trade. As long as this problem remains in our communities, the need to bring as many of these dangerous criminals as possible to justice will continue. But doing this is fraught with danger for ordinary police officers, who when attempting to serve warrants on these criminals often find themselves pitifully outgunned. Therefore, the need for police SWAT teams to serve high-risk arrest and search warrants is likely to remain in America for some time in the future.

14

Interagency Cooperation

On March 15, 1991, a team of three bank robbers held up the Wells Fargo Bank in the West Hills area of Los Angeles. Two of the robbers, heavily armed and wearing disguises, grabbed the money from the tellers, while the third robber, also disguised, stood in the middle of the bank with a stopwatch. According to witnesses, the men worked as a coordinated unit, getting in and grabbing the money, and then escaping before the police could respond. This robbery, however, was only the beginning of a string of robberies, and over the next year, this same gang would hold up eight additional banks and net themselves over $1 million.

Bank robberies, such as the one above, can be either a state or a federal crime, and they are often investigated by both the FBI and the local police. In the case of the "West Hills bandits," as this group of bank robbers became known to the police, the FBI worked very closely with the Los Angeles Police Department in attempting to put the gang out of business. But since this gang of bank robbers was always heavily armed, the police realized very early that apprehending them was going to be a high-risk venture and would require the assistance of SWAT.

Bank robbery in the Los Angeles area is not an unusual event, but a daily occurrence. Each year in Los Angeles over twenty-six hundred robberies take place in the area's 3,500 banks. Therefore, even though the robbers at the West Hills Wells Fargo Bank carried off their first robbery much more professionally than most, it didn't overly concern the police at the time.

However, in April, May, and July 1991, this same gang, again heavily armed and wearing disguises, and again coordinated by a gang member keeping an eye on a stopwatch, hit banks in the San Fernando Valley area of Los Angeles and got away with nearly $224,000. Then, in September, the same gang entered another bank in the area, obviously well cased since they called the bank manager by name, and left with over $436,000 from the vault.

By the time of the September robbery, the police had figured out that the same group of individuals had been responsible for all five of the bank robberies, but they still didn't have a clue to any of the gang members' identities. And while there had been no violence in any of the five robberies, the police feared that eventually either someone would resist or the police would be nearby and respond before the robbers had time to flee. Since the West Hills bandits were always heavily armed, violence would be the almost certain outcome. FBI agents and the robbery investigation unit of the Los Angeles Police Department met to discuss the case and to develop a plan for identifying the members of the gang, including the surveillance of possible suspects. At these meetings, the participants also decided that an FBI SWAT team would be used when the time came for apprehensions to be made.

As the Los Angeles Police Department and the FBI began working to identify the members of the West Hills bandits, the gang itself continued with their robberies, one time disguising themselves as postal workers and even driving a salvaged postal truck, and one time wearing army fatigues. In each robbery, it seemed, the West Hills bandits brandished new, and more deadly, weapons: one time a double-barreled shotgun, one time a submachine gun, and one time an M-16 assault rifle. As the weeks went by and the robbers continued their crime spree, the police worked doggedly trying to identify them.

Finally, persistence paid off. After weeks of work, the police identified two men from the West Hills area who had been buying tens of thousands of dollars worth of weapons and ammunition during the past year, always paying cash for them. The two men, who had only minor criminal histories, lived in an expensive home, yet had no visible means of support. In order to gather intelligence on these two men, the police decided to use plain-clothes surveillance.

The surveillance began on February 18, 1992, and paid off almost immediately. Undercover officers followed and watched one of the suspects as he parked and then moved two vans around shopping-center parking lots in the area of the previous bank robberies. From his actions, the police believed he was preparing for a vehicle switch after a robbery.

For the next two weeks, the surveillance continued. The police followed the suspects as they moved the vans around several more times, and as one of the suspects cased several banks. Finally, this suspect appeared to be paying particular attention to a bank in the Woodland Hills area. The police also cased the location and found it to be perfect from the robbers' point of view, being isolated and out of view, but also perfect from the police point of view, since an apprehension of the heavily armed suspects could take place with a low risk to innocent bystanders.

Along with the bank, however, the police noticed the suspect surveying a parking area in a nearby apartment complex. The police felt certain that this was where a vehicle switch would take place. This spot also appeared ideal for an apprehension, since it was isolated and wouldn't be dangerous to bystanders when the time for the arrest came.

During the next two days, the police followed the suspects as they drove several times from their home to the bank and the apartment parking area. Although in the eight previous robberies there had been at least three other individuals involved, the police didn't observe the two suspects meeting with any of them and didn't know if they usually met with them only after the robbery had been planned out, or if the gang had split up.

On March 6, 1992, the police followed the two suspects as they parked a third van in the parking garage of a large hotel and then moved one of the two vans they had parked at shopping centers to the apartment-complex parking area. Since the van parked at the hotel was registered to one of the suspects, the police felt certain that the two suspects would go first from the bank to the van parked at the apartment complex. The police developed a plan, which would use several teams of FBI SWAT officers, for apprehending the two men as they made the vehicle switch at the apartment complex.

At 3:00 P.M. on March 6, 1992, the Los Angeles Police Department surveillance teams observed the two suspects leaving their home in West Hills carrying large bags. The suspects drove their car to a shopping-center parking lot and switched to the remaining van; then, they headed off in the van toward Woodland Hills. After several detours, they finally pulled in and parked behind the bank they had cased. A few moments later, they climbed out of the van wearing army fatigues and disguises, and carrying weapons they had obviously hidden in the bags.

In order to prevent any nearby police officers from inadvertently disrupting the plans for apprehension, the Los Angeles Police Department's Communications Center had agreed not to broadcast the holdup alarm at the Woodland Hills Bank. The alarm activated only moments after the two suspects entered and announced a holdup.

Spending only two minutes in the bank, the robbers ran out with the money, jumped into their van, and headed toward the apartment complex. Once there, the suspects parked the getaway van next to the switch van, both vehicles facing the parking-facility wall. The FBI SWAT team prepared to move in and make the apprehensions as soon as the two men got out of the vehicle. However, as often happens in events such as these, the unexpected occurred. A pedestrian suddenly appeared near the vans, and the SWAT team had to hold up. The suspects, though, were apparently busy because they didn't notice anything as the SWAT team, once the pedestrian passed by, surrounded the two vans and then blocked any possible movement of the vans with cars. The suspects remained oblivious of what was happening until the FBI

SWAT team identified itself over a loudspeaker and ordered the two men to come out of the van and surrender.

For several minutes, the two suspects seemed confused. While they didn't actively resist, they wouldn't get out of the van either. It was as if they had convinced themselves they were much too smart and clever for the police ever to catch them, and now that they had been caught, they didn't know what to do. In an attempt to show the two men the futility of resisting, the agent on the loudspeaker identified both suspects by name. Finally, seeming at last to realize the hopelessness of their situation, both men came out of the van and surrendered. In the van, the police found an M-16 assault rifle, a revolver, and $150,000 in cash taken from the bank.

Once the arrest of the two robbers had taken place, other FBI SWAT teams positioned near the suspects' home in West Hills served a search warrant on the house. The SWAT officers, once inside, were surprised by the size of the house. The basement, they discovered, had two additional levels that could be reached through trapdoors. In the basement, they found an indoor firing range and also found that the suspects had built security rooms in the house that stored 119 different weapons, with a total value of over $200,000. In addition, the police discovered over 24,000 rounds of ammunition and a considerable amount of survivalist literature, even a six-volume book set entitled *How to Kill*.

The successful apprehension of the two bank robbery suspects in the incident above was accomplished through excellent planning, strong SWAT team discipline, and extensive cooperation between the FBI and the Los Angeles Police Department. As evidenced by the survivalist literature and the huge amount of weaponry and ammunition confiscated by the police, the arrest of these two suspects, if attempted haphazardly, could have been disastrous in terms of injuries or deaths. But by working in cooperation with each other, the two police agencies closed this criminal investigation without a single shot being fired.

There are other reasons besides shared responsibility for a

criminal investigation that cause police agencies to cooperate at SWAT incidents. Often, police agencies work together during a SWAT operation when the incident occurs on the geographical boundary between the jurisdictions of two or more police agencies, as demonstrated in the following incident.

At 11:15 on the morning of May 23, 1994, the Denny's Restaurant on the northeast side of Indianapolis was filled with the sounds of several dozen customers eating and talking. The conversation stopped abruptly, though, and the customers looked over in surprise when a scuffle broke out between the restaurant manager and a young man, followed soon by gunfire. Almost immediately, the struggle stopped, and the manager, blood gushing from a gunshot wound to his abdomen, slumped to the floor. Then, without any warning, another young man, who had been standing nearby watching the struggle, began randomly firing a .357 Magnum revolver at people in the restaurant.

A few seconds later, Alfred Smith lay dead in his wife's arms from a bullet that had passed through his arm and into his chest. Seventy-four-year-old Cecil Williams found himself shot in the left hand and would later lose several fingers from the wound. Justin Basicker, five years old and at the restaurant with his mother and her fiancé, lost the lower part of his face when a bullet shattered his jaw, while Steve Johnson, the fiancé of Justin's mother, received a bullet wound in the back. After a moment of shock, many of the customers and several Denny's employees begin screaming and running out of the restaurant before the two gunmen could stop them.

At 11:20 A.M., the Marion County Emergency Communications Center, which handles all 911 calls for the county, received its first call about the shooting at Denny's. It was initially reported that there had been a holdup at the restaurant and that ten people had been shot. The restaurant's location, though within the jurisdiction of the Indianapolis Police Department, lies only yards away from the boundary between the jurisdictions of the Indianapolis Police Department, the Marion County Sheriff's Department, and the small town of Lawrence, Indiana. The dispatcher immediately sent several Indianapolis Police Department officers to the scene; they found the area in panic and soon discovered from several of the customers who had managed to escape that there were two men with guns inside the restaurant holding twenty to twenty-five people hostage.

The two gunmen inside the restaurant, brothers Tom and Ron Mathisen, had several days earlier fled from their home in Caspar, Wyoming, taking with them over $3,500 that belonged to their employer, an adult book and video store called the Emporium Video Exchange. Leaving a note and some of the money behind for Tom's pregnant wife, the two men first drove to Des Moines, Iowa, where they dumped their car, and then, seeing Indianapolis on a road map, boarded a bus for the city. Although the people in Caspar described both men as being polite and soft-spoken, before leaving Caspar the two brothers had purchased a Ruger .357 Magnum revolver and an AA Arms 9-mm assault pistol. Because both brothers had had a felony conviction for an earlier embezzlement at another place of employment and consequently weren't eligible to purchase the weapons, they had used aliases to buy them. Their original plan for the weapons was to use them to commit robberies on their way across the country, but they didn't carry out this plan and soon found their money running low.

Once arriving in Indianapolis, the brothers checked into a motel close to the Denny's but quickly found that their money was now almost gone. In order to replenish their funds, they planned to rob someone and perhaps even kill the person during the robbery, but as with their earlier plans to commit robbery, the brothers never went through with this one. Finally, on the morning of May 23, with only one dollar left between them, they made a pact that they would go to the Denny's restaurant and, after eating a meal, take some hostages. Then, when the police arrived, they would both go out in blaze of glory.

But as often happens in these types of incidents, the unexpected occurred. The Denny's manager, Robert Doan, bumped into Tom Mathisen near the rear of the restaurant and saw the assault pistol he carried. Believing that Tom meant to rob the restaurant, the manager grabbed for the gun. When the weapon went off, striking the manager, Ron Mathisen panicked and began shooting wildly at the customers in the dining room, sending them diving for the floor or racing out the doors.

"They just started shooting," said a Denny's employee. "They didn't say anything. They just started shooting" (Denny's hostage, 1994, A1).

The fleeing customers immediately raced to nearby businesses and called the police. But in addition to Indianapolis police officers, who immediately requested that the SWAT team be sent, also responding to the scene and assisting in the incident were members of the Marion County Sheriff's Department, the Indiana State Police, the FBI, and the Lawrence Police Department. Since the incident occurred within the Indianapolis Police Department's jurisdiction, and since twenty-four members of its SWAT team and several of its hostage negotiators had quickly responded to the call, the Indianapolis Police Department retained overall jurisdiction over the incident, while the other police agencies assisted.

Lieutenant Jerry Barker, the SWAT incident commander, immediately set up the command post in a large communications van designed and equipped specifically for emergencies such as this. He then began replacing uniformed officers from several police departments on the inner perimeter with SWAT officers. The command post's next steps would have been to gather intelligence on the gunmen and develop an emergency assault plan. But first, another problem had to be dealt with.

"We've found that for any incident like this, in order to free up the command personnel for planning and other duties, you first have to have some type of support mechanism in place to take care of the family and friends of the hostages," said Lieutenant Barker. "They naturally come immediately to the scene, and someone has to comfort and assure them while SWAT is trying to resolve the incident. However, searching for someone or some agency to do this can't be done once the incident begins. An agency has to investigate its resources in the community ahead of time, and have plans already set up for who to call to assist them."

Fortunately, the Indianapolis Police Department had already done this and soon had a number of professionals on the scene to help with the family and friends of the hostages. Comforting and reassuring them were both victim assistance counselors and psychologists from a private company under contract to run the police department's employee assistance program.

The first hostage negotiator to arrive at the scene, Indianapolis Police Sergeant Frank Evans, conferred with Lieutenant Barker and then made initial telephone contact with Tom Mathisen. Sergeant Don Wright, another experienced hostage negotiator, arrived minutes after Sergeant Evans and served as the secondary negotiator, recording the conversations and keeping notes on the progress of the negotiations.

"Tom was really excited and upset at first," Sergeant Evans later told reporters. "He told me that he and his brother had never committed any violence before. So I tried to calm him down and have him tell me his story. At first it was real shaky. He told me he had been in jail once for theft and that he would never go to jail again. He'd die first" (Booher, 1994, A5).

As an experienced negotiator, Sergeant Evans knew that hostage takers often say things like this. He also knew the importance of letting Tom talk and vent his feelings, and so the conversation between them went on for several hours.

Inside the restaurant meanwhile, with blood splattered everywhere, Tom appeared to become more and more remorseful over the shootings. "I'm really sorry it happened," he kept saying over and over. But whether he was really remorseful or not, the police weren't sure. However, during the negotiations, Sergeant Evans did persuade him to release a number of the hostages, including the wife of shooting victim Alfred Smith, who had cradled her husband's dead body in her arms for several hours (see photo on page 242).

The police, however, weren't the real heroes in this case. Even though being held captive, several of the hostages inside the Denny's restaurant performed acts of extraordinary heroism. Steve Johnson, fiancé of the mother of shooting victim Justin Basicker, even though shot in the back himself, picked up five-

year-old Justin and confronted the gunmen, telling them that he was going to take Justin to the hospital. They allowed him to leave with the boy, whom he then rushed to the hospital.

"I wasn't trying to be a hero," he said. "I was just doing what had to be done" (Schramm, 1994, A1).

Also, one of the waitresses, Kelli Grisby, acted as an intermediary between the police and the gunmen, leaving and then reentering the restaurant several times. She also convinced the gunmen to let the children being held hostage have coloring books and crayons, and she did all she could to calm the situation, as did waitress Katherine Fuller.

At 3:40 P.M., reportedly sickened by the sight of the body of Alfred Smith, Tom Mathisen told Sergeant Evans, "We're going to bring the dead body out. We can't stand it." The two gunmen then ordered several of the male hostages to carry the body of Alfred Smith outside but, before allowing them to leave, threatened to kill the hostages' wives if the men didn't return. The men carried the body outside, laid it on the ground, and then returned to the restaurant. Waiting SWAT officers retrieved Alfred Smith's body.

Negotiations between Sergeant Evans and Tom Mathisen then continued, and even though snipers had been set up on nearby rooftops, and even though other SWAT officers had been standing by, waiting for the go-ahead for a forced rescue, the command post held them back, since no violence had occurred since the police had arrived. The command post wanted instead to try for a peaceful resolution. And so, Sergeant Evans continued to talk with Tom Mathisen on the telephone. Using his years of experience as a hostage negotiator, Evans calmly explained to Tom how letting the hostages go and coming out peacefully was the only real manly way to end this situation, and after over four hours of talking, he finally persuaded Tom and his brother to surrender peacefully. Tom, however, made their surrender contin-

←————————————————————————————

Photo of hostages and SWAT officers, taken during the Denny's incident. (Photo by Mike Felder. Copyright 1994 The Indianapolis News. Reprinted by permission.)

gent on the condition that he first talk with his pregnant wife, Heather, in Caspar, and that she be flown to Indianapolis. Denny's management agreed to pay for the flight, while Sergeant Don Wright, the secondary negotiator, called Heather in Caspar and told her what they needed her to say to her husband.

At 5:07 P.M., after Tom had spoken with his wife, and with his and his brother's plan to go out in a blaze of glory apparently forgotten, he and Ron came out of the restaurant and surrendered, leaving behind them an afternoon of terror and bloodshed that few of the hostages will ever forget.

While the hostage incident at the Denny's restaurant was managed by the Indianapolis Police Department, the command post personnel were afterward glowing in their thanks to and appreciation of the other police agencies that had assisted them. The FBI office in Indianapolis, for example, had sent out several of its hostage negotiators to assist. The Indiana State Police had sent out its SWAT team, which had assisted in maintaining the perimeters around the incident. The Marion County Sheriff's Department and the Lawrence Police Department had assisted with traffic and pedestrian control, which, in a lengthy, high-profile case such as this, is no small matter.

This interagency cooperation during SWAT incidents is one of the trends that is likely to continue and to be expanded in the twenty-first century. The state of American society today is such that there is simply no sacred ground left where situations like the Denny's incident cannot occur, and so, police departments, both large and small, must be prepared for them.

"Everyone thinks that incidents like the one at Denny's can't happen in their jurisdictions," said Lieutenant Barker. "Well, they can."

Because of this increased likelihood of a SWAT incident, some small police departments that cannot afford to equip or staff a SWAT team themselves have entered into agreements with nearby large metropolitan police departments, or with the state police, to assist them with SWAT officers if they become necessary. For example, the Lansing, Michigan, Police Department SWAT team has agreements to assist smaller police agencies in three surrounding counties.

"If we have a situation that calls for a SWAT team, we have an agreement with the Harnett County Sheriff's Department," said Chief Butch Halpin of the Angier, North Carolina Police Department in a telephone interview (January 24, 1995). "Fortunately, we haven't had to use them yet, but the other agencies that have seem very pleased with the arrangement."

This type of agreement is very common across the United States. But even large police departments like the Indianapolis Police Department, which has a fully equipped and staffed SWAT team, realize that, by working together with other police departments, by having interagency cooperation, they can accomplish much more than by working alone, as was clearly demonstrated in the Denny's incident. This interagency cooperation is important not just for law enforcement agencies responding to incidents that occur on the boundary between law enforcement agency jurisdictions, as the Denny's incident did, or for agencies that share responsibility for the investigation of certain crimes, as in the Los Angeles bank robberies, but also whenever criminals, while committing a crime, travel through several jurisdictions, as the next incident demonstrates.

In September 1992, a man who had been fired from his job decided to seek both revenge and riches by kidnapping his former boss, along with his family, and holding them for ransom. Recruiting two friends to help him, the man succeeded in kidnapping his former boss, the boss's wife, and the couple's three-year-old child from their home in Coral Springs, Florida. The three men then drove the kidnap victims to a house in Boca Raton, Florida, where the kidnappers instructed the man that he had two hours to return with a large sum of money if he wanted to see his wife and child again. They also warned him not to contact the police if he valued his wife's and child's lives.

One of the three kidnappers then drove the man to his broker to obtain the ransom money. While at the broker's office, though, the kidnap victim slipped away from the kidnapper for a moment and notified the police of what was happening. The police responded immediately and arrested the kidnapper after a short chase. The arrested kidnapper, seeing his precarious position, told the police that the original plan had been to get the money and then kill the three victims. Although cooperating, the arrested kidnapper didn't know the exact address of the house in Boca Raton where the wife and child were being held, only the general area. The husband also didn't know the exact address, but he did give the police a good description of the van that had been used in the kidnapping.

In response to this kidnapping, the Palm Beach County Sheriff's Department activated its SWAT team and put part of them on a standby basis, instructing them to be ready when the house in Boca Raton was located. Other members of the sheriff's department SWAT team were then sent into the Boca Raton area to look for the van described by the husband. After a short, but intense, search, the police found the van driving around a shopping-center parking lot. From the description they had received, the police believed the driver to be the fired worker and leader of the gang of kidnappers. As the van started to leave the parking lot, two cars of SWAT officers stopped it, and once seeing what he was up against, the driver of the van surrendered without incident. Although the officers had hoped to find the two remaining kidnap victims in the van, all they found was a handgun, a Colt AR-15 assault rifle, a shotgun, and a handheld radio. In the pocket of the arrested driver, though, the officers found the key to a hotel room in Fort Lauderdale, Florida.

While this arrest was taking place, the police located the residence in Boca Raton where the kidnap victims had originally been taken, and the SWAT team conducted a hostage rescue mission but found the house vacant. They discovered that the third kidnapper had taken the woman and her three-year-old child to the hotel in Fort Lauderdale.

Since Fort Lauderdale is in Broward County, the Palm Beach

County Sheriff's Department contacted the FBI office in Miami, which sent an FBI SWAT team to the hotel in Fort Lauderdale. Locating the third kidnapper and his two victims, the FBI SWAT team convinced the man of the futility of his position and persuaded him to surrender peacefully and release the two victims unharmed.

In addition to the various interagency cooperative agreements already discussed, another popular and developing interagency trend in police SWAT team use is for several small agencies to form a joint SWAT team, using members and resources from all of the small police departments. An example is the South Suburban Emergency Response Team, which serves the south suburban area of Illinois. This fully staffed police SWAT team is responsible for about 5,000 square miles and a population of 290,000 people. Each small police department contributes both officers and money for equipment, and the team members train together one day a month. In 1991, the team contained twenty-eight officers from fourteen small police departments and was on call twenty-four hours a day.

Unfortunately, however, it sometimes takes an incident that requires interagency cooperation for the police to realize how important it is to have such agreements in place ahead of time, as the following incident demonstrates.

On April 27, 1987, deputies of the Lewis and Clark County, Montana, Sheriff's Department responded to the call of a van overturned in the Holter Lake Recreation Area. Finding the abandoned van and running a computer check on it, the police discovered it was connected with a recent double murder in Colorado. The deputies then immediately began checking nearby campsites for the van's occupants. The deputies not only found the previous occupants of the van, two escapees from the penitentiary at Vacaville, California, but came under intense sniper fire from them, the gunfire keeping the deputies pinned down until evening.

The next day, FBI agents from Salt Lake City and officers from the Montana Highway Patrol, the U.S. Forest Service, and the Montana Fish and Game Service, along with SWAT teams from the Helena, Montana, Police Department and the Lewis and Clark County Sheriff's Department, all began a massive hunt, using helicopters provided by the Montana National Guard. After several days of searching, the police located the two suspects in a cabin next to Holter Lake, and the officers from the various agencies converged on the area.

Upon finding themselves surrounded, the two prison escapees began shooting at the police. One of the two men, however, when firing at the police, accidently shot a hundred-pound propane tank next to the cabin. The gas tank exploded, burned down the cabin, and killed the two prison escapees.

Because of the huge cost of this operation in Montana (near $2 million) and the lack of any clear plan of coordination, the Montana Sheriffs' and Peace Officers' Association soon afterward developed guidelines to help police departments in Montana that find themselves in need of assistance at SWAT-type incidents. Now, any police agency in Montana that needs SWAT assistance from another agency for any reason has clear guidelines on how to obtain it, as well as guidelines on how the cooperation and coordination will work between the agencies.

No matter what the reason for interagency cooperation among police SWAT teams, be it the type of crime, its location, or its seriousness, police departments across the country have found that they can accomplish much more by working together and pooling their expertise and resources than they can by working alone. Therefore, almost everyone involved with police SWAT teams sees interagency cooperation as something that will continue to grow in the coming years. As criminals become bolder and more violent, police SWAT teams find they need to depend on each other and work together if they are to successfully meet the threat these criminals present.

15

Some Failures of SWAT

While in the three decades of their existence police SWAT teams have met with hundreds of successes and have saved countless lives, there have nevertheless been some SWAT incidents that have not ended successfully but have instead ended in unnecessary bloodshed and loss of life. Occasionally in the past three decades, police SWAT teams have gone into operations with bad intelligence, bad planning, bad tactics, or poor leadership. As a consequence, these SWAT operations have met with failure and have ended with individuals being unnecessarily injured or killed.

Whenever anyone thinks of a police SWAT team failure, almost without a doubt the disastrous incident at Waco, Texas, in 1993 comes to mind. This incident was very likely the largest and most widely publicized failure since the creation of police SWAT teams thirty years ago. But before I discuss what went wrong at Waco, I want first to say that the following discussion does not mean, and should not be interpreted as an implication, that any religious sect or denomination is right or wrong, or that anyone's religious beliefs are better or worse than anyone else's. My intention is simply to show how and why the warrant service by the Bureau of Alcohol, Tobacco, and Firearms (ATF) SWAT teams at the Mount Carmel compound of the Branch Davidians in Waco, Texas, failed.

The incident in Waco began in May 1992, when the McLennan County Sheriff's Department contacted the ATF about a large number of suspicious deliveries being made to the Branch Davidian complex, which was located just outside Waco in McLennan County. According to the sheriff's department, there had been several shipments of firearms worth over $10,000, several shipments of grenade casings, a large shipment of black powder, and a smaller one of powdered magnesium (while black powder is an explosive on its own, when mixed with powdered magnesium it becomes a much more powerful explosive). Because the present leader of the Branch Davidians was known to the sheriff's department to have used firearms during violent acts in the past, and because the possibility of unlawful acts being committed through these suspicious shipments fell under the ATF area of investigation, the ATF was asked to look into them.

When the ATF began making inquiries, it found that the present leader of the Branch Davidians was a man formerly named Vernon Wayne Howell, who in 1990 legally changed his name to David Koresh, saying in his court petition that he was an entertainer and wished to use the name David Koresh for publicity and business purposes. Mr. Koresh was well known to the local police. In 1987, the Mount Carmel complex in Waco had been known as Rodenville, after the parents of the leader of the Branch Davidians in 1987, George Roden. On November 3, 1987, the sheriff's department responded to a call at the Branch Davidian complex and found Mr. Roden hiding behind a tree, suffering from a gunshot wound, while Koresh and six of his followers, all wearing combat fatigues and with camouflage greasepaint smeared on their faces, were shooting at him. The sheriff's deputies arrested Koresh and his followers for attempted murder but never convicted them. In 1989, George Roden killed a man and, following this act, was committed to a mental institution. In the leader's absence, Koresh quickly gained control of the Mount Carmel Branch Davidian complex.

During its initial inquiry into the shipment of firearms and explosives, the ATF found that Koresh had also been purchasing parts which could convert some of the weapons that had been delivered to the compound into machine guns. Except under certain conditions, this kind of conversion is illegal. On June 9, 1992, the ATF felt there was enough information to begin a formal investigation. The ATF classified the case as "sensitive," since it involved a religious group. This meant that the investigation would receive a higher degree of oversight by ATF headquarters.

The belief that Koresh and his followers were manufacturing machine guns and explosive devices, however, came not just from his purchase of the necessary parts. The sheriff's department had received complaints from a neighbor of the Mount Carmel complex, a man who had served in a U.S. Army artillery unit. The man complained that, on a number of occasions, he had heard the sound of automatic weapons fire coming from the complex. In addition, a sheriff's deputy, who was on patrol one afternoon near the Mount Carmel complex, had heard a loud explosion and had seen a large cloud of gray smoke coming from the complex.

Although not directly pertinent to the ATF's investigation (though it would be later while the warrant service was being planned), when interviewing former members of the Mount Carmel Branch Davidians, ATF agents heard distressing accounts of sexual and physical abuse of the women and children in the complex. Several former members told the agents that Koresh regularly had sex with all of the women at the complex, no matter how young, and that, when husbands and wives entered the group, Koresh annulled their marriage and would no longer allow the husbands to have sex with their wives. The sex and physical abuse charges were investigated by the Texas Department of Protective and Regulatory Services, but the investigator could not find sufficient reliable evidence or willing witnesses, and so no charges were ever brought. Still, this intelligence alerted investigators that they were dealing with a man who displayed an obviously blatant disregard of others' rights and humanity. What was more relevant to the ATF's investigation was that the former members also stated that they had seen machine guns being operated at Mount Carmel.

After gathering more evidence of illegal weapon and explosive manufacturing, including interviews with gun dealers who had sold the necessary items for this manufacturing to Koresh, the ATF finally felt it had enough probable cause to issue an arrest warrant for Koresh and a search warrant for Mount Carmel. But in order to gain more evidence to present when applying for the warrants, as well as more intelligence that would be helpful in planning how to serve the warrants, in January 1993 the ATF established an undercover operation in a rented house near Mount Carmel. Using the cover story that the agents, who had all been picked because of their youthful appearance, were students at a nearby college, the agents moved into the house and, for a while, kept a twenty-four-hour surveillance on Mount Carmel. However, because of a lack of supervision, the surveillance efforts quickly began to falter and soon became only sporadic.

Eventually, the ATF took all of the information and evidence it had collected to a federal judge, who issued an arrest warrant for Koresh and a search warrant for Mount Carmel. But now that enough evidence had been obtained for the warrants, the problem became the best way to serve them. To decide on this, ATF leaders held a strategy meeting. Unfortunately, while the ATF leaders at this strategy meeting had planned many warrant services, none of the warrant services were even close to the magnitude of what they proposed to do at Mount Carmel. The closest had been an operation against a white supremacist group called the Covenant, the Sword, and the Arm of the Lord (CSA), a group that had maintained a 360-acre fortresslike compound in Arkansas. In this FBI-ATF operation, the government had laid siege to the compound, which contained concealed bunkers and land mines, and eventually, through the siege, had persuaded the occupants to surrender. However, the objective that the ATF wanted to attain in serving the warrants on Koresh's group made the Waco operation much more difficult than the operation in Arkansas. A siege, which had proved successful in the operation against the CSA in Arkansas, would give Koresh time to destroy the evidence the ATF was after. Also, Koresh reportedly had enough food stored in the form of military MREs (meals ready to eat) to last for three months. In addition, Mount Carmel had its own well, and the people lived there with hardly any modern conveniences, so the deprivations of an ordinary siege would be normal for them. The only person at Mount Carmel who enjoyed air-conditioning, heat, a stereo, television, and so on was Koresh. Probably more crucial to the planners, though, was the fact that, unlike the area around the compound in Arkansas, the area around Mount Carmel lacked any significant cover for officers staging a siege, so that a siege would be dangerous for all involved.

The planners at the strategy meeting felt that the service of the warrants would be much easier and safer if Koresh could be arrested away from Mount Carmel. They discussed different methods of drawing him away, including issuing a grand jury subpoena for the sexual abuse of minors and the staging of a school bus or helicopter crash near the compound. But because of poor intelligence-gathering techniques at the undercover house near the compound, the planners discarded this tactic. (They believed that Koresh never left Mount Carmel, while in actuality he did leave on occasion.) Finally, after much discussion of the options, the planners decided on a dynamic surprise entry of Mount Carmel. They also decided that any such enforcement action at the Branch Davidian compound would require the services of several ATF SWAT teams, called Special Response Teams (SRTs).

Intelligence gathered from former Branch Davidian members indicated that the weapons at the facility were usually stored next to Koresh's room, an area off limits to all residents except Koresh and a few of his most trusted aides called the Mighty Men. The intelligence gathered also said that, during the day, most of the men in the compound worked at digging a large pit where a school bus had been buried, this bus forming an underground tunnel that connected the pit to the compound buildings. The planners reasoned that, if they could raid the compound while the men were working in the pit and were therefore separated from their weapons, one SWAT team could hold the men there, while another team could secure the weapons room, and a third team could secure the remainder of the facility. The men usually went to work in the pit, the planners were told, at 10:00 A.M. With this information, the planners developed a strategy that depended heavily on the assumption of the time when the men would be at work, even though the planners made no effort to validate this information. In addition, the raid planners believed that the women at the compound would not be involved in any resistance. They believed this even though an intelligence picture taken of the complex clearly showed a woman holding a rifle. Since over a hundred people lived at the compound, many of them women, this assumption seriously underestimated the number of armed people who would be confronted.

The plan that was eventually developed for the warrant service called for approximately seventy-five ATF agents, in three teams, to approach the Mount Carmel compound while hidden in the rear of cattle trailers, a common sight around Waco. The plan's success depended totally on being able to catch the residents of Mount Carmel by surprise and consequently unprepared to resist. The ATF planners decided to use SWAT teams from their offices in Houston, Dallas, and New Orleans. When the ATF leaders finished the plan, they sent it to ATF headquarters in Washington, D.C., where it was reviewed and approved.

Once the planners had determined the type of operation they would carry out, the ATF had a facility resembling Mount Carmel built at the nearby Fort Hood U.S. Army base. The ATF SWAT teams then used this model of Mount Carmel, constructed in the Military Operations in Urban Terrain (MOUT) section of the base, to practice their proposed warrant service.

Unfortunately, at the same time the ATF was conducting its investigation of Koresh, so was the local newspaper, the Waco *Tribune-Herald*. A reporter who had covered Koresh's 1988 trial for attempted murder, along with another reporter, began developing a series about Koresh and the Branch Davidians that would be published under the title "Sinful Messiah." Because the series contained what the editors felt were shocking revelations of sexual abuse and the amassing of dangerous weapons, they became concerned about the potential of violence against the newspaper's facilities and its employees. Therefore, the newspaper implemented various security precautions, including having the two reporters leave Waco for a bit after the series appeared.

As the reporters writing this series naturally needed to interview a number of law enforcement officers, word of what the newspaper was doing reached the ATF. And so, in what turned out to be a disastrous decision, ATF officials met with newspaper executives and asked that they postpone publication of the series until after the ATF had executed the service of the warrants. They feared that an article of this type would upset Koresh and make him more alert and vigilant. According to the agent who met with *Tribune-Herald* executives, he was told, "The important thing to us is the public's right to have information that they need to know, and that's our job. We're not concerned about where it falls in or falls out in terms of your law enforcement case" (U.S. Department of the Treasury, 1993, 71). This response made the meeting with the newspaper executives a disastrous decision because, not only did the newspaper refuse the ATF request and go ahead with its plans to publish the series, but the ATF had tipped off the news media that it had a major operation under way, which is naturally always big news.

On February 25, 1993, Dennis Green, U.S. magistrate-judge for the U.S. District Court for the Western District of Texas, issued both the arrest warrant and the search warrant the ATF had applied for, and so the plan for a surprise, dynamic warrant service at the Mount Carmel complex moved ahead. Unfortunately, however, because of the ATF meeting with *Tribune-Herald* executives, the word had spread throughout the news media community that something big was going to happen soon at Mount Carmel. A reporter for the *Tribune-Herald* later told the U.S. Department of the Treasury that he had received a tip from a confidential source that something big was going to happen at Mount Carmel between 9:00 and 10:00 A.M. on March 1, 1993 (the originally proposed date for the warrant service). In addition, an employee of an ambulance service hired to be on standby for the warrant service had also told a member of the news media that the ambulance service had been put on notice for March 1, 1993. The media later learned from the same source that the warrant service had been moved up one day.

In addition to these leaks, there were many other clues that something big was going to happen soon, including the ATF's renting 153 hotel rooms in Waco, its procurement of donuts and portable toilets, and its use of a staging area visible to traffic on a nearby busy highway. In addition, on the day of the warrant service, moved up from March 1 to February 28, an eighty-vehicle convoy of government vehicles left Fort Hood and proceeded to Waco, all with their headlights on.

And so, while the ATF prepared for the warrant service, so did the news media. On February 28, 1993, the news media descended on the area of the Mount Carmel compound, some parking so close that they came under fire and had to dive for cover when the fighting broke out. The police also almost shot several news-media people because the officers thought they were part of Koresh's group. This convergence of the news media on the area around Mount Carmel became, indirectly, the cause of Koresh's being alerted to the impending warrant service.

According to the U.S. Department of the Treasury's investigation into the incident at Waco, a local television camera operator sent out by his station to film the ATF warrant service became lost on the morning of February 28, 1993, and, while lost, encountered a local letter carrier driving a yellow Buick with "U.S. Mail" painted on the side. Not realizing that the letter carrier was a member of the Branch Davidians at Mount Carmel, the camera operator, after receiving directions, warned the letter carrier to be careful because some type of law enforcement action was to take place that morning at the Mount Carmel complex, and that there might be some shooting. The letter carrier immediately headed for Mount Carmel to warn Koresh.

The same morning, one of the agents who had been assigned to the undercover house, Robert Rodriguez, visited the compound and learned some crucial information. Early in his assignment, Rodriguez had visited the Mount Carmel complex on the pretext of being interested in buying a horse walker (a device that makes a horse walk in order to cool it down or exercise it) that was on the compound grounds. While there, he had struck up a conversation with Koresh and was invited to join the Branch Davidians' Bible study group, which he did.

During the weeks preceding the warrant service, while the ATF investigation was under way, Agent Rodriguez, still working undercover, had visited Mount Carmel a number of times. But because the first installment of the "Sinful Messiah" series had appeared in the Waco *Tribune-Herald* on February 27, 1993, Agent Rodriguez's superiors ordered him to go to the compound on the morning of the warrant service to gauge whether the "Sinful Messiah" article had upset Koresh enough so that he had increased his security measures. When Agent Rodriguez arrived at the Branch Davidian compound, he was invited to join Koresh, who was apparently not yet aware of the impending warrant service, in a Bible study session, which he did. During the session, however, the letter carrier who had been stopped and warned by the television camera operator arrived at Mount Carmel with his information. Branch Davidian members called Koresh out of the Bible study group and told him what the letter carrier had said.

According to Agent Rodriguez, when Koresh returned to the room he appeared extremely upset, seemed unable to concentrate, and even dropped the Bible he was using. Rodriguez asked what was wrong, and Koresh exclaimed, "Neither the ATF nor the National Guard will ever get me! They got me once and they'll never get me again! They're coming, Robert, the time has come! They're coming, Robert, they're coming!" (U.S. Department of Treasury 1993, 89).

Agent Rodriguez, fearing that the warrant service was going to start while he was still in the compound, told Koresh that he had to meet someone for breakfast. Koresh didn't answer, and when Agent Rodriguez started to leave, he found that several of the Branch Davidians now blocked his exit. Agent Rodriguez again said he had to leave. Koresh walked over, shook Agent Rodriguez's hand, and said, "Good luck, Robert."

Once out of Mount Carmel, Agent Rodriguez hurried back to

report to his superiors at the raid command post what he had just heard. However, when he told them what had transpired, rather than questioning him further about Koresh's knowledge of the impending warrant service, his superiors asked if he had seen any weapons or preparations for resistance. Agent Rodriguez said no, he hadn't.

The ATF leaders in the command post, even though knowing that the success of the operation depended totally on the element of surprise and the necessity of catching the men working out in the pit, decided to go ahead anyway, feeling that the operation could still be successful, but only if they hurried. One of the agents in charge of the warrant service called the ATF's National Command Center in Washington, D.C., and reported that Agent Rodriguez was now out of the compound and that the warrant service was beginning. He did not, however, tell of Agent Rodriguez's revelations about Koresh's knowledge of the warrant service.

The ATF SWAT teams then left the staging area on the route to Mount Carmel. At 9:47 A.M., the helicopters to be used as a diversion that would attract attention away from the SWAT teams got within only about 350 meters of the compound and then had to turn back because they were being fired on by the residents of Mount Carmel. But it was too late then for them to warn the ATF SWAT teams, because the teams had already pulled up in front of the compound in the cattle trailers and were unloading, over forty minutes after Agent Rodriguez had reported his information about Koresh.

One of the first things the agents noticed on pulling up to the compound was no outside activity at all. When one agent said over his radio, "There's no one outside," another agent answered, "That's not good." Then, as the agents entered the compound in full SWAT gear, Koresh opened the front door of the complex and asked, "What's going on?" The agents responded that they were ATF officers with warrants. The door then slammed shut, and bullets burst out through the door from inside with such force that the door bowed outward. All at once, gunfire then also burst from every window of the Mount Carmel compound.

While the other two SWAT teams advanced through the compound on the ground, the New Orleans SWAT team used ladders to climb up onto the roof. Their assignment was to secure the weapons room, though why they were doing it now was questionable, since it was obvious that the weapons had already been distributed. As the agents got up onto the roof, they came under heavy gunfire, and two of the agents were immediately killed. Still, the rest persevered, and three of the agents finally did manage to get inside the weapons room but then were driven back out by heavy gunfire.

On the ground, two other agents also died from gunfire, and a number were shot at repeatedly while lying on the ground wounded. Because of the open terrain around the compound and the intense gunfire coming from inside, the agents who had assaulted the building suddenly found themselves trapped behind any cover they could find. And while agents later discovered several hundred thousand rounds of ammunition inside Mount Carmel, the ATF agents now behind cover on the ground had only what ammunition they carried. In order to conserve it, they could afford to fire only when a clear target presented itself.

In a matter of just a few minutes, four ATF agents had been killed and sixteen wounded. Inside the Mount Carmel compound, two people had been killed and several wounded, including Koresh, who had been shot in the wrist and the pelvis.

A few minutes after the shooting started, a 911 call came into the McLennan County Sheriff's Department, placed from inside the Mount Carmel compound, but the caller hung up before the deputy who answered could speak. Before the caller hung up, though, the deputy heard gunfire in the background. The deputy then called back the number that appeared on the 911 screen. An answering machine inside Mount Carmel responded, and so, the deputy began yelling for someone to pick up the telephone. Someone inside the compound finally did pick up the telephone, and the deputy, knowing about the ATF raid that day, began attempting to negotiate a cease-fire. For the next forty minutes, the deputy tried to act as an intermediary and to arrange the cease-fire, but with little success. Finally, an agent at the undercover house called the compound directly and, after a few minutes, arranged the cease-fire.

This cease-fire, though, almost immediately fell through when the agent in the undercover house insisted that the ATF agents be allowed to retrieve their dead and wounded. The contact inside Mount Carmel insisted instead that the agents leave the compound grounds immediately and unconditionally. After considerable discussion, the contact inside the compound finally allowed the agents to carry out their dead and wounded.

Then, in a move unprecedented in SWAT history, the ATF SWAT teams abandoned the perimeters around the Mount Carmel complex, an action that would have allowed any of the people inside Mount Carmel to escape if they wanted to. Fortunately, however, officers from the Austin Police Department, the Texas Department of Public Safety, the Waco Police Department, the U.S. Marshall's Service, and the McLennan County Sheriff's Department refused to follow the ATF's directives to abandon the perimeters.

The next day at the Mount Carmel compound, where the Branch Davidians still held out, it was feared, and reasonably so, that any further hostile action taken by ATF agents would be seen as revenge, and so the FBI took over the operation in Waco. On March 1, 1993, the FBI moved in, and for fifty days, members of the FBI's elite Hostage Rescue Team negotiated constantly with Koresh and managed, during this time, to win the release of thirty-five individuals from inside Mount Carmel. However, the negotiations at last stalled, and the FBI leadership finally decided that force was the only way to resolve the incident. On April 19, 1993, the FBI pumped tear gas into Mount Carmel. But before the FBI could gain control of the compound, a fire, reportedly set from inside the compound, destroyed the complex, killing more than eighty people, including Koresh.

Conditions within the ATF after the shootout were chaotic. No one in charge at Waco seemed to know what to do, now that the absolute worst-case scenario had come true. A disaster of unprecedented proportions had occurred, and no one knew the appropriate response. (But some of the ATF leaders did do something.)

Once the ATF's part in the obviously failed operation was over, ATF leaders did something very common in law enforcement (and in most other professions, I'm sure). After over twenty-eight years in law enforcement, I have found that, in any law enforcement action that goes very bad, as this one did at Waco, the first thing the people in charge do is CYA, which is a police acronym for "cover your ass." And this is exactly what happened in Waco. Fingers began pointing in every direction. Stories, excuses, and lies began flowing. High-ranking ATF officials began making misleading and false statements about why they had done what they did. ATF leaders at Waco attempted to blame others for the raid's failure. "Additions" and "modifications" were quickly made to the warrant service's written plan so that the actions taken seemed logical. However, as usually happens, the truth eventually came to the surface.

But regardless of the actions that some ATF officials took afterward, the question that needed answering was what went wrong with the ATF warrant service on February 28, 1993. Why was it a failure?

According to the U.S. Department of the Treasury's investigation of the Waco incident, "[The investigation] found disturbing evidence of flawed decision making, inadequate intelligence gathering, miscommunication, supervisory failures, and deliberately misleading post-raid statements about the raid and the raid plan by certain ATF supervisors" (U.S. Department of the Treasury, 1993, 7).

Actually, while all of the problems above were certainly there, the plan for the warrant service itself was fairly well thought out and workable if, and this was a huge if, the conditions the plan depended on had been there. John A. Kolman, retired captain of the Los Angeles County Sheriff's Department, who was asked by the U.S. Department of the Treasury to review the incident at

Waco, agreed on the solidity of the original warrant service plan. "Had the operation not been compromised," he said, "there was a high probability that the tactical plan would have succeeded" (U.S. Department of the Treasury, 1993, B-37).

Lieutenant Robert A. Sobocienski of the New York City Police Department's Emergency Services Unit, who was also asked to assess the Waco incident, concurred. "Based on my twenty-five years of experience with the New York City Police Department, if all of the given facts which led to the decision to conduct the entry were true, I believe the plan had a reasonable chance of success" (U.S. Department of the Treasury, 1993, B-131).

But obviously the plan wasn't successful. And it wasn't successful because several of the conditions on which the plan depended were nonexistent. One of the most important of these conditions was that, at the time of the raid, most of the men would be working in the pit, where they would be separated from their weapons. This circumstance was vital to the success of the plan, even though a later review of the surveillance logs from the undercover house showed that the men had worked in the pit during only fourteen of the thirty-six days of surveillance, and also that 10:00 A.M. was only the approximate time the men began work. Not only was the plan based on this unreliable information, but ATF leaders rushed the warrant service into action fifteen minutes before 10:00 A.M., and did it even though Koresh knew the agents were coming. Had the information about when the men worked in the pit been accurate, it wouldn't have mattered since, once Koresh knew ATF officers were coming, he would have pulled the men back into the compound anyway.

Another condition on which a successful warrant service depended was the belief that the women at Mount Carmel wouldn't be involved in any armed resistance, which they were. The planners of the warrant service accepted their noninvolvement as a fact even though, in the month preceding the warrant service, a picture taken of the compound showed a woman holding a rifle.

But without a doubt the most necessary condition on which the success of the ATF warrant service at Waco depended was the element of surprise. This is a necessary condition for the success of almost all such police actions. To be successful, the police must catch suspects unprepared and separated from their weapons. Police SWAT teams practice rapid-entry techniques repeatedly in order to capitalize on this element of surprise. In Waco, however, the leaders of the ATF SWAT teams knew that they had lost the element of surprise; yet they went ahead with the warrant service anyway, and with disastrous results. Why?

Actually, after spending most of my adult life involved in law enforcement, I recognize the desire, as problematic as it is, to press ahead as the ATF leaders did, even though doing so was extremely hazardous. The warrant service in Waco had been the culmination of an eight-month investigation. A tremendous amount of planning had gone into it, and there had been a tremendous gathering of officers and equipment. There were over 130 ATF agents, drawn from eighteen different cities, in or near Waco, all there for the warrant service. Three ATF SWAT teams (from Dallas, Houston, and New Orleans) and three arrest-and-support teams had been brought together for the warrant service. The agents had trained extensively at Fort Hood. Tensions and adrenaline were high. On the day of the warrant service, the ATF had also gathered members of the National Guard, emergency medical personnel, and police officers from local, state, and other federal law enforcement agencies. At the ATF's National Command Center in Washington, D.C., headquarters personnel were waiting to receive up-to-the-minute data about the warrant service. The cost and effort expended up to that point had been tremendous. To abort the warrant service only minutes before it was supposed to occur would have meant that all that had been done for the last eight months now meant nothing. The pressure to continue would have been intense and overpowering.

Unfortunately, in a situation such as this, calm logic is usually swept aside, and the drive to succeed takes over. As a uniformed street sergeant, I saw this type of attitude and thinking often among my officers, though of course on a much smaller scale. For example, one of my officers would occasionally attempt to stop a motorist for some traffic violation, and the vehicle would speed off. The chase was on. A high-speed vehicular chase through urban areas, however, is an extremely hazardous undertaking, and there are strict rules about when it can continue and when it must be aborted. The weight of the violation must be measured against the danger to innocent people. Often, one of my officers would become involved in a vehicle chase that entered an area heavily populated by pedestrians or a school zone, and if the officer didn't abort the chase voluntarily, I would get on the radio and order him or her to abort it. Usually, the officer would reluctantly obey, but occasionally, an officer would be so caught up in the momentum of the chase that he or she would continue with it even when ordered to abort, even knowing the extreme danger, and even knowing that he or she would face severe discipline no matter how the chase turned out.

This is exactly what happened in Waco. The operation was like a boulder rolling downhill. The momentum had become so great that the leaders couldn't overcome it. Unfortunately, like a boulder rolling downhill, this operation crashed.

In an article in *U.S. Negotiator*, Frank A. Bolz, retired captain of the New York City Police Department and former commanding officer of that department's Hostage Negotiating Team, said, "Perhaps for the supervisors to call off the action so close to it being carried out might have caused embarrassment. Well remember, embarrassment doesn't kill anyone. We can live with, and get over, embarrassment" (p. 41).

Another significant problem that faced the ATF personnel in Waco was that no contingency plans had been made, no plans for what to do if the situation was not what was expected. This lack of a contingency plan was apparent from the fact that, even though the weapons at Mount Carmel had obviously already been distributed, the New Orleans SWAT team assaulted the weapons room anyway, and as a consequence, two officers were killed. And since no contingency plans had been made, when the situation went bad the scene became chaos. Interestingly, several of the experts who reviewed the Waco incident for the U.S. Treasury Department believed that the reason behind this lack of contingency planning for failure was too much success. In the two years before Waco the ATF had conducted over four hundred successful raids. The idea that they might fail may not have occurred to them.

Chief Willie L. Williams of the Los Angeles Police Department, who was asked to review the ATF's actions in Waco, agreed: "After reviewing interviews conducted with ATF personnel who planned the raid on February 28th, and all of those who had support or other roles in the planning, it is my belief that the planners never thought about, nor planned for a partial or full failure of the operation" (U.S. Department of the Treasury, 1993, A-8).

However, in the aftermath of the tragedy that occurred in Waco, many people questioned whether the federal government should even have been involved in investigating a group that was collecting firearms in accordance with its religious beliefs about the impending end of the world. As long as the members were just collecting and firing these arms on their own property, these people said, the federal government should not have intervened.

Larry McMurtry (1993) asked in *The New Republic*, "What were the Davidians doing to provoke [the raid]? Probably they were converting semiautomatic rifles to full auto. That is certainly a crime; even possessing the capability to convert them is a crime. But down here in the Fifty Caliber Belt this particular crime is usually treated about as seriously as spitting on the sidewalk" (p. 16).

In a 1993 article in *The Washington Post*, R. Emmett Tyrell, Jr., wrote:

> No government official has yet explained what crime was being committed by the dimwits of something called the Branch Davidians.... [W]hat provoked the show of force from the crack troops of the Bureau of Alcohol, Tobacco, and Firearms? Was someone caught smoking in a restricted area? Were the faithful of the Rev. David Koresh distilling ardent spirits in an illegal still for one of his holy rites? Was there an illegal drug on the premise or did someone have a shotgun

that ran afoul of government standards? ... If Americans cannot live the life of the rugged—albeit somewhat loony—individualist in the vast reaches of the great West, where can they live normal American lives? (p. B1)

On the opposite side, at the same time the ATF was investigating the charges of illegal weapon and explosive manufacturing, the local newspaper, the Waco *Tribune-Herald*, was conducting its own inquiry on David Koresh and the Branch Davidians. The first of a series of articles about Koresh and his followers, a series that contained allegations of sexual abuse and the amassing of illegal weapons at Mount Carmel, appeared in the *Tribune-Herald* just a day before the ill-fated warrant service at the Branch Davidian compound, an article with a sidebar titled "The Law Watches, but Has Done Little." In addition, an editorial appeared in the *Tribune-Herald* that same day that asked when the law enforcement community was going to take action against Koresh and the Branch Davidians. As often happens in law enforcement, the police were condemned both when they took action and when they didn't.

However, regardless of what some might consider government interference in religious affairs, because of Koresh's past record of violence, as demonstrated by his armed attempt to wrest control of Mount Carmel from George Roden, the federal government clearly had a duty to do something, and particularly when requested to do so by a local law enforcement agency. If the ATF hadn't, and Koresh and his followers had set out on a campaign of violence around Waco, the same people who asked why the government had done something would have demanded to know why the government had done nothing.

And the possibility of this violence is not as far-fetched as it seems. Koresh had often said that his time was coming, and that, when it did, the Los Angeles riots would pale in comparison. He also told his followers that soon they would go out in the world, where they would turn their weapons on the public and kill those who were not believers. And they certainly had the weapons necessary to do so: inside the compound were 57 pistols, 6 revolvers, 12 shotguns, 101 rifles, 44 machine guns, 16 silencers, at least 3 live grenades, and over 200,000 rounds of ammunition—more than enough firepower for any violence envisioned by Koresh.

Violence by various fringe religious groups, incidentally, is much more common than most people are aware. Of course, practically everyone knows about the fate of Congressman Leo Ryan's party and the hundreds of followers of Jim Jones in Guyana in 1978, but this incident, while enormous, was by no means an isolated event. For example, in July 1982, Keith and Kate Haigler hijacked a bus near Jasper, Arkansas. This husband and wife said that they were the messengers spoken of in the Bible, and they had to die so that they could rise from the dead in three and a half days and inspire the multitudes. After the police surrounded the hijacked bus, negotiators couldn't persuade the couple to surrender, and instead, the Haiglers advanced on the police with their weapons ready. When SWAT snipers wounded both of them, Kate turned and killed Keith, then killed herself.

More recently, in January 1990, the police arrested a defrocked minister and his wife and son for murdering five members of an Ohio family. The five people were reportedly killed in a sacrificial ceremony that the defrocked minister believed would cleanse his congregation and allow them to enter a wilderness area, where they would hunt for a golden sword.

The belief that Koresh and his followers were capable of violence, however, is not the real concern. They obviously were. The concern of my discussion is that ATF officials failed to recognize and meet this threat, and that as a consequence, people died. While this failed ATF operation in Waco is certainly one of the most widely publicized SWAT failures, there have been others that are also important to analyze because they, too, have ended disastrously.

In Memphis, Tennessee, in January 1983, a group took a police officer hostage. Although the SWAT team responded to the scene, they were held back for thirty hours, even though the officer could be heard screaming for help as he was being tortured. When the SWAT team finally did assault the hostage site, it was too late. They found the officer dead. While it is always risky to send a SWAT team into a site on an assault-and-rescue mission, there comes a time when peaceful negotiations are not viable and the SWAT team must be sent in. An officer (or anyone else) screaming from being tortured is one of these times.

In June 1978, a mentally ill man in Los Angeles barricaded himself inside his house. When the police SWAT team responded to the scene, it first used tear gas in an attempt to force the man out. Finding that the tear gas didn't work (as it often doesn't on mentally ill people), the police then forced entry into the house, even though the man held no hostages and presented no danger to anyone. When the man came at the officers with a knife, the officers shot and killed him. The man's family sued, and their attorney in the lawsuit claimed that the SWAT team, before assaulting the house, should have first called for someone specifically trained to deal with the mentally disturbed, and that tear gas should not have been used, nor the military assault tactics. The city of Los Angeles apparently agreed and paid $150,000 to the man's family. Since that incident, the Los Angeles Police Department SWAT team's tactics for dealing with the mentally ill have been changed so that another incident such as this will not occur.

In Everett, Washington, in 1992, the local police SWAT team raided a woman's apartment looking for her husband, who had been implicated in an armored-car robbery during which a guard had been killed. While the SWAT team members were rounding up the occupants of the apartment, one of the SWAT officers accidently fired his submachine gun, striking the woman in the neck and killing her. The family members of the woman filed lawsuits seeking over $87 million in damages. The family eventually settled out of court for $1.5 million.

A final incident that received a large amount of bad publicity because of its outcome and questionable tactics was the police assault on the MOVE headquarters in Philadelphia in May 1985. The MOVE organization was a black separatist group, but the discussion here is not meant to evaluate its political or social views, only to discuss the questionable tactics used against it by the police. MOVE was also a group that seemed to be constantly in conflict with its neighbors and the police because the members reportedly shunned bathing, spread garbage and sewage on their lawn, and physically and verbally assaulted their neighbors. (This group had also been involved in a 1978 confrontation with the police that ended with a police officer being murdered.)

In May 1985, dozens of police officers, armed with an eviction notice, surrounded the MOVE headquarters and ordered the occupants to come out. While this number of police officers is seldom called on to serve eviction notices, in this case, considering the MOVE organization's propensity for violence, it seemed an appropriate precaution. Instead of complying with this eviction order, MOVE members, as police officials feared, began shooting at the officers. The police immediately took cover. While the officers had come there to move the group out, gaining access to the building in order to do so, they found, wouldn't be easy because the MOVE group had fortified its headquarters (including constructing what was suspected of being a bunker on the roof of the building). In an attempt to gain entry into the MOVE headquarters through the roof, since all of the doors and windows of the building had been blocked with fortifications that observers said were as thick as tree trunks, the police first tried to knock down the roof bunker with water cannons, but with no success.

The police then developed a plan to use explosives to destroy the bunker and thereby give them a point of entry into the building that would be safer than trying to breach the fortified doors and windows. They hoped to be able to insert tear gas through this entry point first and force the MOVE members out. The police built an explosive device using two pounds of a blasting material called Tovex, an explosive similar to dynamite and often used in mining. They reportedly tested an identical device at the Police

Academy and found it not to be incendiary (fire-producing), a serious concern in any densely populated area like the one where the MOVE headquarters was located. However, it was believed that the police had received intelligence reports that the MOVE group possibly stored gasoline and ammunition in the roof bunker—making the use of any sort of bomb an incredibly dangerous tactic.

Flying over the building in a helicopter, the police dropped the bomb onto the roof bunker. The result was a huge fire that destroyed a complete neighborhood. Sixty homes burned to the ground, and six people, including children, died in the flames. What actually caused the fire, whether gasoline and munitions reportedly stored in the bunker or the bomb itself, will probably never be known because of the total destruction of the neighborhood.

The outcome of this incident is a horrifying warning against using large explosive devices in urban areas. Because of its outcome, this tragedy has been used by some as an example of both growing racial tensions and police aggression. That issue, though, is beyond the scope of this book. The issue at hand is the tactical use of a bomb in a residential area. As this event clearly demonstrated, such a tactic should never even have been considered. Using high explosives in areas where the people live only yards away from each other is a mistake under *any* circumstances.

The mayor of Philadelphia and the police department received heavy censure and criticism after the incident. In response to this criticism, Philadelphia Mayor Goode said, "I don't know that we could have done anything differently. Everything worked until the bomb dropped. The thing we did not anticipate was that there would be a fire" (Stevens, 1985, A1).

The response to the mayor's stance was one of disbelief that he or other officials actually thought dropping a bomb was a sound tactical move.

"Trained public safety officials should have known that the dropping of a bomb onto a row home full of ammunition and other explosives in a tightly compacted area ... is like lighting a match in a room full of gas," said Burton Caine, president of the

Philadelphia chapter of the American Civil Liberties Union (Dvorchak, 1985, A1).

"To bomb a house, not knowing what would happen, doesn't make any sense to me," said New York City Mayor Koch (Koch, 1985, B9).

"Drop a bomb on a residential area?" questioned a neighborhood resident. "I've never in my life heard of that. It's like Vietnam."

All of the incidents discussed in this chapter are terribly unfortunate because they ended in the unnecessary loss of life. After events such as these occur, police departments try to learn lessons so that the same mistakes will not be made again. Because of these incidents, the police have changed many of their policies and procedures, and they have changed their SWAT strategies to protect lives rather than lose them. I doubt seriously if any police department will ever again even consider dropping a bomb in a residential area, and I don't doubt at all that, after Waco, SWAT team leaders will be much more likely to abort missions if they feel the missions have been compromised or are no longer workable, no matter how far along they are in planning and execution. And most police SWAT teams would no longer immediately assault a site where a mentally ill person, who presents no immediate danger to anyone, has barricaded himself or herself.

But like all things in life, failure can breed success, and then, more success can build on this success. While experiencing some failures such as those discussed in this chapter, police SWAT teams have, through building on each other's experiences, both positive and negative, developed strategies and techniques that have met with many more successes than failures.

16

The Many Successes of SWAT

On a bitterly cold February morning, land developer Tony Kiritsis walked into the Meridian Mortgage Company offices in downtown Indianapolis to keep an appointment with mortgage company executive Richard Hall. Kiritsis had lately been complaining loudly to his friends that Hall's company, which held a $130,000 mortgage on some property Kiritsis owned, was trying to bankrupt him by steering prospective developers away from him. Kiritsis had told his friends that he wasn't going to stand for it any longer. The morning of the meeting at the mortgage company, Kiritsis carried two boxes with him, a long flower box, which contained a sawed-off shotgun, and a smaller box, which contained a handgun.

A few minutes after Kiritsis had gone into Hall's office for the closed-door meeting, workers at the mortgage company heard an argument and then what sounded like a scuffle inside the office. Kiritsis is reported to have shouted, "You left me out in the cold! Now I'm going to take you out in the cold!"

Moments later, stunned workers watched as Kiritsis and Hall emerged from Hall's office, the sawed-off shotgun now wired around Hall's neck and pointing at the back of his head. Before they left the office, Kiritsis stopped and telephoned the police, telling them what he was going to do, then marched Hall out of the building and through the downtown area of Indianapolis.

"If you shoot me, he's a goner!" Kiritsis shouted to the police officers who responded to the incident, but who were then forced to stand back as he marched Hall down the sidewalk. Kiritsis had wired the trigger of the shotgun so that if he fell the gun would go off.

After walking several blocks in near-zero temperature, both men in only shirtsleeves, Kiritsis commandeered a police car being used to block traffic in the area. Once they were in the car, Kiritsis forced Hall to drive the vehicle, emergency lights and siren blaring, to an apartment Kiritsis leased on the west side of Indianapolis. The police, in cars and a helicopter, followed Kiritsis and Hall to the apartment area, where Kiritsis warned the police that the door and windows to his apartment had been wired with explosives. He then took Hall inside. When the police questioned friends of Kiritsis, they found that he had indeed recently purchased fifty pounds of dynamite.

The police immediately dispatched the SWAT team to the apartment area, where they set up a command post, established perimeters, positioned snipers, and then waited as the negotiator contacted Kiritsis. For the safe release of Hall, Kiritsis told the negotiator, he wanted a public apology from the mortgage company, and he also wanted a grant of immunity from the prosecutor's office for the kidnapping. The police negotiator said he would see what he could do.

The mortgage company almost immediately did as Kiritsis demanded and publicly apologized. The grant of immunity, however, proved a bit more difficult. At first, Kiritsis demanded grants of immunity from both local and federal prosecution, but he later dropped his demand for immunity from federal prosecution since he hadn't yet broken any federal laws.

The police, meanwhile, worried about Hall's safety. Because Kiritsis had brought the shotgun and the wire to attach it with to the meeting and had obviously set up his apartment as a hostage-holding area, the hostage taking wasn't just a spur-of-the-moment thing, but something he had given considerable thought to. These are often the most dangerous type of hostage incidents, many times really pseudohostage incidents. And so, for sixty-two hours, the police negotiated constantly with Kiritsis, attempting to calm him and forestall any violence, while the SWAT team officers held their positions in the bitter cold, remaining ready to make a forced rescue at a moment's notice, the snipers watching the apartment constantly. Finally, the local prosecutor's office agreed to a grant of immunity (though it would later say that the grant of immunity wasn't legitimate since it had been given under duress).

Thinking he had got everything he demanded, Kiritsis insisted on one more condition. He wanted to hold a press conference before he released Hall. The authorities agreed, and Kiritsis brought Hall into the press conference with the shotgun still wired to his neck. When the television cameras started rolling, Kiritsis demanded that Hall read an apology he had been forced to write during his captivity, but the wire around his neck was so tight he couldn't speak, and so Kiritsis himself gave a twenty-three-minute rambling statement filled with expletives. After this, Kiritsis and Hall walked to the police command post, where Kiritsis freed Hall and surrendered to the police, but only after first being allowed to shoot the shotgun in the air to show that it was really loaded. Afterward, the police discovered Kiritsis's apartment had been booby-trapped with containers of gasoline, but they found no dynamite. Kiritsis went to trial later in the year but was found not guilty of all charges by reason of insanity. He was committed to a mental hospital.

Throughout this incident, which had the potential, because of Kiritsis's fragile mental state, to turn deadly at any moment, the hostage negotiators were able to keep the situation under control by careful and insightful listening to and talking with Kiritsis. Many of the SWAT successes in the last thirty years have come through this proven formula of setting up perimeters to contain an incident, and then allowing the negotiators to persuade the individual initiating the event to surrender peacefully. In this incident, if instead of having this dialogue with Kiritsis, the SWAT team had immediately attempted an assault and rescue, the outcome would very likely have been disastrous.

On April 12, 1992, Linne Gunther of San Lorenzo, California, daughter of Nobel prize winner Owen Chamberlain, sped her white Ford van through the gates of the United Nations complex in New York City, stopping thirty yards from the Secretariat building. Drenching herself and the inside of her van with gasoline, Gunther held a cigarette lighter in each hand and threatened to set herself on fire to protest the use of tax money for military spending.

The police immediately cordoned off the area, and then, negotiators in silver flame-proof suits began talking with Gunther. While the negotiators and Gunther talked, other officers let the air out of her rear tires and placed wedges under the front ones. For the next twenty-four hours, the police attempted to persuade Gunther that she had made her point and that she should now throw away the lighters and come out of the van. She refused, however, and periodically poured more gasoline on herself.

As a part of their attempt to convince Gunther to come out of the van peacefully, the police located her sister, who lived in Florida, and used a telephone hookup to relay the sister's message to her. Gunther also had a brother who lived in Ithaca, New York, and he came to the scene to help the police. Finally, police negotiators, with the brother's help, convinced Gunther to throw away the lighters and come out. The police took Gunther to Bellevue Hospital for observation.

In incidents involving potential suicides, which Ms. Gunther certainly was, successful police SWAT teams know that, after containing the situation, they must protect the public from danger, which the police in this case did by disabling Ms. Gunther's van. After this, negotiators attempt to find and discuss the source of the frustration and despair that has led to the person's suicide attempt, which the negotiators did at great length in this case. While they are doing this, they also usually attempt to find that one thing that will give the potential suicide a reason to live, which in this incident the police did by locating and setting up contacts with members of Ms. Gunther's family.

Police negotiations with potential suicides, however, are very fragile and must be handled delicately. In Henry County, Georgia, the police received the report of a man sitting in a truck on the parking lot of the Calvary Christian Church threatening to kill himself. When the SWAT team and crisis negotiators arrived, they found the man sitting in the cab of a truck, a .357 Magnum revolver cocked and pointed at his chest. More bullets for the gun sat on the dashboard. Although the truck was locked, the man had rolled the windows down a half-inch and was talking with his minister and a friend.

From his family, the police learned that the man had recently confessed to his wife about an affair he'd had with another woman, and apparently, his wife had become so angry she had kicked him out of the house. The man had then confronted his girlfriend and told her that their relationship was over. In her anger at his severing of their relationship, the girlfriend had called his wife and told her all of the intimate details of their affair. The police also learned that the man had recently been in counseling for depression. Although negotiators usually don't like to negotiate face to face if there is any other way, they didn't see one in this case, and so, they went to the truck and asked the minister and the friend to leave. The negotiators then began a dialogue with the man.

Although the man told them he didn't want to live without his wife and children, the negotiators began talking about the life his children would face without a father. As the dialogue continued and the negotiators were able to establish a rapport with the man, they convinced him to roll down the truck windows. Finally, however, the man told the negotiators that he was going to hell and shoot the devil. He then opened the cylinder of the revolver, which the officers saw wasn't loaded, and grabbed for the bullets on the dashboard. But because the windows were now down, the police were able get into the truck and disarm him.

Since they are trained and have experience in working with individuals who are under high stress and on the verge of suicide, police negotiators seldom allow outsiders to join in their negotiations. In this case above, the police asked the minister and the family friend to leave because, while the minister may have been an experienced counselor, he wasn't as experienced as the officers were in dealing with potential suicides, and he might have unintentionally disrupted or even negated the work being done by the police negotiators. Having third parties present during negotiations is often disruptive because these people seldom understand the dynamics of this type of negotiation and may unknowingly interfere with its progress. Also, as the following incident demonstrates, bringing a third person into negotiations may be deadly.

In Jacksonville, Florida, the police arrested a sixteen-year-old youth for drug possession and armed robbery. Although the police thought they had searched him thoroughly, they missed a .25-caliber pistol he had hidden in his shoe. While at the juvenile detention facility, the youth used the weapon to take another inmate hostage. In addition, a twenty-eight-year-old office worker at the detention facility barricaded herself in her office, in order to escape being taken hostage by the youth. Then, though not an actual hostage, the office worker became a captive, since she couldn't leave her office because of the hostage situation.

SWAT hostage negotiators began talking to the youth, whose demand was that he not be put in jail. The youth also told the police that he felt his aunt was responsible for his being arrested, and that he wanted to speak with her. The policy in Jacksonville was not to allow a third party to speak with a hostage taker, and so, the negotiators sent in a tape recording his aunt had made at police request. After listening to the tape, the youth shot the recorder. The youth then said he would free his hostage if he could talk with his grandfather. While this was against department policy, the negotiators felt that denying him this conversation could result in violence to the hostage, and so, they allowed him to speak on the telephone with his grandfather. After the conversation with his grandfather, though, he still would not release the hostage.

The trapped office worker, in the meantime, called her husband and began complaining of chest pains. When the police tried to call her (they could not see her from their location), she did not answer the telephone. The SWAT team then had the fire department knock a hole through the outside of the building and into the office where the woman was barricaded. The police found, however, that she was not having health problems; she was simply scared.

The negotiators informed the youth of what the fire department was doing, but still, he became upset and finally pointed his weapon at his hostage and demanded to speak with his grandfather again. The police once more saw no alternative but to allow this. While on the telephone to his grandfather, however, the youth became so upset that he shot the hostage in the shoulder. As a result, the police, forced to take immediate action, first threw in a flashbang and then charged into the room. The youth, rather than be captured, shot himself in the head. The hostage, though injured, survived.

This incident, though successfully resolved in as far as the hostage and the officer worker were concerned, demonstrates the danger of allowing a hostage taker to speak with a third party. The police are never sure what the hostage taker's reaction to a conversation will be, and in this case, it was deadly. Often, hostage takers want to speak with the very person who has brought on the stress that precipitated the hostage incident, and their reaction to this conversation may well be detrimental to the resolution of the incident.

When dealing with suicidal people, a successful police SWAT team must stay constantly alert to the possibility that the individual is trying to force the police to complete his suicide. In Indianapolis, Indiana, Lloyd Louks found that the divorce he didn't want had just become final. On the evening of the day it did, he purchased a 12-gauge shotgun and went to the Stone, Stafford, and Stone Insurance Company in downtown Indianapolis, where he took hostage the boyfriend of his now ex-wife. When the hostage negotiator began talking to Louks, he found Louks despondent over the divorce and loss of the custody of his two sons.

The negotiator suspected that what Louks really wanted was for the police to kill him. During the incident, Louks tried several times to provoke the police to kill him, once even firing the shotgun into a wall of the insurance company office. The police, however, refused to overreact and finally persuaded him to surrender.

Quite often, along with suicidal people, police SWAT teams are called on to deal with severely mentally disturbed individuals. These people often have a distorted (though true to them) view of reality, and to be successful, a police SWAT team needs to recognize this and not overreact. A case in Tulsa, Oklahoma, demonstrates this need.

The police in Tulsa were called to the home of Michael Majors, who had been diagnosed as a paranoid schizophrenic. A few minutes earlier, Majors had shot and killed his adoptive father and had then barricaded himself in the family garage. Majors believed that he worked for the CIA and that his adoptive father had been a KGB agent who had killed his real father and then assumed his identity. Although Majors had been prescribed medicine to control his aggressive behavior, he was not taking it.

Since Majors had already killed one person and, though barricaded, had no hostages, the police SWAT team could have assaulted the garage and taken Majors by force. This action would, however, have played into Majors's delusions and would very likely have ended in serious injury or death. Instead, the SWAT team set up perimeters to contain the incident and then allowed the SWAT negotiator to talk with Majors. Speaking convincingly with someone who is suffering from delusions is not an easy task, but the negotiator talked with Majors for six hours and finally convinced him to surrender peacefully.

In Latrobe Borough, Pennsylvania, a man, after an argument with his estranged wife, broke into a school for troubled youths and took four people hostage, including a pregnant woman. Dressed in a bright orange hunting jacket and carrying a 30-30 rifle, the man forced the hostages, during their captivity, to read passages from his personal diary. After a four-and-a-half-hour standoff, the police hostage negotiator finally convinced the man to surrender and release the hostages. At his arraignment the next day, the hostage taker told the judge he was sorry.

This case is interesting not only because it was successfully resolved, but also because, rather than involving a mentally disturbed person or a potential suicide, it involved a type of person police SWAT teams find they must deal with quite often. These are individuals who feel that no one will listen to them and that no one cares about their problems. These individuals often take hostages in order to dramatize their need to make others aware of and care about their problems. In this case, the suspect showed this need to share his problems by forcing the hostages to read his personal diary. Police SWAT teams recognize that most of the incidents involving these types of individuals can be successfully resolved simply by setting up perimeters to contain the incident and then allowing the person to vent his or her frustrations to the negotiator. A SWAT assault in these incidents is often an unnecessary risk.

Regardless of the type of person they are dealing with, however, a successful SWAT team's first responsibility at any SWAT incident site is to protect the lives of innocent people. In Torrance, California, a man who had been drinking 151-proof rum all day suddenly picked up a semiautomatic rifle and began firing it out the windows of the apartment he was in, then at the ceiling, and finally toward another apartment. Neighbors called the police, and the Redondo and El Segundo Police Department SWAT teams responded, setting up perimeters around the building while officers evacuated apartments and businesses nearby. When the police attempted to talk the gunman into giving up and coming out, he threatened to "shoot the first officer I see."

While the negotiators were attempting to talk with the gunman, the police manning the perimeters suddenly saw a woman at the window of the apartment above the gunman's. SWAT officers climbed up onto the building next door and held up a cardboard sign that told her to flee her apartment. The police then helped her get out of the upstairs window and across a ladder stretched between the two buildings. A few minutes later, the gunman surrendered peacefully.

In responding to any SWAT incident, the police must find a way, if at all possible, to save not only the lives of innocent people, as the police did in the incident in Torrance, California, but also the life of the suspect. In Tulsa, Oklahoma, a court issued warrants for three felony counts against a man. A police officer, knowing that the warrants had been issued, stopped a car the man was driving on Interstate 44 near Tulsa. When ordered to get out of the car, the driver brandished a shotgun and threatened to kill the officer and himself. The officer retreated and called for the SWAT team.

Even though a police negotiator talked for hours with the man, he couldn't convince the man to surrender. And so, as the negotiator talked through the driver's window, two SWAT officers crept up to the passenger's side, smashed out the window, and then subdued the man without injury.

In some situations, such as the preceding and following incidents, even letting negotiators talk to an individual at length is not enough to resolve the incident successfully, and the SWAT team must occasionally resort to more forceful tactics. In Anaheim, California, a man the police wanted for shooting another man during a barroom brawl barricaded himself inside his apartment. The SWAT team arrived at the scene, and the negotiators attempted to persuade the man to come out and surrender. Although the man wouldn't come out, the police didn't assault the apartment right away because the man was talking to the negotiators.

"As long as he was willing to talk to us," said Anaheim Police Department negotiator Rick Razee, "we talked" (Standoff ends 1990, 41).

The twelve-hour standoff attracted a lot of attention, and many of the neighborhood residents taped the encounter with video cameras. Finally, when negotiations broke down, the police put a K-9 dog into the apartment, and the dog subdued the man long enough for police officers to rush in and overpower him.

It is always difficult for a police SWAT team to know when to agree to concessions in negotiations with suspects, and when to stand firm and take a hard line. It is a call that, if correct, can, as the next case below shows, successfully resolve the incident.

In Grand Junction, Colorado, deputies brought a man arrested for sexual assault and kidnapping over to court from the jail. As the deputies took off the man's handcuffs, the arrested man's wife suddenly rushed forward and shoved the deputies aside, tossing her husband a semiautomatic pistol, while keeping another one for herself. The husband and wife then took three people hostage as others fled the courtroom. SWAT was called.

When contacted by police negotiators, the wife claimed she had explosives, and so, the police evacuated the building and cordoned off the area around the court for a block in every direction. The police also had the electric company shut off the streetlights around the building, so that the hostage takers would not have any close targets to shoot at. Talking with negotiators over a handheld radio taken from one of the jailers, the husband seemed ready several times to surrender, but his wife wouldn't let him and instead threatened to blow up the building. During the standoff, the husband and wife released the hostages one by one. Finally, however, the man's wife, apparently seeing the futility of their situation when the police would not allow her and her husband to leave, shot and killed herself. The husband surrendered peacefully.

In some cases, negotiating is not an option. Sometimes, as in the following incident, only a show of force by the police SWAT team can end an incident peacefully. In Columbia, Missouri, a man armed with a sawed-off shotgun drove to his ex-mother-in-law's home to confront his ex-wife. An argument soon erupted, and in the midst of it, the man tried to shoot his ex-wife with the shotgun. The ex-mother-in-law, however, trying to protect her daughter, jumped in the way and was hit by the shotgun blast, which killed her. Seeing the situation he had got himself into, the man took his ex-wife hostage and then drove to a nearby wooded area.

The police, alerted to the murder and kidnapping, set up roadblocks in the area and began a land and air search for the killer and his hostage. After several hours of searching with no success, a police helicopter finally spotted the man in a creek bed about a mile northwest of the area the police had cordoned off. With the police helicopter guiding them, the SWAT team located the man and, after confronting him, took him into custody without incident. They found the hostage unharmed.

In some incidents, on the other hand, a show of force by the police SWAT team can bring a violent response from a suspect, rather than a peaceful surrender. It is in these incidents, such as the one described next, that the safety and security measures taken by a successful police SWAT team pay dividends.

In Charlotte, North Carolina, two sixteen-year-old girls called the police and reported that they had been raped by a man at the Carriage Inn Hotel on North Graham Street. The girls also told the police that they had escaped while the man was raping a fifteen-year-old girl, whom he still held hostage at the hotel. The police went to the hotel, and when the man answered their knock on the door, the police found he was holding a gun to the head of the fifteen-year-old girl. The man fired several shots at the officers before slamming the door shut.

The police department dispatched the SWAT team to the hotel and had the guests evacuated. Although no officers were hit during the five-hour standoff, the man fired about fifty shots out a window at them with an assault rifle, most of the shots hitting a police car. Hostage negotiators, however, finally convinced the man to surrender and to release his hostage. The police charged the man with three counts of first-degree rape, three counts of kidnapping, and felony assault on a police officer.

Occasionally, situations appear too risky to leave to negotiations, and a tactical solution must be considered immediately. In

La Verne, California, a man fleeing a botched robbery at a children's clothing store ran into a nearby McDonald's restaurant and took nineteen people hostage. SWAT rushed to the scene and set up a command post in a nearby high school. On the perimeters, SWAT officers with binoculars watched the movements of the hostage taker. The man, they saw, had forced some of the hostages to lie on the floor under the tables. Recalling a similar situation that had resulted in the killing of twenty-one people at a McDonald's in San Ysidro, California, just a few years before, the police realized they couldn't simply wait outside and hope for a peaceful resolution. The SWAT command post had a SWAT officer dress up in a McDonald's uniform and slip into the restaurant. When they felt the time was right, the SWAT team, using flashbangs, assaulted the restaurant. When the assault began, the SWAT officer disguised as a McDonald's employee leaped over the counter and tackled the gunman. All of the hostages escaped unharmed.

Sometimes, even though a police SWAT team follows proven procedures and takes all of the proper precautions, the use of firearms becomes necessary in order to resolve an incident successfully. In Bensalem Township, Pennsylvania, the police received an urgent call. Two men had kidnapped two women in Philadelphia, tied up one and left her at the kidnapping site, and then brought the other to the American Motel on Route 1 in Bensalem Township. The kidnappers, the police learned, had already contacted the boyfriend of the kidnapped woman and demanded $10,000 for her safe return.

The police set up a command post at the motel, established perimeters, and were waiting for more SWAT team members to arrive before taking any action. However, it often happens in SWAT incidents that the suspects don't do what the police want them to. Before the remainder of the SWAT team could arrive, one of the suspects left the motel room and got into the kidnapped woman's car. Knowing they couldn't let him drive away, the police ran toward the car, yelling for him to stop. The driver tried to run down the officers with the car. The officers shot at the car, their bullets flattening one of the tires, shattering two windows, and, amazingly, shooting the gearshift lever into neutral, which stopped the car and allowed the officers to arrest the driver.

The remaining kidnapper, believing that the police had just killed his partner, came out of the room and gave up. The kidnapped woman escaped unharmed. Both men later pled guilty and received prison sentences.

This chapter of SWAT successes was undoubtedly the one I enjoyed writing the most, but it was also the most difficult one to write. I had to choose from among hundreds and hundreds of SWAT success stories and decide which few I would include. My definition of success was that the police SWAT team resolved the incident with no innocent parties being seriously injured or killed once the SWAT team had arrived. Whether or not the instigator of the SWAT incident died, either by his or her own hand or at the hands of the police, did not become part of my definition of success. In most of the incidents described, when the instigator of a SWAT incident died it was his or her own decision.

Many of the incidents I decided against including in this chapter were not really remarkable. Someone had been drinking and got into a fight with his spouse or girlfriend. A weapon was produced, and perhaps shots were fired and hostages were taken. The police SWAT team was called, the man surrendered, and the event was over. Nothing remarkable. That is, unless you happened to be the hostage and didn't know if you were going to live out the evening. Nothing remarkable, except for the fact that police SWAT teams are able to successfully resolve incidents like this hundreds of times every year. That is indeed remarkable.

However, police SWAT teams' ability to do this, and to do it successfully over and over, isn't accidental. It happens only because police SWAT teams use sound, time-tested techniques and methods. Police SWAT teams have built on each other's successes and use methods and techniques that have been shown to work over and over again.

Police SWAT teams have also met with considerable success because the teams are made up of highly motivated volunteers who willingly put in many extra hours of work every year honing and perfecting their skills. While all law enforcement is inherently dangerous, SWAT duty is at least doubly so. Still, these officers volunteer every day to put their own lives at risk in order to save others. This is the mindset that has made police SWAT teams successful.

17

The Future of SWAT

In his 1979 book *SWAT*, Phillip L. Davidson of the Metropolitan Police Department of Nashville-Davidson County, Tennessee, wrote, "Taking hostages. This is the crime of the future" (p. 117).

Mr. Davidson couldn't have been more prophetic. Hostage taking has now become so commonplace that many people would find it hard to believe that, thirty years ago, very few police departments in the United States had ever had to deal with this particular crime, and that now every police department in the United States, no matter how small, has to be prepared for it. How did this happen?

As I discussed in Chapter 1, this change in our society began as hostage incidents and other spectacular crimes started receiving more and more media attention. When this happened, their numbers, through imitation, began to grow. And as anyone who has been watching the news for the last several decades knows, this is true not just of hostage taking, but also of other spectacular types of crime, such as aircraft hijacking, mass murder, serial killing, letter bombing, product tampering, and a host of other heinous acts. The more publicity these acts have received, the more their numbers have grown.

"In just the last four to five years, we have quadrupled our number of call-outs," said Indianapolis Police Department SWAT Tactical Commander Stephen Robertson.

In fairness to the news media, no one can really expect them not to report the news. That is their job. And crime, particularly spectacular crime, has always been big news. Consequently, few people in law enforcement expect that this trend of crime imitation will stop anytime soon; rather, most believe it will continue to grow. And so, we have come full circle. The very thing that brought about the original formation of police SWAT teams is also likely to be the impetus for their continuation and growth in the future. SWAT is here to stay.

But while police SWAT teams are here to stay, law enforcement experts do expect a number of changes in the SWAT teams of the future. For example, because of the enormous cost of equipping and maintaining a fully staffed SWAT team, particularly for small and mid-sized police departments, the future is likely to see more mutual-aid SWAT teams, in which small and mid-sized police departments band together to form a SWAT team made up of members from all of the police departments. In addition, for areas where there are not enough small or mid-sized police departments to form a mutual-aid SWAT team, experts forecast an increase of small and mid-sized police agencies contracting for SWAT services from nearby large police agencies. Some law enforcement experts also foresee the formation of many more regional SWAT teams that serve even larger areas than mutual-aid SWAT teams, a present example being the South Suburban Emergency Response Team discussed in Chapter 14, which serves five thousand square miles in the south suburban area of Illinois.

But there is something else that many law enforcement authorities believe will bring about changes in future SWAT teams, and that is court decisions. As more and more appellate courts begin looking at and judging SWAT actions, SWAT teams will be forced to reach for ever higher standards of performance. Some of this reaching for higher standards will come through better training, and a trend that experts believe is likely to continue to grow is neighboring SWAT teams training together. This shared training, police departments have found, not only saves money but allows

SWAT teams that are likely to have to work together in the future to know each other's capabilities, and consequently to feel more comfortable working together. Some of this reach for higher standards of performance will also come from new technology, which will range from newer, more effective weapons to exotic computer programs that can, for example, immediately assess a person's potential for violence. And the future will almost certainly see more integration of female officers into SWAT teams. This is just a natural progression in a profession where woman have finally begun to be accepted as equals.

Edward J. Tully (1994), a retired FBI agent and now director of research for the National Executive Institute Associates, prefaced an article in *The FOP Journal* about the future of policing by writing, "Violent minded youths, individuals affected by drugs, the inherent violence of drug distribution networks, mindless youth gangs, and an increase in the number of others prone to violence combined to produce record levels of homicides in twenty-two metropolitan areas (and countless smaller cities) in 1993" (p. 14). With this preface for his reasoning, Mr. Tully went on to say that he foresaw the formation of more SWAT-like tactical teams, equipped with the best armament and technology available. These teams, he predicted, will be used in the future not just for specialized SWAT-type incidents, but also to control the behavior of unruly groups in America's cities.

Whether America will be forced to resort to this type of policing in the future remains to be seen, but it is undeniable that the world is becoming more and more violent. Every day, Americans witness criminals becoming more bold and increasingly vicious, and every day, we watch in amazement and fear as more and more people mimic the violent incidents they see played and replayed on the news.

"SWAT will be a critical necessity for security in the future," said former FBI SWAT commander Cal Black. "It will become a necessity because the bad guys are getting more and more heavily armed every day."

Fortunately, though, we are not totally powerless and at the mercy of society's violence-minded individuals. As long as there are dedicated police officers who are willing to put their lives at extra risk to rescue others, SWAT will be there.

References

Aubrey, Rodd, "Tape Proves Prison Guards Still Alive, Official Says." *Indianapolis Star*, 19 April 1993.

Baker, Al, "The Ultimate Negotiator." *The Tactical Edge* (Winter 1992): 42–46.

Bolz, Frank, "Frank Bolz Responds to 'Negotiating Waco.' " *US Negotiator*, (Winter 1994): 41.

Booher, William J., "IPD Sergeant's Role as Hostage Negotiator Was Key." *Indianapolis Star*, 24 May 1994.

Chappel, Robert, *SWAT Team Manual*. Boulder, CO: Paladin Press, 1979.

"Coast Man Kills 20 in Rampage at a Restaurant." *New York Times*, 19 July 1984.

Davidson, Philip, *SWAT*. Springfield, IL: Charles C Thomas, 1979.

"Denny's Hostage Ordeal." *Indianapolis Star*, 24 May 1994.

Downs v. United States of America, U.S. Court of Appeals, Sixth District, 8 August 1975

Dvorchak, Bob, "Five Dead in Gutted MOVE House; Mayor Vows to Rebuild Area." *Indianapolis Star*, 15 May 1985.

"Ex-Letter Carrier Kills 3 at Michigan Post Office." *The Tactical Edge* (Winter 1992): 62.

"Former CHP Officer Killed after Terrorizing Tax Office." *The Tactical Edge* (Summer 1993): 58.

"Gunman Massacres 20 at McDonald's before Being Slain." *Indianapolis Star*, 19 July 1984.

Heal, Sid, "Minimum Performance Standards." *The Tactical Edge* (Winter 1991): 19–21.

"Heavily Armed Ex-Marine Uses Tower as Fort." *Indianapolis Star*, 2 August 1966.

Jacobs, Jefferie, *SWAT Tactics*. Boulder, CO: Paladin Press, 1983.

Kinney, Terry, "Inmates Free Prison Guard After Airing Demands on TV." *Indianapolis Star*, 17 April 1993.

"Koch Rejects Bombing Tactic." *New York Times*, 15 May 1985.

Kolman, John, *A Guide to the Development of Special Weapons and Tactics Teams*. Springfield, IL: Charles C Thomas, 1982.

Komarow, Steve, "Police Kill Man in Capital Siege." *Indianapolis Star*, 9 December 1982.

Leo, John, "Treating Felons as Celebrities." *Indianapolis Star*, 31 August 1993.

McMurty, Larry, "Return to Waco." *The New Republic*, 7 June, 1993.

National Institute of Justice. *Report on the Attorney General's Conference on Less Than Lethal Weapons*. Washington, D.C.: U.S. Government Printing Office, 1988.

Paddock, Richard C., "Three Hostages, Three Gunmen Die in Sacramento Store Siege." *Los Angeles Times*, 5 April 1991.

Paddock, Richard C., "Hostages Recall Terror of Siege in Sacramento." *Los Angeles Times*, 6 April 1991.

Price, Richard, "Senseless Deaths of 21 Shock Us All." *USA Today*, 20 July 1984.

Ravo, Nick, "Gunman Surrenders After Holding 4 for a 2nd Day on 101st St." *New York Times*, 6 March 1987.

Schramm, Susan, "Family Friend Ignored Danger to Help Bleeding Wounded Boy." *Indianapolis Star*, 25 May 1994.

"Standoff Ends as Suspect Gives Up," *The Tactical Edge* (Spring 1990): 41.

Stevens, William K. "Six Bodies in Ashes of Radicals' Home; Assault Defended." *New York Times*, 15 May 1985.

Strentz, Thomas, undated. *The Stockholm Syndrome*. Special Operations and Research Unit, FBI Academy, Quantico, Virginia.

"Survey Results." *The Tactical Edge* (Winter 1994): 58.

Tully, Edward, "Difficult Days, Nights of Terror." *The FOP Journal* (Fall/Winter 1994): 14–28.

Tyrell, R. Emmett, "Crystals in the Waco Crucible." *Washington Post*, 4 April 1993.

U.S. Department of the Treasury, *Report of the Department of the Treasury on the Bureau of Alcohol, Tobacco, and Firearms' Investigation of Vernon Wayne Howell Also Known as David Koresh*. Washington, D.C.: U.S. Government Printing Office, September 1993.

Waldron, Martin, "Whitman Told Doctor He Sometimes Thought of 'Shooting People.'" *New York Times*, 3 August 1966.

Williams, Mike, "Case Study: Chattanooga, Tennessee." *The Tactical Edge* (Spring 1983): 32–33.

Index